Transforming the Robocops

To Ben,
  Roboprof and colleague extraordinary,
    with best wishes,
      Maurice.
Amstelveen, March 2006.

Transforming the Robocops

Changing Police in South Africa

MONIQUE MARKS

UNIVERSITY OF KwaZulu-Natal PRESS

Published in 2005 by University of KwaZulu-Natal Press
Private Bag X01
Scottsville 3209
South Africa
Email: books@ukzn.ac.za
Website: www.ukznpress.co.za

© Monique Marks 2005

All rights reserved. No part of this publication may be reproduced or transmitted in any form or by any means, electronic or mechanical, including photocopying, recording or any information storage and retrieval system, without prior permission in writing from the publishers.

ISBN 1-86914-043-5

Typesetting: Trish Comrie
Cover photograph: Graeme Williams (South Photographs/africanpictures.net)
Cover design: Sebastien Quevauvilliers, Flying Ant Designs

Printed and bound by Interpak Books, Pietermaritzburg

Contents

Foreword *by Professor Maurice Punch* vii
Foreword *by Superintendent Faizel Ally* x
Acknowledgements xiii
Abbreviations xv

1 Introduction: *The Challenge of Changing the Police* 1
2 Issues in Police Organisational Change 13
3 From Green to Blue: *The Origins of Durban POP* 31
4 Durban POP in 2001 66
5 Me and my Uzi: *Stepping into Durban POP* 83
6 Half-measures? *Training, Policy and Recruitment* 113
7 New Methods, New Motives? *Durban POP and its Public* 142
8 Shifting Gears or Slamming on the Brakes?
   Management and Supervision 180
9 Division in the Ranks 216
10 Conclusion: *Contradictions of Police Organisational Change* 241

Notes 256
Select Bibliography 264
Index 285

Foreword

This is a stimulating, insightful and valuable book about the sharp end of policing; it also informs us about transition in a key institution in South African society. It is a new-style ethnography by a female within a previously male stronghold, on a subject that was rarely accessible for research, and within a society in transition. Police Studies has been considerably enriched by these explorations of new areas in diverse societies and by the proliferation of women researchers (with Maureen Cain in the UK and Susan Erlich Martin in the USA as early pioneers).

Monique Marks has researched the Public Order Police (POP) in the South African Police Service (SAPS). POP was appallingly bad; it was the strong and vicious arm of the apartheid regime and operationally it was simply crude, violent and unthinking policing. In this highly readable book, Marks discusses the 'miracle' of transition that is transforming South Africa without major violence; reveals the dilemmas for a woman researching such an action-oriented unit; analyses organisational change, drawing particularly on the work and ideas of Janet Chan; and examines what post-apartheid policing has meant for POP. This is an impressive piece of work showing wide reading, extensive field work, use of several sources to gain data and serious thought on interpreting the material theoretically.

The primary thrust is on organisational change, with an assumption that it is difficult to change police culture. In the literature there is a tendency to focus on the conservatism of the police organisation and on resistance to change; at the same time in several societies, police have been through two decades of attempting substantial change. And Sir Ian Blair, of the Metropolitan Police Service of London, has stated that change is now the name of the game and that senior officers in Britain are more than willing to ride the waves of change.

So this leaves us with the key question: has all this changed 'police culture'? Perhaps we should avoid the assumption that there is a universal culture and that it is shared throughout the organisation and across national cultures; the police organisation is better seen as a 'matrix' with many sub-cultures in a segmented and loosely coupled system. There is a generic cop culture, which Reiner (2000) and many others have written about, but there is also variety shaped by the social structure of the work in diverse units and altered by varying cultural settings (Chan, 2003).

If we look at Marks's observations of POP, for instance, then there has been substantial change. The old-style of public order policing was to see operations as a form of 'combat' in a war (e.g. with military-style training, equipment and institutional structure). This was, and is, clearly attractive to certain people who want simplicity, solidarity, action and unambiguous leadership. The nostalgia for this that emerges in her interviews with them is also a form of rationalisation – their occupational 'stories' are of a world lost, and their 'dirty work' is posed in a vocabulary of necessity and of 'war'. In some ways these tough guys seem to find it easy to unburden themselves to a woman.

The structure, uniform, equipment, training, and leadership have changed considerably. In some respects so has the work of POP, as it is now used largely in its secondary role as a heavily armed support group within conventional policing. POP is also a microcosm of the transition and change within the SAPS. That road is one of rising expectations, increasing demand and constant change; there has been something of a 'miracle' but now people expect more miracles. In South Africa the SAPS is supposed to be engaged in a paradigm shift. But crime is high, this has an ethnic element, 'normal' policing is in many areas impossible, and there is ambivalence at the highest levels about tackling crime. This means that when POP is being used for general policing tasks, albeit at the sharp end, some of its members can indulge in old-style abuses because they go in mob-handed, in potentially dangerous situations against stereotypical opponents, and with little chance of exposure (and the record of fatal police violence against suspects and others in South Africa is still unacceptably high).

The key issue is that the SAPS is in the middle of transition; and that change is going to be constant. There have been substantial changes in expressed mission, in structure and leadership, in racial composition, in chances of promotion, etc. This is an earthquake with a lot of side effects. In POP the whites are leaving, the Indians are moving up and the blacks are pretty much still the foot-soldiers (but with some exceptions). These changes are bought at the cost of considerable frustration within the organisation. Before, in the SAPS, but especially in POP, the culture was almost tribal, with unquestioning loyalty and strong solidarity. Now you have a more 'modern' organisation with, for example, female officers concerned about their children and adjusting their work accordingly, and in a sense their commitment to the organisation in order to support their domestic situation. Part of this painful transformation of a beleaguered 'tribe' is related to the fact that this is enforced change from pariah status, with external experts and observers pushing the process (rather than the more gradual and co-ordinated movement for change elsewhere in Western Europe and North America).

*

In essence, Marks provides us with an insightful and rich case study illustrating the transformation of POP, which in turn illuminates change within the SAPS. And the prime image is of an organisation in the middle of transformation, with all its growing pains, and with a long path of transition and permanent change ahead. Elements of the resilient police culture will always remain fixated on the unusual and the unlikely, with a predilection for action and for 'head-banging', but modern policing is rooted in professional, accountable and restrained conduct within the rule of law and geared to the needs and demands of citizens. Doubtless it is difficult to alter that traditional, primal view of police work but this research shows that major change is possible and that police culture can be changed too, even in a complex and difficult environment. This book forms, then, not only a significant contribution to Police Studies but also a valuable addition to research on 'transitional' societies.

Professor Maurice Punch
Mannheim Centre
London School of Economics
and Amstelveen

Foreword

The first time I met Monique Marks was when she asked me to address her final-year Sociology class at the University of Natal on the topic of public order policing. So began a relationship between her and the members of Durban Public Order Police (POP). The unit itself at that time was also looking for somebody like her, somebody who had a research and teaching interest in the police, to come in and give a different perspective about transformation in our unit. A lot of pressure had been placed on us from the national level about transforming as fast as we could. This meant that the potential was there from the beginning to develop a mutual relationship where the unit could benefit from an outsider coming in. I remember the unit commander at the time stating that he would welcome Monique coming in to help the unit understand things from a non-police point of view. I was surprised about this because we had always been such a closed organisation, never wanting people from the outside to scrutinise us. So it was somewhat unusual that Monique was given access to do research in the unit. She came into the unit at the right time.

I think that Monique was able to penetrate the unit because of her general open and transparent way of dealing with members. She earned the respect of members by going out on operations and engaging directly with them rather than just asking questions and interviewing them. Over the years, Monique was exposed and exposed herself to all functions in the unit, from those that were high risk to those that were more boring. This was important because members felt frustrated in some of their activities. They were going through a very uncertain time themselves.

Monique spent time in the unit when things were somewhat tumultuous. From 1996 onward, the unit was expected to make dramatic changes from operating as a unit whose focus was to stabilise the country using hard-handed tactics and where no effort or resources were spared in quelling internal resistance. After 1994, there was a sudden drop in protest activities and the unit had to focus on other issues such as maintaining peace and public order. In 1996, for the very first time in our unit's history, we had a policy document to govern our conduct and our procedures. We were trying to get acceptance from the communities that we were serving, to become more legitimate in the work that we did. Prior to this, if we saw a crowd, our main objective was to disperse them. Suddenly we had to protect the very rights we had suppressed and protect the people we were used to repressing. We had to take the first steps toward change. We had to step back and show that our style and our mindset had changed.

One of the first things that we experienced was the taking away of our camouflage uniforms. We were suddenly just regular police. This was very difficult for the members. Many left, as they could not accept the changes in the unit. White members in particular left and went to other specialised units where they felt that the old style of policing was still being entertained. Those that remained have changed over time. It took a long time for members of the unit to develop confidence in new styles and equipment. But at the end of the day, they had to change. It was a matter of adapt or die. But the change was not smooth. Even though there was a momentum of positive change, troubling conduct persisted. Members feared acting in new ways. They still perceived crowds as the enemy. Most of the work of the unit was in the townships and many still saw the townships as very dangerous. They felt betrayed that they were expected to take a soft approach in a very harsh environment. They had defence mechanisms that they developed in the precarious work environment and old tactics were hard to let go of. As democracy took hold and things settled down, different styles emerged. The problem was that they were still expected to operate from time to time in high-risk environments and it was difficult for them to then shift to softer styles of policing.

Was transformation a success in the end? Yes and no. Yes, in the sense that we developed a structure and a new training system and police who can now manage events in line with international standards. We have had a fair number of international events that we have policed very successfully. But the answer is also 'no' in the sense that there were problems with the way in which members behaved from time to time. The transformation process itself was not watched over and it was often the press that brought problem behaviour to the fore. Individual actions were still taking place. Many police in the unit still opted for quicker solutions in their daily policing. The University of Durban-Westville incident recorded in this book is an example of this. Nobody was ever really held accountable for this incident in the unit.

Now we are undergoing another change process in the unit. Since 2001, we have shifted from being a specialised unit to a more generalised unit. We have again refocused our attention and changed our name. The unit is now called the Area Crime Combating Unit and focus has shifted from crowd management toward the combat of crime. Now we are beginning to draft another new policy that will change our identity again. But, to be fair, a lot of the lessons learned in the transformation process will be carried through. As a unit we have already walked the rocky road of change and we know the difference between good and bad policing.

The change that we went through in the unit and that is discussed in this book is very historic. Nobody has documented anything about the daily experiences of actual members of the unit going through dramatic change. This book gives us a voice, but also gives the police an opportunity to mirror our experiences and reflect on them. In my view, police members and South Africans at large need to understand the context of this transformation and the difficulties involved in transforming police organisations in South Africa and beyond. This book will also serve as a reference for other police agencies.

What the police tended to do was to keep the public in the dark about what was going on in the unit, even though they were key stakeholders in the process. This book will enable the public to understand what we were trying to achieve and to reflect on the problems the police confront. Finally, I think that this book will be used in the future by the police organisation in South Africa as a way of reminding themselves about the foundational period of a hopefully new and better police service.

Superintendent Faizel Ally
Training Manager of SAPS Area Crime Combating Unit
National Head Office, Pretoria

Acknowledgements

My deepest gratitude goes to all the members of the Durban Public Order Police unit (as it was then known) for allowing me to participate in their daily working lives. In particular, I would like to thank individual members of the unit for their constant support of, and engagement with, my research. Faizel Ali took me out into the field and, with great patience, helped me to understand the ins and outs of the unit. He also kindly wrote a foreword to this book. Others from the POP unit who need special mention are: Mike Malimela, Chris Swart, Percy Govender, Msamano Majola, Fanie Masemola, Trevor Reddy, Gerald Singh and Naas de Beer. Thank you for taking me along with you, fetching me, advising me, reading my work, and making me feel like part of your team.

I would also like to thank Vernon Hunter, the Provincial Unit Commander at the time, for his candidness and for making me feel my research was valued. Thanks also to Sakkie van Rensburg, Vernon Day and Colin Armstrong at the SAPS Headquarters in Pretoria for generously providing me with documentation, reports and statistical data whenever I needed them. Thanks also for always saying yes to my phone requests for interviews, even when these were on the spur of the moment. Your names do not appear in this work, since all POP officers' names used here have been changed, but each of you has contributed to this book in very direct ways.

I would also like to thank my colleagues in the Faculty of Human Sciences and the Sociology Programme at the University of KwaZulu-Natal for always taking an interest in my work and for their patient support of all my endeavours (crazy as they must have seemed). Thanks to Bill Freund for reading and commenting on my work and for providing encouragement along the way. A special thanks to Gerhard Maré for his careful reading of this manuscript and for creating the space in my departmental commitments for me to go out into the field and to write this book. Ari Sitas provided me with important insights and has always been a motivating force. Charles Crothers was always available, from both near and far, to share valuable perceptions.

More recently, my time on the staff of the Regulatory Institutions Network (RegNet) at the Australian National University has been an immense privilege and has broadened my insights into policing and security in ways I never imagined possible. RegNet is in every way a ceaseless flow of new ideas. I particularly want to acknowledge my RegNet colleagues in Security 21 who have jolted my thinking and understanding of the world of policing. They are – in no particular order – Clifford Shearing, Jennifer Wood, Jenny Fleming, Peter Grabosky and Nina Leijon.

I cannot thank David Newmarch enough for his careful, creative and skilful editing of this book. David has an amazing ability to work magic into words and I have found his interventions truly dazzling!

Many thanks also to Maurice Punch for supporting the publication of this manuscript and for writing a foreword to this book. His work and unique style of writing have inspired me over the years.

This book is dedicated to all those people who were victims of policing brutality in the old South Africa, and to those police officers who were themselves brutalised by apartheid.

*

Parts of this book have already been published in some form in the following journals:

The British Journal of Criminology
Society in Transition
The Journal of African and Asian Studies
Policing and Society
Current Sociology

I would like to thank the editors and editorial boards of each of these journals for allowing me to republish material that has appeared in their journals.

Abbreviations

ACCU	Area Crime Combating Unit
ANC	African National Congress
AWB	Afrikaner Weerstandsbeweging
BOF	Black Officers' Forum
BVPI	Best Value Performance Indicators
Cosatu	Congress of South African Trade Unions
CRASH	Community Resources Against Street Hoodlums (US)
CSO	Community support officers (UK)
IFP	Inkatha Freedom Party
IRA	Irish Republican Army
IRIS	Incident report information system
ISD	Internal Stability Division
ISU	Internal Stability Unit
KZP	KwaZulu Police
LAPD	Los Angeles Police Department
MK	Umkhonto we Sizwe
NP	National Party
PAC	Pan-Africanist Congress
PCAS	Policy Co-ordination and Advisory Services
POCOC	Provincial Operational Co-ordinating Committee
POP	Public Order Police
POPCRU	Police and Prisons Civil Rights Union
POPU	Public Order Police Unit
RDP	Reconstruction and Development Programme
RUC	Royal Ulster Constabulary (Northern Ireland)
SACP	South African Communist Party

SAP	South African Police
SAPS	South African Police Service
SAPU	South African Police Union
SSC	State Security Council
SWAT	Special Weapons and Tactics (US)
UDF	United Democratic Front
UDW	University of Durban-Westville
WCAR	World Conference Against Racism

1

Introduction
The Challenge of Changing the Police

On this road of change and transformation an enormous amount remains to be done ... What the situation requires of us, on the one hand, is to give due recognition for such changes as have taken place; on the other hand, it also requires us to acknowledge that both the rate and the scope of change still leave quite a lot to be desired (Nelson Mandela, 1996).

IF SOUTH AFRICA'S democratic transition in 1994 was indeed the 'miracle' it has so often been called, its revered icon Nelson Mandela nonetheless warned his fellow citizens from the earliest days of the new democracy that while societal and institutional 'transformation' was assured, the process was likely to be slow and contradictory. Mandela's caution was that, yes, they should welcome the great strides that had been made, but be under no illusions about the obstacles to change that still remained.

Ten years on, there is vigorous debate about how far reforms have penetrated South African institutions and how well the new democratic state has been able to deliver on its many promises (Freund, 1999; Marais, 1998; Glaser, 2001; Daniel et al., 2003). And though a decade may not be time enough 'to unravel the disparities bequeathed by 300 years of white domination and more than 40 years of apartheid rule' (Daniel et al., 2003: 2), sufficient time has passed to make some initial appraisals of political, economic and institutional changes.

Of all the national institutions undergoing transformation, none calls for sharper scrutiny than the South African state police, with their notorious history, their critical new responsibility for securing a safe environment for the new democracy, and their residual capacity to obstruct its hopes. So the question persists: 'Have the police in South Africa *really* changed?'

It is a not an easy question to answer. Certainly, even the most cursory review will confirm that far-reaching changes have taken place. The structure, uniform, equipment and training of the police are different in very visible ways. Police station charge offices are plastered with posters proclaiming a community-oriented service ethic, which is reflected too, in the more courteous reception that members of the public can, generally speaking, expect from the officers on duty. There has also been a dramatic increase in the number of women and black personnel who occupy high-ranking positions in the new South African Police Service (SAPS). And, most significantly, police violence during protests and demonstrations is now the exception, where before it had been, all too literally, the rule of the day. However, this is not the full story. The South African media continue to report instances of excessive force by SAPS members, notwithstanding the official agencies that are now in place to hold the police to account. POPCRU, the Police and Prisons Civil Rights Union, still takes to the streets to demonstrate against institutional racism in the police service. And community members continue to express outrage at the dubious professionalism of police interventions. So the question remains: is it really possible to change the police in South Africa – or indeed anywhere?

Police reform in transitional societies

Police reform, like any institutional transformation, is certainly possible but perhaps more than with any other institution, it is likely to have contradictory outcomes. Police organisations are characteristically bureaucratic with strict rules and entrenched structural hierarchies that get in the way of change (Rippy, 1990; Ray, 1995; Dean, 1995). Quasi-military management produces a style of supervision that is a 'disincentive to [the] risk-taking and creativity necessary for [an innovatory] problem solving orientation of policing' (Williams, 2003: 125). These organisational impediments are compounded in transitional societies still extricating themselves from the residue of authoritarian rule. All too often police in these societies do attempt to put the past behind them, only to be shackled anew by high levels of crime with clamour from all sides for the old strong-arm tactics. Signing up to a new declaration of rights has not precluded governments from calling up the old machinery of control in the name of 'security'.

The difficulties of police reform in transitional societies has been well documented. Pustintsev (2000) studied the (failed) process of police transformation in post-communist Russia, where leadership rhetoric and signing of agreements did little to appease public indignation at continuing police incompetence and abuse. During the first nine months of 1997 in St Petersburg alone, 3 366 Russian police officers were disciplined for misconduct, 1 541 were arrested for serious crimes and 721 complaints of police brutality were registered (Pustintsev, 2000).

The uncertain outlook for police reform has also been noted in other former Soviet bloc countries. In Hungary and Lithuania police transformation looked to be under way in the early 1990s, but by the end of the decade 'was running out of steam' (Koci, 1998: 307). New emphasis on police accountability, the rule of law and human rights all notwithstanding, the Hungarian police still turned out to be keeping members of the opposition under surveillance, and in both Hungary and Lithuania moves toward greater centralisation and militarisation undermined the commitment to civil liberties (Koci, 1998). Similar failures have been documented in the case of Bosnia-Herzegovina, where provisions of the 1995 Dayton agreement were intended to pry police forces loose from long histories of implication in military operations and human rights violations and make them conform to internationally recognised standards of policing with respect for rights and freedoms. There was screening of all officers already in service, with dismissal of those found to have perpetrated human rights violations, yet it has to be concluded that policing reform has still not made significant headway (Dominique, 2003).

And we can add to this list the numerous cases of ongoing police violence in such democratising states as El Salvador and Guatemala, along with Brazil and South Africa, which demonstrate that democratic constitutions and elections do not translate automatically into democratic policing. Police forces stubbornly retain their authoritarian structures and procedures, their proclivity for abuse, their bigotry towards minorities both in society and in their own organisations (Du Toit, 1995; Huggins, 1998; Shearing, 1995; Seleti, 2000).

Mozambique provides a good example of imperfect police reform in a southern African country in transition to democracy. Here, the 1992 General Peace Accord opened up new opportunities for the transformation of the police: a National Police Affairs Commission was established to monitor human rights commitment by the police, and police monitoring was also part of United Nations involvement in peace-building initiatives. Yet the reports continue of police corruption and brutality, inefficiency, bribe taking, complicity with criminals and rights violations. Trying to understand the persistence of these abuses, Seleti concludes that 'police identities in Mozambique are rooted within a powerful social structure that reproduces hegemonic relations of inequality. The images of the police as corrupt are embedded in routines of social and political life' (2000: 366).

Baker, who conducted fieldwork in Mozambique in June 2002, agrees with Seleti's analysis, but adds a number of other contributory factors: the legacy of civil ruin, a dearth of democratic politics; the absence of a real social movement to act as a counterbalance to the state; and low consciousness of human and civil rights among the Mozambican population. Added to this is a social context blighted by weapon proliferation and an increase in organised crime. Meanwhile the police organisation itself must also contend with a serious shortage of resources. Desks are often shared by three officers, there are no facilities for ballistic testing, and there is a perennial shortage of vehicles for police operations. The final impediment comes from the government itself which continues to view the 'primary role of the police in terms of regime support, rather than as providers of the order and protection of the law for citizens' (Baker, 2003: 156). Democracy, Baker concludes, has brought only minor changes to the force, compromising broader national commitment to reformed standards of governance.

Baker notes that policing may actually worsen in new democracies. He argues that

> police effectiveness has fallen since their hands are now more tied by human rights considerations. There has certainly been a greater freedom of movement of nationals and foreign crime networks that has facilitated crime ... Perhaps most significantly, new democracies have seen a breakdown of community and/or state structures that inhibit crime, whether as a result of the collapse of state authoritarian practices or the deep seated contempt for state law and violent responses to the state that those practices have provoked (2003: 144).

What the Mozambican case illustrates is that legacies of police culture and operational routine – in a context of broader social inequalities – are not the only obstacles to police reform in transitional democracies. Rachel Neild (1999) has reviewed the abortive attempts at police reform in many countries from Latin America to Asia and

Africa. She concludes that common features contributing to these failures are lack of money, lack of motivation, the resilience of old paramilitary habits and a generalised cop culture of incompetence in the face of high crime rates – compounded in transitional societies by the general context of poverty and disorder.

But police organisations trying to cast off a totalitarian past are not the only ones that struggle with reform. Police reform seems to be difficult even in countries with a long history of liberal democracy. The Los Angeles Police Department (LAPD) is a case in point. In 1991 the LAPD attracted heavy condemnation for brutality and racism after a black citizen, Rodney King, was severely beaten by four LAPD officers while being wrongly arrested. Reforms recommended by the subsequent Christopher Commission of Enquiry included more community-oriented policing, improved training, and civilian oversight. Measures were correspondingly set in place, yet the problems did not go away and the LAPD continues to provoke censure time and again.

In October 1999, the LAPD was hit with another major scandal when horrifying tales emerged of misconduct by officers based at Rampart police station. Rampart is a poor inner city neighbourhood populated by a mix of Latino immigrants and Korean shopkeepers and home to many violent gangs. Responding to high levels of gangsterism and drug-related crime, the local police formed a paramilitary unit which they called CRASH (Community Resources Against Street Hoodlums), and it was members of CRASH who were subsequently accused of raping a woman while on duty, beating suspects to the point of causing severe injury and even death, fabricating evidence in cases of false arrest, planting drugs on suspects, theft of cocaine, witness intimidation and planting guns on unarmed suspects (*Los Angeles Times*, 22 October 1999). Although these incidents had been going on since 1997, the Rampart CRASH unit remained protected by a code of secrecy and by supervisors who turned a blind eye. A Board of Inquiry concluded that the Rampart scandal 'devastated' the relationship between the LAPD and the public and 'threatened the integrity of the entire criminal justice system. Distrust, cynicism, fear of the police, and an erosion of community law and order are the inevitable result of a law enforcement agency whose ethics and integrity have become suspect' (LAPD Board of Inquiry Final Report, 2001: 13).

The British police have also been slated for their lack of resolve in implementing reforms. Over a period of two decades extensive changes have been set in motion affecting management systems, training and equipment, and more recently the introduction of uniformed community support officers (CSOs) to patrol the streets, and at every point the initiatives have been thwarted by 'reform resistant' police members (Savage, 2003: 172). According to Savage, the police service has been the most effective organisation within the public sector in 'resisting reform and subverting modernisation' (2003: 171). The Police Federation, which represents rank-and-file police, has resisted almost every aspect of the government's police reform agenda and made it very difficult to carry out. Whether or not the Federation buys into the latest Police Reform Bill (2003) has yet to be seen. The Federation has already made it clear that it does not support the CSO programme and it is likely that a watered-down version of the Reform Bill will materialise.

These examples raise a number of questions about police reform: Why do police persist with old and unreconstructed modes of behaviour despite reform initiatives? What role do police supervisors and managers have in implementing police organisational change? In what ways do historical legacies and memories impact on attempts at police reform? What mechanisms would be most effective in bringing about police organisational change? And how can lasting police cultural change be brought about?

A South African police special unit from the inside
This book attempts to answer these questions through an examination of the change process in the public police agency in South Africa. But the book is not about the entire police agency. It is a case study of one specialised unit, the Public Order Police (POP) unit, in a large South African city. It follows the story of transformation in the Durban public order unit (it had various names at various stages of its history, but 'Durban POP' is how it is remembered in this book) through ethnographic notes of observations and conversations that span a four-year period from 1996–2001. By immersing myself in the Durban POP unit I tried to discover how rank-and-file and senior police officers experienced, evaluated and responded to the transformation process that was taking place in the unit. Ethnographic case study was the focus I adopted, on the principle that while it may be feasible to assess structural change and even make comments about behavioural change from 'the outside', it is very difficult to interrogate more hidden values and beliefs without entering the everyday life spaces of those we are trying to understand.

Why did I select Durban POP as a case study? This was really a confluence of opportunity, political priority and theoretical judgement. The unique opportunity that arose for me to participate in the life of Durban POP is recounted by Superintendent Faizel Ally in his Foreword to this book. As the police in South Africa (and the POP unit in particular) entered a dimension of drastically changed and unsettling circumstances after the transition to democracy, police managers felt more than a little perplexed as to how to steer an organisation towards new objectives, new principles and new expected outcomes. For the first time in their history, South African police opened their doors to 'outsiders' who might help them find their way through the unfamiliar political geography of the new South Africa. Such an invitation would have been inconceivable under the old dispensation, least of all from a paramilitary unit such as POP.

Police transformation moved to the top of the agenda in the 1990s when the formally negotiated political settlement first began to be thrashed out in the multi-party forum (which included the apartheid National Party and organisations of the liberation movement) that debated how to 'dismantle the old undemocratic and repressive forms of social control in the society' (Levin, et al., 1994: 1). In August 1991, a new South African Police Strategic Plan came into effect, aimed at 'improving police-community relations by improving the SAP's image, service and organisational efficiency' (Rauch, 1991: 1). In 1994, the Safety and Security Green Paper was drawn up, which set new priorities: democratic control over the police service; accountability of the service; community consultation and involvement; demilitarisation of the service; and the need to improve the quality and professionalism of the service (Van Kessel, 2001). The Green Paper stressed that the police service must at all levels, including the higher echelons, represent the diversity (especially racial) of South African society. Creating a 'new' police service in South Africa also involved the complex task of amalgamating eleven existing police bodies into a single national service.

While the entire police service had to be transformed as part of the broad project of state democratisation, the unit engaged in public order policing, with its notorious history of unrestrained brutality, stood out as one of the sections most in need of fundamental reform. Additionally, public order units are highly visible: they police high-profile public events that attract media attention, and the way protests and demonstrations are policed is, in many ways, a shop window of state commitment to human rights and freedom of expression (Della Porta, 1998).

POP was arguably the unit that underwent the most comprehensive process of change within the SAPS. It was the first unit to develop a new policy document (in

1996) outlining the objectives of change and the principles and procedures required to put such change into effect. All members in the unit participated in retraining programmes that were guided and evaluated by multinational advisory teams. The Public Order unit embarked upon its process of organisational transformation in 1995, soon after the democratic transition. Previously known as the Riot Unit, later as the Internal Stability Division, this was the unit responsible for the policing of protests, demonstrations and any kind of situation deemed to be public disorder. Before the political transition, white men with strong allegiance to the apartheid government dominated this unit at all levels. Black officers were generally confined to the lower echelons of the hierarchy and had little authority or influence. The unit was heavily militarised and highly centralised in its organisation. Its members were widely perceived by (mostly) black South Africans as thugs and murderers in uniform.

Considering the sort of reputation the unit had acquired for itself, the new government decided that a 'new' renamed and refashioned Public Order Police unit had to be crafted. This unit was to be demilitarised/civilianised, community- and service-oriented, representative of the broader society, accountable and non-partisan, and committed to human rights. Its modus operandi had to change from repressive to tolerant, from reactive to preventative, from confrontational to consensual, from rigid to flexible – bringing it into line with international trends in public order policing (Della Porta and Reiter, 1998). And it was the changes taking place in public order policing internationally that provided an additional academic impetus for the study presented in this book. I was curious to explore parallels between the South African case and public order police transformation elsewhere and hoped thereby to contribute to debates about the possibilities and challenges of shifting the behaviour and value systems of paramilitary policing units.

For reasons already mentioned, the scope of this book is confined to one specialised police unit located in South Africa's third largest city. But the book is also confined by the time period in which the research was conducted – a stage in the lives of a group of police officers working together in public order policing. My ethnography of Durban POP ended in 2001, seven years after the transition to democracy and five years after new policies and training programmes were launched nationally in the unit. Being located in the unit during this time gave me the chance to observe the implementation of change mechanisms and to reflect, together with the unit members I grew to know, on whether transformation objectives had been realised.

The end of this study coincided with the onset of another change that was to affect the unit. In 2001 SAPS management decided it was time to revamp the unit once again. This involved changing the name, the identity and even the very role of the unit. Henceforth it was to be the Area Crime Combating Unit (ACCU), retaining essentially the same personnel as POP, but with its primary function being crime prevention, not crowd management. The paramilitary configuration of the unit, it was believed, would provide a basis for ACCU to 'hit hard at crime', tackling more serious and recurrent crimes occurring within particular police jurisdictions. How successful this recent change has been and what it has meant for the self-identities of members of the unit falls outside the scope of this book but would be a fascinating subject for future police ethnographies in South Africa.

The prospects for police reform in South Africa
My experience of Durban POP leads me to conclude that police transformation may not necessarily be quite as elusive an objective as sometimes supposed. The same authoritarian, bureaucratic and hierarchical character of police organisations that would seemingly impede organisational change may in fact be able to facilitate it. Police managers and supervisors are quite literally able to command desired forms of conduct. Judiciously exploited, the hierarchies of status and authority in most police organisations have the potential to promote change at a speedier pace than in most other organisations. Police generally follow top-down instructions without question and if they are told to change the way they do things, they generally comply, provided they feel they have the capacity. However, as this book will show, a top-down approach to organisational change may be effective in the short term but change brought about this way is likely to be mechanical, perfunctory and contingent on immediate circumstances. To achieve more enduring organisational change, the basic assumptions and values of police members need to change. As we shall see, and as Australian police scholar Janet Chan has pointed out, fundamental police organisational change requires a fundamental change in existing police culture (Chan, 1996).

Following Chan, my own observations confirm that the key to understanding police practice and values will always be the cultural knowledge, in its various dimensions, that police officers hold on to. This cultural knowledge is deeply embedded and it informs police rationales, their understanding of what they do, their ways of seeing the people they interact with and the methods they use. For real and fundamental change to occur in police organisations, it is these core values and assumptions that have to be transformed, and that is far easier said than done. It means changing the way police work is seen by police officers themselves, it means changing the way officers are rewarded for the work they do, and ultimately it means changing the very nature of police work itself and police workplace relations. In all of this, the role of supervisors and managers will be critical. I argue that for significant change what is needed are, paradoxically perhaps, both directive leadership and participatory management styles. Directive leadership and supervision provides rank-and-file officers with the guidance they need to be confident about changing the way they do things. Participatory management practices, on the other hand, allow individual officers to feel that they have a stake in the change process rather than being, as more than one Durban POP member[1] put it to me, mere 'Robocops' in an organisational machine. This in turn builds morale and commitment to the service, without which, organisational change will go nowhere. Participatory management traditions also have the potential to transform existing cultural knowledge pertaining to power relations and democratic practice.

My time with Durban POP unit did lead me to think that police transformation is a real possibility – and in some circumstances perhaps inescapable. There may be dinosaurs in the police who face towards the past, yet ultimately they too have to shift or they will find themselves marginalised by the very organisation they have helped to shape. But change processes in police organisations don't work smoothly, nor did they in Durban POP. For some they come as a devastating upheaval and for most they create unintended consequences. Along the way, rudiments of police culture may remain stuck, surfacing in unusual circumstances and at unpredictable times.

As the world around the police is transformed, their organisations are compelled to refashion themselves too. Indeed, the public police throughout the world are undergoing an 'intense period of self-questioning' (Bayley and Shearing, 1996: 586). They are, as Bayley and Shearing point out, re-examining their management styles, their accountability structures and mechanisms, their strategies, their organisational form, and even their objectives. The entire project of policing is undergoing dramatic changes as private policing and community-based policing enterprises expand in both democratic and democratising societies; the state police are losing their exclusive grip on the policing enterprise. But despite the fact that the 'state's monopoly on policing has been broken' (Bayley and Shearing, 1996: 586) in recent decades, it is still important for policing scholars to review the possibilities and limitations of (state) police organisational change. This is because so long as (relatively) sovereign states continue to exist, the public police will be mandated with the important functions of 'regulating public space, and processing that minority of crimes which can be cleared up, acting as the initial filter into the criminal justice system' (Reiner, 1992a: 270). Moreover, while wealthier citizens may be able to minimise their contact with the public police through their capacity to 'buy' security, poorer communities will continue to rely on the public police for most of their security requirements (Bayley and Shearing, 2001). It is for these reasons that it is important to theorise and evaluate attempts by the public police to democratise and clean up their acts.

Intentions of the book
This book follows the narrative of Public Order policing in Durban from its origins to what was in many ways the end of the story in 2001, just before Durban POP was reborn as the ACCU.

An initial theoretical chapter lays down some of the necessary parameters, derived from international police studies, for the historical and analytical explorations that follow. The next two chapters present what was, in nearly all respects, the shameful record of South African and Durban public order policing up to the extraordinary moment of turnabout in the nation's political, moral and psychological history, and then look past that moment to profile the men and women who made up Durban POP in the initial years of the new dispensation. Then comes the chapter that tells my own tale of (rather unexpectedly) stepping into the Durban POP narrative. I think it will convey something of the personal intensity of the experience for me, but I also present it as a seriously considered account of the methodological and ethical issues that researchers who step into the world of the police must take on board. The next four chapters, together with a final chapter of concluding reflections, are the ones in which I work through the implications of what my own research uncovered – research that, as things worked out, was interwoven with what came to be a close relationship of interaction both with working officers on field operations and with their superiors and with some of their policymakers in a time of intense planning and reconstruction in the national policing endeavour.

I have written this book in the hope of contributing to debate on police transformation, particularly in transitional societies. I also hope that it will convey some insight into the 'miracle' of transition in South Africa and the contradictory record of institutional change since the end of apartheid. The twists and turns should have been no surprise, but looking back on the path of change in an institution that in its day impinged so cruelly on life and death for South Africa's citizens may, perhaps, point to ways in which the long road ahead can be made less bumpy and unpredictable.

2

Issues in Police Organisational Change

POLICE ORGANISATIONS DO not on the whole have a reputation for enthusiastically embracing transformation, yet in reality, like any other organisation in contemporary society, they are constantly refashioning themselves to meet new circumstances and challenges. The changes are not always dramatic or fundamental but they are unavoidable nonetheless. Police are, in fact, perhaps more than other organisations, constantly obliged to adapt to new demands in confronting urgent social issues of crime and public disorder. And, as the most public face of the state, they are under continual pressure for their policies and their practice to reflect evolutions and changes in government and the forms of state.

In the past three decades, state police agencies in a number of countries have shifted toward a policing style that emphasises working partnerships with 'client' communities, problem solving rather than reactive policing, and increased accountability and transparency. Internally, police organisations have sought to introduce more participatory forms of management, less hierarchical organisational structures, and increased representation of minorities (Reiner, 1992b; Marks, 1997; Marenin, 1996; Mainwaring-White, 1983). These trends have been spurred on, in general, by three factors: global trends towards privatisation; more widespread democratic governance; and the realisation that traditional police strategies have not been effective in the fight against crime (Bayley and Shearing, 1996). More recently, however, police agencies have had to realign their resources and practices to meet international threats of 'terror', which has, in some instances, led to a remilitarisation of police modus operandi and the de-prioritisation of localised community safety. State pressure to get a grip on terror and international crime may also lead to a reclaiming of privatised policing functions by the state police.

Fundamental organisational transformation in police agencies is regarded nonetheless as extremely difficult, if not impossible, to effect. As we shall see below, the very nature of these organisations, at both the formal and the informal level, presents an obstacle to change. The theorisation of police transformation, moreover, remains limited (Mastrofski and Uchida, 1993: 354). In this chapter I attempt to outline a framework for understanding police organisational change. This framework provides a basis for analysing the changes that took place in the Durban Public Order Police unit, but will hopefully also indicate a schema for understanding change processes in other police agencies.

Drawing on the work of Australian policing scholar Janet Chan, there are four main theoretical points that underpin this study. Firstly, police organisations can and do change. I argue, controversially perhaps, that the hierarchical, command-driven nature of police organisations can actually facilitate change processes. Secondly, for behaviour to change and new values to be installed in police organisations, 'deep level' cultural change needs to occur, and the cultural knowledge of the police has to alter. To make this happen means having to shift many of the most basic assumptions and beliefs of police members; their 'stories' and their memories must be transformed. Thirdly, changing police organisations means fundamentally restructuring the way police work is organised, both in terms of how that work is evaluated and given recognition, and in terms of police labour-management relations. A change in the nature of work in police organisations represents a change not only in the structure, but also in the culture of the organisation. Finally, police organisational change will always be constrained where the social, political and legislative policing environment is unaccommodating.

The nature of police organisations – built to resist change?

Police organisations are usually conceived of in Weberian terms: typically rational bureaucratic entities that are stable and resistant to change (Albrow, 1970; Thompson and McHugh, 1990). They are seen as operating generally on a military-style ranking system with a strong emphasis on rule-bound behaviour enforced through a variety of disciplinary consequences (Bayley, 1994; Manning, 1977; Vollmer et al., 1951). Conceptualisations like this are hardly surprising when leading police authorities resort, as they so often do, to classical organisational theories in constructing police agencies with the emphasis on 'specialisation, limited spans of control, unity of command, elaborate policy and procedure, and position descriptions' (Kuykendall and Roberg, 1982: 242).

The (dominant) Weberian approach to understanding and managing police organisations creates various difficulties for change programmes. Police services tend to prioritise 'doing things right' rather than 'getting the right thing done'. They reward those who follow the rules rather than those who achieve results and take risks (Bayley, 1994). This makes police members reluctant to go beyond the call of duty and take creative initiatives. Officers are inclined to be more concerned with ostensible process than with the actual goals of an intervention, leading in turn to over-conformity to rules and regulations, and to reactive rather than proactive responses to problems. Relationships within the organisations become depersonalised with lower-rank officers tending to see laws and regulations as imposed from above and stripped of moral meanings (Van Heerden, 1982). Compliance on the part of low-ranking police officers may then be driven by purely instrumental incentives such as promotion, increased responsibility, or an opportunity to be in a command position. All this can make the intrinsic structure of the organisation a barrier to its achieving its own objectives (Bayley, 1994).

The Weberian understanding of police organisations is undoubtedly useful and helps in comprehending the limits of police organisational change. However, I would like to propose a somewhat more optimistic way of viewing the relationship between the formal component of police organisations and the capacity to bring about change. In the first place, the very fact that lower-ranking officers are bound by rules, legislation and lines of command means that behavioural change initiated or decreed from above is more likely to happen. It is unlikely that police in lower ranks would blatantly ignore such instructions. The behaviour change may be superficial and driven by extrinsic reward systems, but orders and instructions can nonetheless be an important *starting point* for police transformation. The typical organisational structure of the police lends itself to top-down initiation, at least, of reform. The real problem is how to ensure that change so introduced actually takes root and is 'bought into' by all police members of all ranks.

Aside from the rather pessimistic prognosis of the Weberian perspective, there are two other more fundamental problems with this account of police organisations.

Firstly, the view that contemporary police organisations are typically modern bureaucratic organisations is in any case too simplistic and by now rather out of date. Police organisations, some would argue, are better seen as 'mock' or 'symbolic' bureaucracies: only at first sight do police organisations 'seem bureaucratic in a strict Weberian sense' (Johnston, 1988: 52). There may indeed be strict division of labour, a clear hierarchy of ranks, a distinct career structure, but there is also a deep occupational culture that intervenes and shapes what 'real police work' is (Albrow, 1970). Perhaps the most unique feature of police organisations is in fact the high level of discretion that frequently prevails, particularly at the lower levels. This wide discretion is supported both by the law (in which there is seldom no room at all for interpretation) and by the immediate practicalities of day-to-day policing (Pike, 1985; Reiner, 1992a; Bent, 1974). And this discretion is plainly a deflection from notional organisational ideals of strict linearity of command and clear demarcation between superiors and subordinates.

Secondly, and perhaps even more to the point, police may indeed carry out their work along rationally bureaucratic lines of operation but the notion of police organisations as 'pure bureaucracies' ignores the multitude of informal dimensions also at play within these organisations. The inevitable web of organisational arrangements and interactions very often means that actions taken by the police in a given situation are driven less by rules than by an officer's own 'common sense theory of policing' – a common sense derived from basic assumptions, general police culture, and immediate task demands (Manning, 1977). The upshot is that police roles, functions, and conduct are always mediated by the day-to-day experiences of policing and the informal relationships within the organisation.

The informal dimensions of police organisations are at least as important in shaping police behaviour and organisational change as the more formal dimensions. In recent decades, following a general pattern in organisational studies (Blyton and Bacon, 1997; Winslow, 1998), these informal dimensions – in particular the notion of 'police culture' – have had a lot of attention from police scholars, and conceptions of occupational culture are presently very much the centre of focus in the sociology of policing (Brewer, 1991). The term 'police occupational culture' acquired its widespread currency from policing scholars who observed that laws and court decisions are limited in their ability to shape the behaviour and decisions of the police (Skolnick, cited in Ray, 1995). Reiner, building on Skolnick's work, contends that the legal framework governing policing is a permissive one which 'leaves considerable leeway for police culture to shape police practice in accordance with situational exigencies' (1992a: 108). Police culture has the potential to subvert, deflect, and distort managerially defined structures and practices. So while law and policy are by no means obliterated by police culture, they are refracted in one or another direction according to the way they resonate with the existing police culture.

Police culture

There are many typologies of police culture in the policing literature. Holdaway, for example, maintains that there are certain 'essential features' of police culture. These include a 'perception of the world as a place that is always on the verge of chaos, held back from devastation by a police presence. In this police view, people are naïve and potentially disorderly in all situations; control, ideally absolute control, is the fundamental police task' (Holdaway, 1989: 65). Bayley is equally pessimistic in his approach to what he calls the police 'occupational ethos'. According to Bayley, though police workers may claim to be professionals they are in fact more like blue-collar workers who resist taking responsibility and need constant supervision; rather than embracing discipline and accountability, they resent these and regard them as punishment; they work for monetary incentives and resent working where there are no clear material rewards; this is an ethos heightened by a working environment inclined to be 'sleazy', possibly dangerous, and conferring low social status (Bayley, 1994).

McConville and Shepherd (1992) argue likewise that all police organisations to some extent share a 'common police culture'. And when police tell themselves they are the 'thin blue line' separating chaos from order in society, that is also a motivation for policing to be aggressive and action-centred. Craving speed and excitement produces a disinclination for more predictable and less adventurous forms of police work. There is also an argument that a common police culture emerges because police organisations attract a particular 'personality type' – generally from the lower middle class, usually white, with a liking for action, and a leaning towards conservative values (Bent, 1974).

The notion that there is a common or intrinsic police culture and a corresponding police 'personality' is certainly open to challenge. Reiner, who has developed arguably the most influential model of police culture (or what he calls 'cop culture'), insists that police culture is 'neither monolithic, universal or unchanging' (1992a: 137). The form it takes will depend on the kind of people who make up a particular police organisation, the situations and problems they confront, the diverse philosophies that govern police organisations, and the wider cultural beliefs in a society. Even within a single police organisation it will be possible to detect what Brewer refers to as 'lines of fissure' in the occupational culture between different sub-groups of police based on rank, race, function, religion, and gender (Brewer, 1991).

Cop culture may not be monolithic, universal or static, but Reiner does nevertheless note certain core characteristics. These stem from the nature of the work police do and include:

- **a sense of mission**: police see their work as not just a job but a vocation, a mission to protect innocent victims from evil forces that could harm them.
- **cynicism**: the police are exposed to the harrowing side of society and consequently become hardened and bitter.
- **hedonism**: police work is regarded as fun, exciting and challenging.
- **a search for excitement and action**: routine work gets a low priority. Police like work that is action-oriented and promises thrills.
- **machismo**: there is a strong masculine ethos in police organisations with a climate of sexism and anti-gay intolerance.
- **suspicion of outsiders**: the police are always suspicious of the outside world and constantly on the lookout for danger and signs of trouble.
- **isolation from society**: the police tend to be isolated from the rest of society, both at work and outside of the workplace, and they find it difficult to interact with people who are not part of the policing world. That fosters close solidarity within the organisation while to outsiders the police present the impersonal face of authority.
- **moral and political conservatism**: the police have a generally conservative world-view in line with dominant ideologies in a given society. They value stability and order and are uncomfortable with any threats to the status quo; they are likely to be antagonistic toward individuals or groups that challenge the status quo. They incline to prejudiced and stereotypical views of their fellow citizens. There is also evidence in some countries of police support for right wing political groups.
- **pragmatism**: the police see themselves as having to get a job done with the least fuss possible. They are generally anti-theoretical and concrete in their thinking and shy away from innovation and experimentation, preferring to stick to tried and tested practices and principles.

Pragmatism, conservatism and isolation are all intrinsically obstacles to change. Police pragmatism dictates a preference for doing things the way they always have been done rather than experimenting with new and untested approaches. Conservatism inclines police to embrace things as they are rather than actively engage in a new ordering of society. Stereotyping and prejudice render the police intolerant of incorporating new (mostly minority) groups into their own organisational body, and reinforce differential treatment of the communities they serve. What complicates matters further is that police culture itself, if not static, is still relatively enduring or 'fixed' – in Reiner's terms, 'a patterned set of understandings which help police officers to cope with and adjust to the pressures and tensions which confront the police' (1992a: 109). For police work brings with it endless pressures and stresses that render coping mechanisms necessary: vulnerability to allegations of misconduct; unreasonable demands from communities; physical danger; incompatible expectations; and public misunderstandings of the role of the police (Goldstein, 1990).

Reiner's concept of cop culture has been very influential among policing scholars, including those who have studied the police in South Africa. Brogden and Shearing (1993), for example, have made use of Reiner's concept in trying to understand the horrific brutality of the South African police in the years 1948–87. They see police behaviour during the apartheid era as a product both of normative expectations and practices within the SAP (police culture) and of the formal rules that governed policing. Both were geared primarily toward the maintenance of white domination, but police culture was the 'agency that control[led] and direct[ed] police behaviour in South Africa' (1993: 42). Brogden and Shearing comment that the SAP police culture contains 'all the elements universally found among rank-and file police' (1993: 43). They add that to understand police culture in South Africa one also has to understand the Afrikaner host culture that fed that police culture. This host culture embraced very particular religious and political and also technological discourses, which were inculcated throughout the police force via processes of recruitment, training and indoctrination.

The terminology is now well established in the policing literature, but a number of problems have been raised regarding conceptions of 'cop culture'. Some argue that 'police culture' has become overused and reified as a concept. Fielding, for example, regards the term as 'extremely slippery and unuseful' (1989: 86). He finds it simplistic to assume that this police culture is something all new police recruits are subjected to and imbibe. New recruits, Fielding argues, do not enter the police as ideological blank slates, they come as individuals with their own world-views and experiences. Individuals may accommodate or resist police culture; when police culture (whatever this may be) is introduced to the new recruit, he or she decides what to internalise. But even when aspects of cop culture are internalised, they do not in any direct way determine police behaviour. Culture only shapes attitudes and predisposition; it does not determine them. The extent to which cop culture influences individual police officers, and the form this influence takes, is dependent on each officer's own experience of his or her work, as well as his or her individual motivations and commitments.

Fielding's contribution is very useful in alerting us to the fluidity and malleability of police culture. It also forces us to explore simultaneously both the impact of collective features of policing on the individual police officer as well as the way the individual officer influences and responds to the organisation. Police officers in this view are actors (not cultural dupes) who negotiate and rework existing norms, values and practices in police organisations. But they do this, Fielding argues, within the existing institutional and symbolic framework of the organisation.

Another critic of the way police culture has been understood is Herbert (1998), who maintains that there is a mistaken tendency to view police culture as autonomous and consequently to undervalue the importance of formal rules, policies and laws in determining police behaviour and providing boundaries. Police culture itself, he believes, is composed of both informal and formal aspects of policing that cannot easily be separated. In Herbert's view, police culture is based on multiple normative orders or sets of rules and practices. Normative orders are oriented around a central value, and one of the fundamental normative orders of the police is a basic valuing of the law. The law structures police action, and as the continual point of reference for police behaviour, the regular source of justification for what the police do, it has to be seen as an intrinsic element in police culture. Herbert's emphasis is an important caution against analysis that too readily divorces the formal from the informal dimensions of policing.

But perhaps the most penetrating criticism (framing many of the assumptions in this book) comes from Schein who argues that in organisational studies generally, the term 'occupational culture' is used very vaguely. Indeed, Schein argues, what 'culture' actually signifies is left unexamined: simply a term that loosely indicates norms, values and ways of thinking and reacting. His own position is that sets of values, traditions, orientations, styles of thinking or ways of doing business are more appropriately to be seen as the artefacts rather than the constituents of culture (see also Van Buskirk and McGrath, 1999). Culture, Schein insists, incorporates these elements, but far more deeply embedded (and perhaps less conscious) is another level of organisational culture, which is the 'set of shared, taken for granted implicit *assumptions* that a group holds' (1996: 236). Culture, in this view, becomes entrenched in memories, stories, and 'tried and tested' practices in the field. Unlike values and norms, which are relatively perceptible, assumptions are seldom questioned. Members of an organisation may then not even be aware of their 'culture' until they are confronted with another one. Consequently, Schein argues, attempts at organisational change have to move beyond statements of value change to challenge more basic suppositions about the world and about the workplace which organisational members share (1996). Because, in the police, the culture is so solidly embedded, police reform means having to dislodge a lot of very deep-rooted and cherished articles of faith.

Understanding police cultural change

Theorists of police culture seldom take account of these deep-level components that Schein writes about. Two notable exceptions – Della Porta and Chan – have been very helpful for my own thinking about the history and evolution of Durban POP and need to be looked at here.

Della Porta sees police culture as integrally bound to the nature of the *knowledge* that underpins what police do, relating both to their own work and to the environment in which they work. In her view, police culture includes the images that police have of their own role along with their assumptions about external reality, which in turn includes their views about the public they police (1995a: 2). These images and assumptions constitute the key components of police knowledge. Police knowledge is the real foundation of policing, fundamental to the collective identity of the police, and it functions as a filter for the types of practices the police employ (Della Porta and Reiter, 1998). Police knowledge, then, provides a long-term underlying influence on policing styles and practice. For example, on-the-spot decisions in crowd management situations are often determined by stereotypes that the police have about particular groups of people and situations. These stereotypes are frequently congruent with dominant political discourse. Such stereotypes can become 'guidelines for police interventions' (Della Porta and Reiter, 1998: 14). And while police culture is fairly impervious, it can also change if there are historic turning points (such as dramatic shifts in government) and if the police environment changes (Della Porta, 1995a).

Della Porta (along with her co-authors) takes up Schein's emphasis on the centrality of basic assumptions and beliefs to police organisational culture. She underlines the significance of police self-perceptions and of their constructions of the external reality for what they actually do in their everyday practice, though she also insists on the importance always of context – the organisational framework of the police and the wider conditions of the prevailing environment – for any understanding of police culture.

Janet Chan provides the account of police culture that I have found to be the most useful of all. She explicitly adopts Schein's approach to organisational culture, emphasising that it is something both deeply embedded and difficult (though not impossible) to change. She is in agreement with Della Porta that police culture should be viewed as shared organisational knowledge shaped by a given political and social order. Police culture, as she describes it,

> ... contains basic assumptions about descriptions, operations, prescriptions and explanations about the social and physical world. At the same time, members of a group operate in a particular social and political context that consists of certain structural arrangements of power, interests and authority. Police practice is then the product of interaction between this shared knowledge and the structural conditions (1999: 105).

This shared cultural knowledge informs police rationales, understandings of actions, ways of seeing the people they interact with, and their use of tactics and strategies.

Borrowing from Sackman (1991) Chan identifies four dimensions of police cultural knowledge:

- **axiomatic knowledge**: the basic rationale for policing and why things are done the way they are – the police mandate. This would relate most closely to what Reiner calls the police 'mission' (1992a).
- **dictionary knowledge**: the categories according to which police perceive their environment (black townships, white suburbs, sporting events . . .) and the people they come into contact with (blacks, environmentalists, trade unionists, drug dealers . . .).
- **directory knowledge**: how police go about doing their work and the processes that are to be followed – the methods that are used.
- **recipe knowledge**: the menu of acceptable and unacceptable practices in particular situations. Recipe knowledge also refers to what is normative – embedded, for example, in police value systems.

Each of these four dimensions of cultural knowledge is fundamental to the way police go about doing their work and the choices they make. They endure because they have emerged as ways of understanding and coping with the external environment. As we shall see in this book, established ways of coping are reinforced time and again either because they provide good solutions to problems or because they assist in reducing anxiety in uncertain situations. Newcomers to the policing occupation 'typically learn the culture through anecdotes and "war stories" told by more senior officers' (Chan, 1999: 112). For police organisational change to happen, the stories that police tell must change (Shearing, 1995; Chan, 1999). The difficult question to answer is: How can police individuals and collectives actually create new stories and memories and what is needed for police to abandon nostalgia for the bad 'good old days'? It is one I attempt to tackle in the final chapter of this book.

Chan stresses that accounts of police culture should allow for the possibility of both change and resistance: police culture should not be regarded only as an impediment to change. It is also potentially a space for creativity and new kinds of interpretation – although, since police culture is a 'deep phenomenon', change is never unproblematic. As we shall see, police organisational change is possible, but it is limited by deeply held values and assumptions as well as by environmental constraints.

A final very important point made by Chan is that in understanding police culture it is important to examine the interaction between what she refers to as the *field* (objective, historical relations or the structural conditions of police work) and the *habitus* (dispositions, established ways of perceiving and acting). Chan reminds us that 'members of a group operate in a particular social and political context that consists of certain structural arrangements of power, interest and authority' (1999: 105). It is the interaction between this 'field' and the shared cultural knowledge of the police that gives rise to police practice or 'habitus'. Changes in cultural knowledge need to be supported by changes in the field in order for real behavioural change to take place. Change in field and change in habitus reinforce one another.

Though the elements of Chan's schematisation may not all be new, her synthesis of debate in the policing literature is invaluable for the caution it gives against accepting shallow, oversimplified notions of cop culture if one wants to think seriously about what is realistically possible in police reform.

Police organisational change: possibilities and limits

Brogden and Shearing argue that there are traditionally two approaches to transformation in police organisations. One is to tighten the rules and legislative framework, focusing on the formal component of police organisations. The other gives priority to the informal component of police organisations, 'meet[ing] police culture head on and attempt[ing] to change it directly' (1993: 96). Few would argue that rule-tightening is an adequate mechanism for organisational change, but with rules and regulations always of so much consequence to police organisations and their members, it is important to know how these need to be 'exploited' to bring about change.

The formal structure of police organisations gives police managers and supervisors considerable power and influence. It follows that a top-down approach to police organisational change must have some value. Police managers and supervisors are quite literally able to order certain forms of conduct, at least in the immediate term, meaning that the distinct levels of status and authority in most police organisations, judiciously employed, have potential to push change at a speedier pace than in many other organisations. It makes sense, therefore, to propose that change should be initiated from above and that the police leadership should provide focal ideas as to where the change process is heading, what is to be achieved, and how to achieve it. Police leaders are also in a good position to dismantle old and discredited practices and encourage new and appropriate ones.

However, there are limits to what a top-down, management-defined change process can achieve. Police culture, as we have already noted, while not fixed is nonetheless deeply embedded and can all too readily subvert change initiatives. So how can (or does) the culture change?

Nearly all the literature recognises that this is the key question, yet there is still very little in the way of constructive suggestion. But before we try to come up with some answers, there is a prior question to be considered: How exactly do we measure or evaluate organisational change in the context of organisational culture? What constitutes *effective* change?

Evaluating change in police organisations is complicated for a number of reasons. In the first place, measures of performance or of 'good policing' are limited; performance indicators for the police have long been a thorny issue. Evaluating police performance is difficult because it involves both internal organisational processes and external public functions (preventing disorder and crime) which are notoriously difficult to measure. Nor is this a difficulty unique to police agencies; figuring out what has changed is complicated in any organisation. It may be easy enough to judge whether structural change has taken place but it is another matter to say whether individuals have changed, or what degree of change there has been in the more informal components of an organisation. Change can also be uneven: it may occur in some areas and not in others.

Organisational theorists Ogbonna and Harris (1998) suggest three aspects of organisations to scrutinise in assessing change: are there changes in the material manifestations of the organisation (the structure); are there changes in the behaviour of organisational members; and are there changes in the values of the members of the organisation?

Behavioural and structural changes, Ogbonna and Harris suggest, are easier to observe; change in values (including assumptions and beliefs) is a good deal more opaque. Organisational values may be 'reinvented', 'reinterpreted', or 'reoriented'. Reinvention refers here to the 'recycling of existing values so that they are presented as aligned with newly espoused values' (1998: 290); existing values become camouflaged in the rhetoric of new values, but new values themselves are not readily accepted. Reinterpretation refers to the development of ideas that are modified but still remain broadly in line with presently espoused values; new values then are partially accepted and there is a maintaining of at least some aspect of the old existing values. Finally, reorientation refers to the 'seemingly unquestioned adoption of newly defined values replacing existing value sets' (1998: 291). What mostly happens, Ogbonna and Harris suggest, is that members of an organisation that is in a process of change either reinvent or reinterpret existing value systems.

These distinctions remind us, then, on the one hand that behavioural change may signify mere compliance rather than actual commitment to a new value system, and on the other, that change at the level of either structure or behaviour doesn't automatically translate into change in the value system. And organisational change that doesn't really extend to the value system may be extremely fragile. With the embeddedness of (cop) culture as a further factor to contend with, it is to be expected that a top-down and rule-tightening reform strategy will in all likelihood deliver no more than limited change at the structural and behavioural level, representing mere compliance rather than a thoroughgoing reorientation of values and belief systems (Ogbonna and Harris, 1998).

How then is systematic and lasting and genuine reform, change at the deeper level of values, to be set in train? At this point we return to the work of Janet Chan for the help I think it provides in tackling this question.

Chan's account of police culture suggests that what is required for police organisational change is 'deep level' change. This would entail change in the cultural knowledge of the police: by implication, change in the most basic assumptions and beliefs of police members. Change in cultural knowledge may not translate directly into structural change (which is in any case easier to achieve) but it does signify behavioural and value changes.

In Chan's schema, axiomatic cultural knowledge should be the most important target for change in the *habitus*, given that it encompasses the rationale that police subscribe to in their work. This involves changing assumptions about the essential objective and mandate that drives reform of policing strategies and methods.

There are a number of ways in which change in axiomatic knowledge can be brought about. In the first place, there needs to be a clear statement of new objectives and principles and the reasoning behind them; the fundamental rationale for the existence and functioning of the police organisation may need to be redefined. New desired outcomes must be defined that can be appropriately measured. Nor will the rhetoric of mandates and mission statements on its own supply the mechanisms to actually put into effect the new methods and strategies that comprise reformed directory and recipe knowledge. Police need to grasp the positive reverberations of doing things in new ways and this requires positive feedback from police managers and supervisors when changed approaches are attempted – and, if possible, positive reinforcement too from the recipients of police services. Police need to see that new methods do actually work. All this will mean a fundamental rethinking of systems of reward and of indicators of 'good' performance (Bayley, 1994).

It is equally important, however, that change in dictionary knowledge accompanies change in axiomatic, directory and recipe knowledge. Positive new ways of defining and viewing the situations police find themselves in and the people they come into contact with may flow automatically from new methods and strategies. However, as this book demonstrates, beliefs and stereotypes about groups of people and their circumstances are often very difficult to transform since they are all too likely to be reinforced not only by on-going sub-group dynamics within the police organisation but also each time a tricky or abrasive encounter takes place between police and specific communities. The stereotyping will fade only as police officers come to appreciate diversity both within their own immediate organisation and within the broader police environment.

Sustained behavioural change in police organisations also calls for close supervision because of the high levels of discretion and autonomy that operate in the way police go about their day-to-day work. Changes in values, beliefs and assumptions are difficult and slow to realise in the first place and it takes conscious effort to maintain them; behaviour easily reverts to the old ways so long as existing cultural knowledge persists. Rank-and-file officers (especially in the early stages of transformation) need guidance and oversight when they tackle sensitive operations. Goldstein (1990) stresses how important good frontline supervision is when the experience police have of their daily working lives is so crucially shaped by the direction that their supervisors at this level provide. This means that wherever possible frontline supervisors need to be visible and present when rank-and-file members are 'on the job'.

All these changes in cultural knowledge or *habitus* need to be supported by change in the *field*. Chan has stressed that police culture cannot be separated from the social, political and economic context in which it develops, nor from the structure and composition of the police organisation itself. If *field* is not changed in support of changes in *habitus*, *habitus* will revert to what there was before. For example, if police supervisors attempt to change cultural knowledge (such as which methods are acceptable and which are not) and the changes they give orders for are contradicted by training or policy (both of which are part of the *field* of policing), officers may simply refuse to go along with those orders. Additionally, if institutional racism persists as a feature of the organisational field, it will in all likelihood be extremely difficult for officers to change their attitudes and demeanour towards minorities. Without oversight mechanisms and systems to ensure accountability, abuse and misconduct may likewise persist despite attempts at developing new value systems. Equally, disempowered and dispossessed population groups may lack means and confidence to challenge police misconduct. The Durban POP story in this book demonstrates how difficult it is to effect change in the police *habitus* when there are deficits in the transformation of the *field* – poor dissemination of new policy, deep social cleavages (based on race and gender) within the police organisation, and limited capacity for mobilisation and contestation on the part of the communities themselves who are most affected by police wrongdoing.

Cultural change and the organisation of work
I have emphasised the importance of supervision and pointed out advantages in a

top-down approach for the early stages of transformation. At the same time, for police to embrace new value systems there has to be an environment where all officers, regardless of rank, can make a contribution to the process; excluding the rank-and-file is likely to leave them feeling disillusioned, manipulated, frustrated and demotivated (Washo, 1984). They may comply with reform directives, but they will do so grudgingly (Brown, 1993). Some may resist change completely if they feel that it poses a threat to self-definition and self-esteem (Hogg and Terry, 2000).

Drawing rank-and-file police into decision-making runs contrary to traditional police management practices in which the favoured mode is command and control. Even though, in day-to-day practice, individual officers exercise a surprisingly high degree of discretion in what they choose to do, communication typically still flows downward, rank takes priority over knowledge, and a plethora of rules, directives and regulations cover every aspect of activity (Bayley, 1994: 64). Put more bluntly, 'the dominant form of policing today continues to view police officers as automatons' (Goldstein, 1990: 27). For Goldstein this means that officers are expected to conform, they are treated impersonally, and they get rewarded only if they unthinkingly comply. Make that a paramilitary unit, and you have the archetypal Robocop production line.

It is unlikely that police services will ever really abandon linear ranking systems but there have been attempts (mostly in Western Europe and North America) to move toward more participatory forms of management (Rippy, 1990; Goldstein, 1990; Bayley, 1994). Partly this is the result of police organisations 'buying into' corporate practices that encourage a flattening of organisational structures to allow more scope for participatory management (Fleming and Lafferty, 2000). This is a shift that goes along with a broader commitment by the public service in recent years to codetermination practices, modelled to a large extent on German industrial relations policies and practices (Lawrence, 2000).

An altered style of management is also likely to be important in the evolution of new organisational culture. Wilms has argued that real commitment to changed culture will only develop when workplace practices and relations are transformed. The key to successful organisational transformation in the workplace (both in the private and the public sector), Wilms believes, is the development of new management-worker relationships. Transformation requires 'fundamental changes that can emerge only after the systems of production and the underlying cultures have been altered' (Wilms, 1996: 282). Any cultural change in an organisation requires change in the way its members relate to one another. Participatory, person-centred management entails more than simply a change of heart on the part of management. It means comprehensive revision of the way the work process is organised, which in turn will, potentially, modify the entire occupational culture – values, assumptions and ways of coping.

Participatory management has been the subject of growing attention in theories of organisations and work, in South Africa and abroad (Beckhard and Harris, 1987; Ahrne, 1994; Wilkinson, 1989; Adler and Webster, 2000). It promises, as Johanson puts it, that 'when members of an organisation are allowed to participate in decision making that relates to changes in their work environment, they are more positive toward change than those who are simply ordered to change their work processes' (2000: 393). For members to feel committed to organisational change, and to the effectiveness of the organisation more broadly, they need to feel a sense of ownership in the organisation and have the perception that its future and theirs are tied together. The dominant message in organisational management theory is that democratic leadership is better both for morale and productivity, and for communication and decision-making.

Participatory management is a relatively new concept for police agencies and the question that invariably gets asked is whether it undermines the rank and command system. The system of rank is, at least in theory, based on skill, expertise, and most of all, authority, none of which need be called in question by the new system of management. If there is agreement on the credentials that put someone in a position of authority (authority rather than power), then an open, inclusive management style should give that authority even greater legitimacy, conducive to increased trust and respect, and willing, not just grudging, compliance.

Goldstein (1990) has argued that transformational initiatives in police organisations (like a shift to problem-oriented policing) present an opportunity to rethink management issues and styles. In a programme of change much hinges on rank-and-file involvement at the level where so many of the problems present themselves: the boredom and lack of challenge associated with most police work; the lack of dignity accorded to low-ranking police officers; the feeling on the part of police officers that they are achieving little; and the lack of opportunity for upward mobility. These problems can be alleviated if officers of whatever rank feel a sense of importance and self-worth and have freedom to think and act independently within acceptable boundaries. Policies are needed to help officers see the benefit of their work; to provide positive feedback; to mark out clear career and promotion pathways. All these must go hand-in-hand with ensuring the 'active participation of employees in the development and implementation of policies and programmes' (Goldstein, 1990: 154). None of this should imply diminishing the authority of supervisors and managers, but it does put a new emphasis on creativity, mutual respect, and open communication between all ranks. It means that supervisors must play a role as facilitators and guides; and a support role also requires constant contact with rank-and-file members.

Can the police change?

Changing police organisations is a difficult, though not impossible task. It is, arguably, relatively easy to *modify* police behaviour in a very short period of time given the structured rules and hierarchies of police organisations and a police culture that encourages compliance. However, behavioural change spurred on by managerial directives and rule-tightening, while useful and even effective in altering behaviour in the short term, generates behavioural change likely to be both superficial and erratic. Long-term, sustainable transformation requires fundamental change in police culture and in the organisational and environmental field in which the police work.

The Durban POP story tells us that to block regression to old and discredited ways, change needs to happen at all levels of cultural knowledge and in the structural field in which police work. More than simply altering policy and training, this means fundamentally transforming the belief systems and work practices of both managers and rank-and-file police. As we shall see in the chapters to follow, without changing embedded assumptions, values and beliefs, any attempt at police organisational change is likely to be short-lived and perfunctory, while treasured memories of the past persist and stories glorifying bygone golden days of policing go on being recalled.

In this book I try to capture something of the importance of stories and memories for police in the Durban POP unit and how these stories shape actions and reactions. I think it will demonstrate, too, that police officers do not simply imbibe 'police culture'. Rather, they are social actors who interpret and shape their social environment. Police are active decision-makers but their actions are guided by the assumptions they learn and the possibilities that exist for them. Armed with new cultural knowledge and bolstered by a supportive structural environment, police will hopefully be able to put the old behind them and step out to meet the challenges of the new.

3

From Green to Blue
The Origins of Durban POP

Nay' i-meloyelo *(ma)*	Here comes the mello yello (*Mama*)
sesisengozini (*mo we ma*)	we are now in danger
Nay' i-meloyelo	here comes the mello yello
Mama mus' ukukhala	mama don't cry
Ngoba kuzulunga ma	because we will be ready
Nay' iBotha	Here comes the [president] Botha
Sesisengozini	we are now in danger
Nay' iVlok	Here comes Vlok
Sesisengozini	we are now in danger
Mama sul' inyembezi (*we ma*)	Mama stop lamenting
ngoba sizonqoba ma	because we shall overcome
Mama sengiboshiwe	Mama I've been arrested
mama duduzeka (*we ma*)	Mama be comforted

IN THE 1980s township youths chanted this freedom song in defiance of the endemic presence of the paramilitary police storming into the townships in the 'mello yellos' (*izimeloyelo*), the big yellow and khaki-green military vehicles used by the police responsible for riot control and public order. These vehicles (Casspirs and Nyalas) were armoured for protection against landmines and small-arms fire. The Casspir is normally armed with single or twin 7.62 mm machine-guns. Some Casspirs mounted 20 mm cannons. There is a firing port facing each seat in the vehicle. 'Mello Yello' was a caffeine-loaded soft drink from the Coca-Cola stable in a lurid yellow can.

The song gives us the bitter conjunction of two wildly diverse social processes where the anodyne neverland of branded marketing morphs into the brutal actuality of paramilitary intervention. In these years it was young people, defiant and on the streets, who generally bore the brunt of riot police attentions – in or out of the menacing vehicles. And it was their mothers who wept (and whom they tried to comfort) when the mello yellos thundered along the township roads.

The Casspirs and the Nyalas came to symbolise the militarised, violent, ruthless policing of public order at the height of apartheid. During the apartheid years and well into the 1990s sweeping definitions of public disorder were writ large in legislation and policing policy. Public order legislation seemed 'to include all political activity outside of the narrow limits which the state [considered] legitimate, where "political" in itself was defined widely to include economic, industrial and social activity' (Brewer et al., 1988: 178). These definitions were far-reaching in their consequences for security policy. Brutal and partisan public order policing was set firmly in place as the order of the day – and in later years remained stubbornly resistant to change even when the political order turned entirely on its head.

This chapter outlines the history of public order policing in South Africa from the initial establishment of the South African Police (SAP) in 1913 through to the programme, set in motion in 1995, for eventual transformation of the specialised public order policing unit.[1] In each period incidents have been selected to illustrate the nature of both protest and policing. The chapter aims to convey the conjunctions across these decades between the nature of the state, political protest and resistance, and the policing of public order. This history will stand as backdrop for the ethos, the make-up and the disposition of the agency (and its personnel) responsible for the policing of public order. It will set the scene for our attempt to understand the potentialities and the difficulties of transformation.

Early days
For most of the twentieth century, the policing of public order in South Africa moved by and large in a diametrically contrary direction to what was happening in Western Europe and more particularly in Britain. From the 1930s through to the 1960s the British police were concerned to cultivate an image of friendly protectors and crime fighters. There were very few restrictions on public protest, and when crowds needed to be policed, inoffensive push-and-shove methods were considered adequate. A very different picture, however, developed in the colonised world. In these countries,

the state police were the agency with principal responsibility for enforcing the laws of the colonies, regulating indigenous population groups and protecting settlers and their property. Crime was relegated to a secondary concern as energies were directed at controlling local populations and repressing any form of resistance disorder (Killingray and Clayton, 1989).

When the SAP was established in 1913 it was shaped by colonial polity and the administrative legacy of frontier wars. From its inception, the force had a disciplinary ideology and a militarised administrative structure (Nasson, in Killingray and Clayton, 1989). The ethos was that of 'policeman-cum-soldier': an emphasis on military discipline, a confrontational thrust, and comprehensive paramilitary-style training in riot control and counter-insurgency (Van der Spuy, 1990). Policing in the early part of the century was also shaped by what Van der Spuy has called an 'emergent ethnic and political mobilisation of Afrikaner nationalism' (1990: 90). Few national institutions, least of all the police, escaped this influence, and so was set in train the long drawn-out struggle within the SAP between resurgent Afrikaner nationalism and British settler hegemony. While the early police bodies were largely made up of men of British origin, by the late 1920s the majority of rank-and-file policemen were drawn from rural Afrikaner communities, leading increasingly to internal fragmentation and contested organisational loyalties.

Internal friction between British colonial authority and Afrikaner nationalism was certainly in itself a significant dynamic in South African policing history, but it masks an even more significant feature pervasive in national policing from its inception until the 1990s: categorical intolerance and repression of black resistance. It could well be said that the history of policing in South Africa is indeed the history of public order policing, insofar as that means, as Van der Spuy puts it, 'a history of the policing of large collectivities of black people, such as black industrial strikers, tribal groups at war, factions on the mines' (1990: 92), along with black demonstrators and protestors. Little attention was paid to 'normal' crimes, certainly, when persons from the black majority were the victims.

From the 1920s onward, the police played a key role in the ordering of South African society through their enforcement of segregation laws. The 1923 Urban Areas Act decreed that black people could reside in urban areas only if they were 'economically active', and were to be regarded principally as a labour reserve at the disposal of whites (Posel, 1991). So began the formalised geographical segregation of racial groups, with the police commissioned to make sure that black people stayed in their designated areas by arresting any black persons without a 'pass book' authorising them to be in the urban areas. In 1948 the National Party (NP) was voted into power by an essentially white electorate with a mandate, diligently pursued for the next two decades, to ensure the segregation of racial groups in South Africa and once and for all confirm white domination. A sequence of policies was set in place during the course of the 1950s which together formed the cornerstone of apartheid, including the Population Registration Act (1950), Job Reservation and Separate Amenities Act (1953), the Group Areas Act (1950), and the Bantu Education Act (1953).[2]

The promulgation of these Acts created the impetus for massive urban protest and boycotts led by formal political organisations such as the African National Congress (ANC) and the South African Communist Party (SACP). In 1952 the ANC embarked on a Defiance Campaign to challenge apartheid segregation and white supremacy. The government responded with mass arrests and police raids on the homes of anyone involved in resistance politics; 8 500 people were arrested and sent to prison.

But government reaction went beyond arrests. The Criminal Law Amendment Act of 1953 decreed that 'any person who committed any offence by way of protest, or in support of any campaign against the law could be sentenced to a whipping of ten strokes, a fine, three years in jail, or a combination of any of these penalties. On a second conviction, whipping or imprisonment as well as a fine were obligatory' (Karis and Carter, 1977: 6). The Act also provided for serious punishment of anyone who used 'words' calculated to cause someone to commit an offence as a means of protest. A second piece of legislation in the same year, the Public Safety Act (1953), empowered the Governor General to declare a state of emergency if he thought public order was under serious threat. During states of emergency, a person could be summarily arrested and detained; the state's only obligation was to submit the names of those detained to parliament within 30 days. The police, naturally, were the body responsible for making the arrests and securing the convictions.

Despite the government response, the Defiance Campaign was revived in 1955. There were three main wings to this campaign: boycotts of Bantu Education, anti-pass protests, and demonstrations against forced removals and relocations. There followed yet another Act restricting civil liberties: the Riotous Assembly Act of 1956, which authorised the minister to act whenever he was satisfied that a person was 'promoting feelings of hostility between whites and non-whites' (Karis and Carter,

1977); meetings of more than ten black people were prohibited unless special permission was granted beforehand. For the next decade and beyond, the police actively harassed black people who were not carrying passes, arrested them for minimal or no offences and forcibly removed many thousands of black families from their homes in urban areas and relocated them in outlying rural districts.

In 1956, 156 prominent activists were arrested and charged with treason. For the next four years, the state tried to prove that they had been involved in a countrywide conspiracy to violently overthrow the state. The trial finally ended on 29 March 1961 with a 'not guilty' verdict but the stage had been set for more complete and systematic repression of protest and mass organisation in the 1960s.

The sixties: zero tolerance
Internationally, the policing of protest in this decade witnessed some interesting changes. British police cultivated, as we have already suggested, the image of the friendly, civilianised officer; as late as 1968 'the dominant image of policing political protest . . . was of lines of bobbies with arms linked, pushing and shoving against lines of demonstrators, with whom they were in "eyeball-to-eyeball" contact' (Jefferson, 1990: 1). This consensual, non-forceful style of policing was possible, according to Jefferson, because the post-war period in Britain was characterised by political stability and an emphasis on state compensation for a citizenry that had been socially and economically impacted on by the war. The state, following Keynesian principles, focused on employment creation with an accompanying welfare net. People of all classes felt they had a stake in the system under a legitimate government – or did so at least until the 'golden era' began to fade toward the end of the 1960s with rising inflation, new fiscal strictures, and waning state hegemony.

Elsewhere in the world, public order policing had begun to assume more militarised forms. In the United States, Special Weapons and Tactics (SWAT) units were formed to deal with potentially dangerous situations: intensively trained, in military-style uniforms, armed with automatic weapons (Brewer et al., 1988). Protests and demonstrations were heavily policed, in turn provoking riotous situations. During the Detroit riots of July 1968, more than 7 000 people were arrested (most of them black) and 43 were killed. In France, the Compagnie Républicaine de Sécurité killed five demonstrators in 1968 (Roach and Thomaneck, 1985). In China, the police, often together with the military, were sent in to restore order by force during the period of the Cultural Revolution (Brewer et al., 1988). In each of these countries and others, governments were challenged, particularly by minority and dispossessed groups, but nowhere was the legitimacy of the state more in question than in South Africa.

The 1960s in South Africa was the time of 'Grand Apartheid' as the NP government attempted to consolidate its domination through a strategy of divide-and-rule. The main project of the state in this period was to achieve white 'Afrikaner hegemony' (Uys, 1989: 206) through the economic and social promotion of Afrikaners and the 'separate development' of other racial and ethnic groups.

In April 1960 the two main liberation movement organisations, the ANC and the Pan-Africanist Congress (PAC), were banned in an attempt 'to repress all forms of opposition, although non-violent and legal, in the country as a whole' (Truth and Reconciliation Commission, 1998: Chapter 3, 163). In 1963 and 1964 almost the entire leadership of the ANC and PAC inside South Africa (including Nelson Mandela) were arrested, charged with high treason, and sentenced to life imprisonment. The message was very clear that protest and resistance would not be tolerated, yet despite the mass arrests and the bannings the liberation movement continued to protest openly against the pass laws and the Group Areas Acts that restricted black people to designated urban areas. It was during this period, too, that the ANC established its military armed wing, Umkhonto we Sizwe (MK), and began an underground campaign of active resistance.

Police actions at this time were essentially driven by the ideological assumption that Africans were rightless subjects. The overriding emphasis was on 'law and order' policing, and the police were the most important institution for upholding the apartheid social order, enforcing the influx control regulations along with more general political repression. Fighting 'communism' and 'terrorism' were the overriding priorities and police ruthlessly put down protests and demonstrations.

The 1960 Sharpeville massacre was the turning point in the apartheid government's categorical intolerance of collective resistance. On 21 March a crowd of 20 000 township residents gathered in Sharpeville to protest against the pass laws. A police line of some 70 men was ordered to load their firearms in preparation to shoot. Then, with no actual order to shoot having been given, they fired into the crowd and 69 protestors were killed, most of them shot in the back (Jeffery, 1991).

In the years following Sharpeville, stakes were raised acutely in what was, for the police, virtually preparation for civil war. The Terrorism Act of 1967 authorised police to conduct themselves as if they were indeed in a state of war (Dippenaar,

1988), and combating 'terrorism' developed into more than just a geographically internal police function, with deployment of SAP personnel, particularly from the mobile units, on the Rhodesian, South West African, and Angolan borders.

Service on border duty thrust police officers into unequivocally military situations of engagement where deadly force was employed as a matter of course and rarely, if ever, investigated – inescapably reinforcing the prevailing credo that the SAP were fighting a war with no boundaries. The 'threat' to public order came from both outside the country and from within and the same uncompromising tactics were considered equally legitimate in either arena.

Within the country's borders meanwhile, following the banning of political parties and the imprisonment of leaders, there were during the 1960s relatively low levels of public protest against the apartheid state. 'The main threat to the political system', as Rauch and Storey review this period, 'was deemed to be from the liberation struggles and nascent democracies in neighbouring states' (1998: 4). So while there was substantial police deployment on the country's borders and beyond, no specialised, dedicated unit had yet been established to deal with public order problems.

Embryonic precursors for such units first materialised in the early 1960s in the form of mobile units. The first of these anywhere in the country was set up in Durban under the command of Captain Visagie (Barnard, 2000), who was at the time based in the Durban Area Commissioner's office. In 1963 Visagie proposed that there was a need for police officers trained specifically for the containment of riots. In the Durban area, station supervisors selected personnel from their stations to be trained in riot control and subsequently called upon 'when the need arose' (Barnard, 2000: 28). These officers got together once a month to train in formations and drill at the old Mobile Stores Unit in Wentworth. According to Barnard, the 'foresight' of the Durban Area Commissioner's office meant that Durban SAP, during the late 1960s, was available for mobilisation to deal with riotous situations. Similar units began to be established throughout the country, but not yet as part of any broader SAP planning. Local mobile units were formed in response to local needs with no particular uniformity in the process:[3] 'each Division was more or less left to its own methods of crowd control based on local conditions and knowledge' (Rauch and Storey 1998: 19).

During this period, three principal Acts governed the policing of riots and public order:

- The Riotous Assembly Act 17 of 1956. This conferred wide powers on magistrates and the Minister of Justice to control and prohibit public gatherings. Section 2(1) of the Act enabled a magistrate with the authorisation of the Minister to prohibit a public gathering if he/she were of the opinion that it represented a serious threat to public peace. 'The Minister of Justice had wide (and practically unchallengeable) discretion to prohibit particular public gatherings from taking place, or to prohibit a particular person from attending a public gathering ... Once prohibited, mere attendance at such a prohibited gathering was not an offence, but all actions relating to the organisation of a prohibited gathering were criminalised' (Rauch and Storey, 1998: 9). If a prohibited gathering did take place, the police were empowered to disperse the gathering by force.
- The Suppression of Communism Act 44 of 1950. Section 9(3) of this Act gave the Minister of Justice power to prohibit a particular gathering, or to ban gatherings generally in any area and for any period specified by him. Neither the size nor the location of the gathering (indoor meetings included) limited the Act's application.
- The Public Safety Act 3 of 1953. This Act gave the police wide latitude in their application of the legislation and allowed them to act with impunity against those engaged in protests or demonstrations, providing indemnity against civil or criminal prosecution for members of the security forces who acted in 'good faith'. In practice, this meant that the police and the military were placed above the law and rather than the police being responsible for providing evidence for the legitimacy and legality of their actions, the 'onus was on the victim to show that a policeman acted in bad faith when he fired recklessly into a crowd, or failed to fire a warning shot, or neglected to use less drastic forms of "coercion"' (Haysom, cited in Rauch and Storey, 1998: 17).

These three Acts (enacted in the 1950s but enforced most zealously in the 1960s) provided an exceptionally permissive legislative framework for the use of force in crowd situations, from which it was just a short step to regular use of excessive force without question or reflection. The policing of protest was in many respects approached quite simply as warfare. Protests were regarded as having been organised by communist agitators who had to be silenced in the most 'effective' way possible. The legislation and practices that evolved in the 1960s set the stage for public order policing for the next two decades.

Natal was an epicentre of political activism during this period. A military high command of the ANC's military wing MK was established in 1961 in the Natal region and an active sabotage campaign began in December of that same year with an attempt to bomb the Durban offices of the Department of Bantu Education. The Durban Post Office, telephone services in Durban, tax offices and a railway line were also targeted in this campaign. As a result of these activities, Natal was particularly hard hit by the imposition of restrictions, bannings, detentions, arrests and banishing orders (Truth and Reconciliation Commission, 1998: Chapter 3).

The seventies: a new turn in protest policing

In the 1970s public order policing globally came under the spotlight as policing of crowds became increasingly aggressive and specialised paramilitary units multiplied. This was true of both developed and developing countries. The Israeli police and military, threatened by the internal resistance of Arab Israelis, responded forcefully to public demonstrations. In March 1976, for example, Arabs protested against the expropriation of land in the Galilee and Negev areas. Six demonstrators were killed when the military were called in to assist with the policing of the crowd (Brewer et al., 1988). In the United States, the proliferation of SWAT units gave rise to growing concern at the militarising effect this would have on policing in general (Kraska and Paulsen, 1997).

In Britain there was widespread consternation at heavy-handed police responses to protests and demonstrations. In 1974 a university student, Kevin Gately, was killed during an anti-National Front demonstration at Warwick University (Gregory, 1985). In 1975 widespread violence erupted between minority communities and the police during the Notting Hill Carnival, sparked off by a massive presence of the Special Patrol Groups, heavily armed mobile police units (Rollo, 1980). The police were met with a hail of stones and bricks and, inadequately equipped and poorly trained, had to grab dustbin lids for protection. In April 1979 a civilian, Blair Peach, was killed when police tried to handle a counter-demonstration by the black community in Southall against a National Front meeting.

A number of British policing scholars have tried to explain this change. Gregory (1985) argues that it was an increase in Irish Republican Army (IRA) activity and terrorism, serious and widespread industrial disputes, and the eruption of race-related conflict that gave rise to this response. Jefferson (1990) on the other hand, focuses on the issues that triggered the protests in the first place and how these issues in themselves influenced the response of the state. He locates these issues in the crisis of hegemony facing the British state from the late 1960s as unemployment grew under the law-and-order political dispensation of a newly elected Tory government. Police militarisation was both a symptom and an outcome of a breakdown in hegemony.

In South Africa, too, the state entered into a period of serious economic and political crisis. 'By the mid 1970s,' in Mark Swilling's summary of the state of affairs, 'townships were facing a crisis of reproduction: inadequate urban services, rising unemployment as a result of the recession, and declining real wage levels as inflation rose' (1988: 4). In neighbouring Angola and Mozambique, popular liberation movements won political independence, inspiring a revitalised politics of resistance in South Africa. The emergence in this period of the Black Consciousness Movement betokens, for Alf Stadler, the 'collapse of any significant belief among Africans in the possibility of a liberal resolution to the South African crisis' (1987: 171). In the workplace too, resistance intensified and the black trade union movement expanded, paving the way ultimately for new and liberalised industrial policies.

The state responded to this crisis with a two-pronged strategy. On the one hand, efforts were made to try to legitimise the political and social order; legislative and administrative structures were remodelled and supposedly liberalised, and opportunities for blacks in education and the economy were expanded. On the other hand, 'the state's repressive apparatus was strengthened, and both the military and police acquired expanded powers and resources' (Stadler, 1987: 161). Both strategies, seemingly contradictory, were aimed at restoring state control and ending internal resistance to state authority. Neither succeeded, and the challenge to the state intensified.

By the early 1970s the police in South Africa began to see the need for a 'specialized capacity to control unrest' (Rauch and Storey, 1998: 5) in a climate of growing resistance to apartheid. New mobile units were established throughout the republic, positioned at divisional level and commanded by an officer with divisional level authority, usually of the rank of Major. This divisional head would command the mobile unit over and above the other work he was responsible for. General Marais, a member of the original mobile unit from its inception, explained to me how these Divisional Mobile units operated:

Each divisional head had a number of vehicles and some equipment which was placed at a store somewhere to be used when the need arose. When trouble came, it was the Divisional Officer's job to mobilise members. The districts would then be informed and would have to allocate members who would be sent out. There was no ongoing and specified training for these members. Nobody belonged permanently to the mobile unit. It was all very ad hoc at the time. Members would be called to operate in the mobile units, they would be equipped and sent out to the trouble spots. They would then come back to their stations.[4]

Initially officers were not permanently based in the mobile units but this began to change after the June 1976 Soweto uprisings – a critical turning point in the policing of crowds and public disorder. When thousands of Soweto school children took to the street on 16 June 1976 to protest the use of Afrikaans as the medium for instruction in schools, the SAP were caught completely unprepared. They confronted the school children with automatic weapons and close on a thousand people were killed in the six months that followed. Murphy Morobe, a Soweto school student from that time, captured the brutality of that fateful police response and the ensuing chaos when he remembered 16 June in a statement 20 years later (23 July 1996) to the Truth and Reconciliation Commission:

> The police came out with the dog and let loose the dog that came charging at us . . . It was a real dog that bit some of the students there and I think that really raised the anger of the students that we were not doing anything that we thought warranted that kind of reaction from them . . . That dog was then killed by students who sought to protect themselves from it. At that time the police started opening fire, you know, and sure there was taunting of the police . . . Once the shooting began it was at the time that other schools were approaching us from the back of the police that were perched on the hill facing us . . . it was the first time that many of us had experience of tear gas . . . One of the things that always remains a painful one was the fact that most of those policemen that came out of the van were actually black policemen . . . There was no attempt whatsoever, you know, to tell us to disperse . . . It was a matter of them stepping out of their vehicles, taking positions alongside their vehicles and sending the police dog into us. He might have shouted, you know, but any well-trained policeman who respects human life would know

that he or she would have to do that in such a way that the people for whom that announcement is meant, hear it (www.truth.org.za/hrvtrans/soweto.morobe.htm).

The SAP was not equipped to deal with a domestic uprising on the scale of the 1976 uprisings. 'The policemen who faced massive protest marches at the time were ordinary police officials drawn from nearby stations, possessing no special skills in training or handling crowds' (Rauch and Storey, 1988: 10). The brutal force used by the police and the catastrophic human costs provoked outcry from all sectors of South African society. For the SAP it was abundantly evident that the dynamics in the black townships had changed utterly and that they would have to drastically rethink their riot control structures and strategies.

A commission of enquiry chaired by Mr Justice Cillie concluded that 'so far as manpower, equipment and mental attitude were concerned, [the police] . . . were completely unprepared for such a mass demonstration' (Cillie Report, cited in Jeffery, 1991: 28). Given the inadequacies in capacity, intelligence and readiness in the face of the uprisings, it was decided that the SAP required easily identifiable and mobile Riot Units able to respond swiftly and effectively to future instances of collective action.

As had been the pattern in the 1960s, regular police members at station level were assigned to these units and given training. There were at the time no formal selection criteria and the decision as to who would be assigned to the riot unit was left to the discretion of the Station Commander. Those chosen were often the most violent, undisciplined and unproductive policemen whom station commanders were most willing to dispense with.[5] They were drawn from all race groups, but the command structure was entirely white.

Each unit fell under the command of a Divisional Commander, and the unit for each division was allocated a number: the Durban Division unit was Riot Unit 9. Following the events of June 1976, each Divisional Commander was instructed to send a team of commissioned officers on a six-week course at a new SAP training base at Maloeskop in the Eastern Transvaal. These officers were trained as instructors and made responsible in turn for training other personnel around the country in crowd or riot control. This 'train the trainer' approach represented the first attempt at planned, decentralised training in crowd or riot control.

General Marais, the first Durban West Riot Unit District Commander, describes the training at Maloeskop Police College as 'very basic'. According to his account, the South African Defence Force was centrally involved and conducted training in counter-insurgency. Marais claims that some of the trainers were sent to Israel for training in counter-insurgency where they learned 'how to do things like chase a bus and how to attack a bus'. Trainees were taught how to use the riot control equipment with which the SAP was then issued and they studied the legislation that pertained specifically to 'riot control'. There was little training in the range of strategies that were being developed internationally in police work of this kind. The objective of the training was 'to ensure that a member would emerge from the course with the knowledge of what gatherings should be dispersed, when to disperse them, and how to use weapons to disperse them' (Rauch and Storey, 1998: 26).

The vehicles most frequently used during this time were Land Rovers – the notorious armoured vehicles came later. Unit members were issued with steel helmets, kit bags and batons. More significantly, they were also issued with lethal weapons such as shotguns and rifles (Jeffrey, 1991). No shields were available at this time. Members were trained in how to use tear gas and gas masks, and in the use of military formations developed by the old Rhodesian Police force. Members from the Durban area were trained at the Wentworth Training Centre once a month, and sent regularly to the Maryvale Shooting Range for shooting practice.

The events of 1976 led to more systematic and coherent planning for localised Riot Units and a more structured approach to training. At the same time, there was a concern to establish a more permanent component for riot or crowd control. In late 1979 a new national unit was formed, called the Reaction Unit, which was in effect a riot unit at national level. The particular brief for the Pretoria-based Reaction Unit, also known as Unit 19, was to deal with counter-insurgency and riot control situations. Unit 19 was responsible for rapid deployment to unrest points anywhere in the country that the local mobile Riot Units were unable to contain.[6]

The formation of local mobile riot units around the country, along with the establishment of the national Reaction Unit, was an initial stage in the development of a separate specialised unit within the SAP to deal with all crowd situations. Officers selected to serve in the mobile units were not the only ones who received training in riot control and counter-insurgency. After 1976, all police had to be prepared for potentially riotous situations and it became policy for all personnel to undergo crowd control and counter-insurgency training. It was a kind of call to arms: South Africa faced 'total onslaught' by evil communists; it was time for extreme measures; and over the next eight years SAP manpower levels rose by close on 30 per cent (Brewer, 1988: 259).

During the 1970s, Durban was once more the setting for both major resistance and repression, ushered in by the 1973 Durban strikes that affected 150 establishments. The University of Natal Medical School was one of the chief institutional bases of the Black Consciousness Movement and many Black Consciousness supporters were arrested in Durban and charged under the Terrorism Act. The 1976 Soweto uprising soon impacted on Durban too, setting off a wave of protest among the youth (Stadler, 1987). The security forces in Durban responded with arrests and detentions and there were widespread allegations of torture. A series of treason trials also took place in Natal during this period and in 1976 Harry Gwala, a significant liberation movement figure in Natal, and nine others were charged under the Terrorism Act (Truth and Reconciliation Commission, 1998: Chapter 3).

The eighties: riot policing at its zenith
Globally in the 1980s public order policing came in for a good deal of reappraisal, both organisationally and politically. As greater powers accrued to police themselves and old-fashioned 'push-and-shove' gave way to baton charge and water-cannon, relations between police and public grew increasingly tarnished (Roach and Thomaneck, 1985; Morgan and Smith, 1989).

Fundamental to the review of public order policing in Britain was the Scarman Report of 1981. This report was commissioned following the violent urban commotion of the early 1980s, for which the catalyst had been the 1981 riots in Brixton in south London, a rental area since the 1950s for Caribbean immigrants. In April 1981, Brixton police conducted raids in full riot gear in an attempt to enforce unpopular housing policies. In the eyes of many in the local community, they were an occupation force and in the few days that followed, violent conflict erupted between the police and black youth. Between 10–12 April, 145 shop premises were damaged. On the evening of 11 April, nearly 300 police officers and at least 45 members of the public sustained injuries. Many police and other vehicles were destroyed. Police attempted to disperse the crowd, but widespread looting ensued. Police did confine themselves to the use of batons but it became clear nonetheless that they were not properly trained, equipped or deployed (Pike, 1985).

The Brixton riots came to symbolise the need for a fundamental shift in the conception of public order policing, and the report by Lord Scarman's commission was the culminating response to demands for high-level review of police strategy. The aim of the Scarman report was to provide suggestions for widening of the scope 'that the police have to de-escalate potentially riotous situations' (Brearley and King, 1996b: 56). Scarman identified a number of problems internal to the police themselves that had contributed to the violence in Brixton: police racial prejudice; inflexible, unimaginative strategy; over-reaction to disorderliness; delay and lack of vigour in dealing with disorder; poor equipment and training (Pike, 1985).

The report called for better training and equipment, better communications, a review of tactics, and much greater stress on planning and negotiations (Brearley and King, 1996b). Aside from its insistence on proper procedure – pre-planning, negotiation, proper assessment, and comprehensive evaluation and debriefing – a number of important principles were identified as 'good practice'. These included the development of co-operative relations with communities, a graduated police response, minimum force, tolerance, and situational appropriateness – principles founded on acceptance of the rights and liberties of the individual and essentially a restatement of early 'Peelian' principles in British policing, which had traditionally stressed accountability, co-operative relationships with communities, impartiality, and minimum force (Pike, 1985).

The Scarman Report did not produce immediate changes in Britain, and confrontations continued between police and minority communities in the immediately following years, with no automatic transformation in police behaviour or police-community relations. But the report did place firmly on the agenda the need to develop new forms of public order policing.

The Report was directed at the British police, but its influence extended to police forces worldwide, particularly in the liberal democracies, in response to widespread and 'vociferous domestic protest and increased international pressure arising from the wider acceptance of the norms governing human rights, equality, and justice' (Brewer et al., 1988: 235). Implementation of the Scarman suggestions hinged, however, on a number of variables which included 'the nature or changing of the state, the cleavages that [existed] within society, the specific functional specialisms of the police force concerned, and the organisational structure and lines of accountability within the force' (Brewer et al., 1988: 234).

The authoritarian nature of the apartheid state, legally enforced racial segregation, and the unassailable authority of the SAP meant that the Scarman Report had scant impact on policing in South Africa. By the middle of the 1980s, the South African state was confronting its greatest crisis of legitimacy as internal resistance escalated and much of the world severed social, political and economic ties. In a desperate attempt to hold on to power, repression was intensified and the government insulated itself from outside influences and criticism. Policing of crowds and demonstrations grew even more ferocious and international trends counted for very little.

From 1982 onward, oppositional political mobilisation escalated dramatically, especially in response to implementation of the Black Local Authorities Act in 1983 (Seekings, 1988), which sought to devolve the government of black townships to local authorities without resources, capacity or legitimacy. The anger of township residents mounted as local councils increased rents, evicted defaulters and demolished shacks, and it was fuelled further by inadequacy of services and widespread corruption. Initially protests were peaceful, but when residents' demands and concerns were ignored protests escalated from confrontation to violence (Lodge, 1991) and the violence spiralled as the security forces responded with tear gas, rubber bullets and even live ammunition (Steytler, 1989). In April a nationwide school boycott began, precipitated by the extremely poor matriculation results and the refusal of the authorities to readmit pupils who were over the stipulated school-going age (Lodge, 1991). This set school-going youth free to take up oppositional activities that became the backbone of community struggles (Seekings, 1988; Hyslop, 1988; Johnson, 1989).

Township resistance stiffened markedly in the second half of the decade following the formation of the United Democratic Front (UDF) in August 1983. In Tom Lodge's assessment, 'the UDF inspired an insurrectionary movement . . . without precedent in its combative militancy, in the burden it imposed on government and in the degree to which it internalised hostility toward apartheid' (1991: 29).

Restrictions on protest and assembly were expanded yet again and the Minister of Justice acquired still further power to prohibit gatherings. New legislation 'granted sweeping discretionary powers, closed any loop-holes that had previously been exploited, and extended the range of criminal offences associated with gatherings, while reducing the restrictions on the use of force to prevent and disperse crowds' (Rauch and Storey, 1998: 10). The most important legislation governing the policing of public order at this time was the Internal Security Act of 1982. This gave wide powers to the Minister of Law and Order to control and prohibit public gatherings: he had authority to prohibit any gathering if he deemed this necessary or expedient; police officers had authority to order a crowd to disperse and to use force to secure compliance.

The Internal Security Act authorised use of force including recourse to firearms and other lethal weapons in policing of protest and assemblies, and while it stipulated that lethal force should be used for crowd dispersal only if lesser means had proven unsuccessful, or if violence appeared imminent, these provisions had little effect in curtailing the use of force. Perhaps the most fundamental problem with the Act was that it (intentionally) provided for no means other than dispersal to deal with a prohibited gathering or assembly. To make matters worse, the Act required that a warning be given only once, and police were no longer obliged to inform the public that force might be used to disperse the gathering (Rauch and Storey, 1998).

The Internal Security Act was used in conjunction with Section 49(2) of the Criminal Procedures Act of 1977. This Act allowed the SAP and other police agencies (such as the mining police and private security firms) to use any force that was deemed 'necessary' under a given circumstance to overcome resistance or to stop a fleeing suspect; justifiable homicide was an acceptable plea if a fleeing person could not be stopped or arrested. It also provided for the detention of a suspect for a period of 48 hours, even without good cause being demonstrated. These Acts, taken together, gave the police wide powers to arrest, detain, and to use deadly force with almost no liability or accountability.

Despite the brutal response of the South African police, mobilisation and protest continued and indeed intensified during the course of the decade. The violence spiralled as resistance grew and the police crackdown intensified. The scale of the challenge to public order (provoked by the state itself) meant that 'riot control in South Africa was not a "skill" restricted to a specialist or elite squad' (Brewer et al., 1988: 177). Instead, the entire SAP was now geared towards front-line counter-insurgency action with ' "normal" crime . . . a secondary problem as the police concentrated on the struggle against "ideological criminals" ' (Cawthra, 1992: 6).

In 1984 Defence Force units were sent in to black townships to help quell unrest, marking very plainly the military dimension to the imposition of apartheid. Evans and Phillips describe the moment when the troops went in:

On the night of Saturday 6 October 1984, South African Defence Force troops entered Joza township outside Grahamstown. By the next morning they had moved into Soweto outside Johannesburg as well . . . Within two weeks Operation Palmiet was launched. At four in the morning, a 7 000 strong contingent of policemen and soldiers entered the Vaal township of

Sebokeng outside of Vereeniging. While troops cordoned off the streets, the police conducted house-to-house searches in an attempt . . . 'to root out revolutionaries'. By the end of the day, they had arrested 350 residents . . . A new phase of conflict in South Africa had begun: a phase in which the lines of battle shifted from the borders of Namibia to the black townships of South Africa . . . (1988: 117).

Working now in tandem with the military, the police themselves grew increasingly heavy-handed and more and more overtly paramilitary in their operational style. This shift represented a critical stage of polarisation in the battle between the apartheid state and the liberation movement (Evans and Phillips, 1988).[7] The State Security Council (SSC) called for a strategy of counter-insurgency against what they called the 'communist onslaught' of the liberation movement.[8]

From 1984 onwards the SADF and the SAP operated jointly on a continual basis in township operations, signalling that the SAP alone was no longer able to contain the intensifying resistance. The brutality of the police and the military during this period was unremitting. Between September 1984 and December 1985 alone the security forces were responsible for the deaths of 628 people in township operations. 'Allegations of rape, assault, murder, theft, the besieging of schools, the disruption of funerals and church services and the demolition of shacks' by the security forces were commonplace (Evans and Phillips, 1988: 130). In the townships of South Africa, this was indeed now virtually civil war.

On the 21 July 1985, a State of Emergency was declared in 36 magisterial districts. The Emergency, which lasted for eight months, gave soldiers and policemen, regardless of rank, 'absolute authority to arrest, interrogate, search homes, and confiscate possessions. The commissioner of police could declare night and daytime curfews, close any building or business property, regulate the news, and restrict access to any area defined by the regulations' (Lodge, 1991: 78).

A string of new offences, punishable by prison sentences of up to ten years, was simultaneously promulgated. These included innocuous acts such as verbally threatening to harm another person; preparing, printing, publishing or possessing a 'threatening' document; hindering officers in the course of duty; destroying or defacing any notice of the emergency regulations; disclosing the names of any persons arrested by the security forces before their names were officially confirmed; causing fear or panic or weakening public confidence; and advising people to stay away from work

(Johnson, 1989). These regulations effectively criminalised any activity that could be construed as political. It also empowered the police to act against collective groups of people in almost any setting – students at school, workers in a factory, mourners at funerals, and participants in peaceful demonstrations. Within the SAP, 'black South Africans were stereotyped as criminals and threats to the state' (Brewer et al., 1988: 270).

The State of Emergency also conferred indemnity from civil and criminal prosecution on all security force members and officials in the prison services as long as they acted in 'good faith'. If a member of the security forces acted under the command, direction, or instruction of a superior officer, his actions were deemed to be in good faith. These virtually unrestricted powers were used extensively by the police and the military and at enormous human cost. In 1985 alone, a total of 512 African adults and 187 African juveniles were killed in police shootings; 2 312 people were wounded by the police (Brogden and Shearing, 1993). During the same period 18 966 people were detained for 'unrest offences'; 22 per cent of those detained were under sixteen years of age (Brewer et al., 1988). Only rarely was the brutality of police operations subjected to public scrutiny. This was largely due to the 1958 Police Act which prevented the publication of what it called 'untrue material' relating to police misconduct. The intensity of the force which the police employed can be measured by the ammunition and equipment they were issued with. Standard issue for police in riot control operations during the 1980s included:

- R1 rifles – either single or automatic shot with a lethal range of 150 m;
- R5 rifles – hypervelocity single or automatic shot, lethal at 150 m;
- Uzi hand machine-carbine – either single or automatic shot, lethal at 100 m;
- tear gas – used to incapacitate people or disperse them from a particular location;
- wooden sticks, truncheons, and later, plastic batons;
- stopper guns – used for firing tear gas rounds or rubber bullets; and
- 12 bore Musler shot-guns – used to fire a range of ammunition which included both rubber bullets and pellets.

The use of live and lethal ammunition was an integral part of riot control. Some of the equipment may have been labelled 'non-lethal' – tear gas, rubber bullets, batons – but all of these are lethal if used inappropriately. As Rauch and Storey (1998) point out, tear gas inhaled in a closed environment can cause death by asphyxiation. A rubber or wooden baton used to strike a person's head can cause death with a single blow. Both rubber bullets and pellets are lethal if fired at vulnerable body parts and at short range. The distinction, then, between lethal and non-lethal ammunition is almost irrelevant, and the consequences of its use depended on the intent of the police officer using the equipment.

The Mobile Riot Units were ruthless in dealing with township residents who protested against apartheid legislation, or even gathered for funerals, or celebratory events. Lethal weapons were used as a first, rather than a last, resort (Hansson, 1989), in a policy of maximum rather than minimum force. The police offered three main justifications for this use of force: the fact that most protests and demonstrations were illegal; the volatile and violent nature of such events; and the fact that the legislative framework governing the policing of crowds provided little scope for the use of negotiation in resolving conflict.

From 1985 onwards, the SAP tried to involve as many allies as possible in crushing resistance: homeland police, right-wing vigilante groups, and new black police bodies. In 1985 the SAP started to train the various homeland police forces[9] in counter-insurgency and riot control. 'This [was] not only an attempt to prevent infiltration by guerrillas but also reflects how unrest [began] to occur in rural areas' (Brewer et al., 1988: 261). Homeland police were heavily involved in the suppression of resistance movements. The KwaZulu police, for example, played an active role in controlling political and industrial unrest, and, in particular, in actions against political opponents of Inkatha (Brewer et al., 1988). There were also persistent reports of homeland police collaborating with well-armed clandestine vigilante groups.

The SAP, for its part, actively cultivated relationships with right-wing vigilantes. Where there was not outright collaboration there would be tacit approval. And where there was no vigilante presence already on the ground, the SAP had little compunction in fostering and encouraging it. It would also seem that many vigilantes were paid informers who acted under the direction of the SAP. Haysom (1990) argues that the main objective of the SAP in colluding with or supporting vigilantes was to destabilise and 'disorganise' local communities. Put more strongly, he asserts that vigilantes allowed the police to operate effectively at a distance in a low-intensity war.

The SAP also made a number of other desperate attempts to increase their manpower (particularly with regard to 'riot' situations) and at the same time claim some kind of legitimacy by creating new black police agencies. In 1984, 32 township authorities were granted the power to have their own police bodies. Recruits were trained separately from the SAP, and, initially, these new Municipal Police were 'charged with protecting the lives of African councillors and guarding municipal installations and government buildings, thus freeing the SAP to concentrate on policing township unrest' (Brogden and Shearing, 1993: 81). It was not long before they were directly and actively involved in unrest suppression operations.

Brogden and Shearing argue that the Municipal Police in fact became responsible for much of the direct and forceful repression of anti-apartheid organisations and individuals while the SAP withdrew to a more supervisory role. The Municipal Police were, not surprisingly, very unpopular in the black townships. They 'soon earned themselves pejorative labels in townships, where they were called variously "greenflies" (a reference to the flies that buzz around faeces), "Amstels" (after the beer bottles) and "sunlights" (after a soap commercial on TV2 promising a faster response to your washing up problems), "magodolos" (the opposers), "magundawane" (wild rats) and "Zulu boys"' (Brogden and Shearing, 1993).

A second surrogate police body was established in 1986: the SAP-financed Special Constables or *kitskonstabels* (Afrikaans for 'instant police'). These were given three six-week training courses and were used to supplement the SAP where they were overstretched. At the passing-out parade of the first set of *kitskonstabels*, the head of the national Counter-Insurgency Unit made it clear that their role would be to act against those whom the security forces identified as 'leftist' or 'radical' (Brewer et al., 1988: 263). 'Recruits required no educational qualification, and included many illiterates. Equipped with shotguns, and dressed in functional blue overalls, they were allocated the tasks of foot patrol and riot control' (Brogden and Shearing, 1993: 83). Paid by the hour as temporary employees, they were not eligible for any of the usual SAP personnel benefits. Their utility to the SAP was to be the scapegoats for the violent policing of the townships. Township residents laid hundreds of complaints against the *kitskonstabels* whom they claimed were often drunk on duty and extremely aggressive.

Far from deterring the liberation movement, the heavy-handed approach of the security forces during the first State of Emergency is more likely to have fuelled rage and discontent as the count rose of detentions, arrests, harassment, and deaths.

The 1985 State of Emergency was lifted on 7 March 1986 but there was only a short interval before a new State of Emergency was declared on 12 June 1986. Announcing the second State of Emergency, the government made it clear that it had no intention of making concessions and would take even stronger measures to put down resistance. Arrests and detentions continued and resistance organisations were forced to operate in increasingly clandestine ways (Marks, 1993).

In 1986 a new centralised/unitary and permanent Riot Unit was created with local units directly under its control. The Riot Unit was the first dedicated public order (or should that be disorder?) policing formation in the SAP. Initially, the core of the 'new' unit was the old Reaction Unit. As time went by, members from the decentralised Mobile Units in the districts were also brought in on a permanent basis. They formed part of the new Riot Unit but were locally based. All new recruits were then sent to Maloeskop Training Centre for three months' training. This included infantry training, weapons training (rifles in particular), use of tear gas, recognition of explosives and land mines – and, for the first time, use of shields. Officer training for junior, middle and senior management included crowd control and counter-insurgency warfare courses.

The Riot Unit was divided into companies on military lines and controlled from the SAP national headquarters in Pretoria, but based in the respective regions. Unit 19 (formally Unit 19 of the old Reaction Unit) continued to operate from Pretoria and was deployed when there was a capacity problem at the local level, although the command structures at national and local level remained completely separate. Equipment for the new Riot Unit now included proper anti-riot gear, but unit members resisted using it 'in favour of the raw force they seemed to prefer' (Cawthra, 1992: 11). With this sort of predilection, and a general lack of accountability and supervision, the Riot Unit soon acquired a reputation as one of most problematic and brutal security units in the country (Brogden and Shearing, 1993).

The second half of the 1980s was a time of massive security presence in the townships: raids, roadblocks, disruption of gatherings and meetings, cordon searches, thousands of detentions, and the deaths of hundreds of activists. Communities were ripped apart and the detentions and arrests lead to a potentially serious leadership crisis, particularly at local levels (Marks, 1993; Plasket, 1989). The Riot Unit had a leading role in planning and carrying out these operations, creating space in turn for surrogate forces to move into the townships and cause further disarray while the security forces took a back seat (Plasket, 1989). Instead of breaking up gatherings, the police became more proactive. They banned rallies, meetings, even mass funerals, or they set restrictions on the numbers who could attend and how they should conduct themselves (Friedman and Webster, cited in Plasket, 1989).

The entry into the picture of the new surrogate security bodies and the collaboration with right-wing vigilantes enabled the police to 'sub-contract their dirty work' (Plasket, 1989), which meant in turn that they could modify their general strategy towards the resistance. Increasingly the police themselves began to abandon direct maximum force and withdraw from the townships leaving in place the vigilantes and the surrogate forces to shift the balance of power. The police could then re-enter the townships to 'sort out' what they would now portray as inter-community conflict.

But they were selective in the 'malefactors' they targeted, for the most part acting against supporters of the UDF and the Congress of South African Trade Unions (Cosatu) and in favour of vigilante groups or parties not antagonistic to the apartheid state, such as Inkatha. This invited allegations not merely of partisanship but of active collusion, as a 'third force', in fuelling community conflict (Maré and Hamilton, 1987). Most serious was the problem of SAP collusion with Inkatha in KwaZulu-Natal where Inkatha and the UDF battled for power bases and territory.[10]

Collusion between the police and Inkatha was also taking place at other levels. In 1988, 300 Inkatha recruits were deployed as special constables in the Pietermaritzburg area after undergoing training organised, indications suggest, by Riot Unit 8. These special constables, once deployed, soon acquired a reputation for 'acts of extreme brutality' (Truth and Reconciliation Commission, 1998: Chapter 3, 196).

The Trust Feed massacre in the Natal Midlands on 3 December 1988 was a notorious instance of intervention by the Riot Unit and the special constables. Inkatha-aligned gunmen opened fire on a house where people had gathered for a night vigil, mowing down thirteen of them aged between four and sixty-six. Both the Riot Unit and the New Hanover Station Commander, Brian Mitchell, had been given prior warning of the pending attack. Instead of taking steps to protect residents of Trust Feed, they rounded up and detained local UDF supporters the day before the attack. Only two people survived (Truth and Reconciliation Commission, 1998: Chapter 3). Captain Mitchell later admitted during the Trust Feed trial that he 'had ordered four black special constables to kill UDF supporters in Trust Feed on 3 December 1988. The killings had been planned by him in conjunction with Mr Jerome Gabela, the chairman of Inkatha in the community' (Jefferey, 1997: 257).

Aside from the obvious collusion, particularly on the part of the Riot Unit, with Inkatha during this period, police also used the emergency regulations to crush UDF-aligned resistance. Between June 1987 and April 1988, 1 100 UDF supporters had been detained (Jefferey, 1997). In Natal alone, between 1983 and 1989 the South African police had killed over 800 people (Truth and Reconciliation Commission, 1998: Chapter 3).

Into the nineties – putting on a professional face

In February 1990, the South African political arena was transformed at a stroke when the State President, F.W. de Klerk, unbanned the ANC and all other black opposition political parties. And at once, in the entirely new political dispensation all players now found themselves in, all the emphasis was now on working towards a negotiated settlement. Crucially, the police were identified early in the negotiations as a key institution that had to be transformed for a new democracy to come into being with due promise of national stability and legitimate assurance of law and order (Shaw, 1994; Marks, 1996).

The transformed political climate was not, however, accompanied by a decline in collective protest or public disorder. On the contrary, protest intensified at the still appalling conditions in the black townships and the catastrophic vacuum in local government, while political parties and trade unions wrestled to consolidate their constituencies. Political conflict underwent a dramatic shift that produced sharply increased levels of violence in many parts of the country but most especially in Natal and KwaZulu in ferocious rivalry between the ANC and the Inkatha Freedom Party (IFP).[11]

A hundred people died in Natal and KwaZulu, on average, each month between July 1990 and June 1993: 3 653 deaths in total. For the most part, this violence resulted from local contests for political and territorial ascendancy. Tens of thousands were affected by the violence, which brought death, injury and in the end, mass displacement of communities. Hostel dwellers, who were usually IFP-aligned, engaged in massacres of neighbouring township residents. In many of these incidents, the KwaZulu Police (KZP) were implicated in grave human rights abuses against people seen as ANC sympathisers. KZP members were regularly spotted transporting IFP supporters to the scenes of attacks (Truth and Reconciliation Commission, 1998: Volume 2, Chapter 7). Members of SAP Riot Unit, particularly in the Natal Midlands, were also involved in selling guns to the IFP, and in siding with the IFP against the ANC.

Perhaps the most scandalous incident in Natal during this period was the Seven

Day War that took place between 25 and 31 March 1990 in the Vulindlela and Edendale valleys. Armed Inkatha supporters invaded the valleys, killing 200 ANC supporters in just seven days. The Riot Unit seems to have taken orders from Inkatha warlord, David Ntombela, and was directly involved in the attack. Director Danie Coetzee was on duty during the Seven Day War and acknowledged to the Truth and Reconciliation Commission that he had made no attempt to disarm Inkatha members (Truth and Reconciliation Commission, 1998: Volume 2, Chapter 3).[12]

The violence in Natal/KwaZulu spread to the Transvaal where 4 765 killings were recorded between July 1990 and June 1993. More than 200 township residents were killed on the East Rand in large-scale massacres perpetrated by hostel dwellers. Over the next twelve months violence continued to intensify (Truth and Reconciliation Commission, 1998: Volume 2, Chapter 7). In the four months leading to the 1994 elections, KwaZulu and Natal experienced the worst wave of political violence in the region's history. Fearing an ANC majority both nationally and provincially, the IFP sought to prevent their opponents from canvassing support, particularly in the KwaZulu 'homeland' areas. In one instance, '15 ANC supporters were massacred by IFP supporters as they prepared for an election campaign' (Jeffery, 1997: 419). The IFP was aided by the SAP who continued to transport large quantities of weapons on behalf of the IFP (Truth and Reconciliation Commission, 1998: Volume 2, Chapter 3).

Violence took the form of night-time massacres, drive-by shootings, military-style attacks on commuter trains, and assassinations. Massacres and killings were carried out by large groups of men wearing red headbands and wielding anything from iron rods to automatic weapons, although the incidents often gave the impression of being unplanned and random. And all through this virtual reign of terror, allegations never ceased that a 'third force' involving the security forces was behind much of the violence, intent on escalating it to derail the political negotiations. In evidence to the Truth and Reconciliation Commission, one SAP member, Wayne Swanepoel, confessed that he and others in his unit were involved in throwing people from trains in an attempt to get the ANC and the IFP to blame one another (Truth and Reconciliation Commission, 1998: Volume 2, Chapter 7).

Many deaths also resulted from the continued use of force in public order policing. Estimates by the Human Rights Commission were that 518 people were killed in the course of public order policing operations between July 1991 and June 1992 (Truth and Reconciliation Commission, 1998: Volume 2, Chapter 7). The Truth and

Reconciliation Commission concluded that there was little change in the policing of demonstrations after 1990 (Truth and Reconciliation Commission, 1998: Volume 2, Chapter 7).

Between 1990 and 1991, police statistics record 10 889 gatherings, the majority of which were 'not authorised' (Jeffrey, 1991). For the most part, gatherings were still deemed illegal, and this meant that gatherings and protest actions were still exposed to the customarily brutal interventions of the Riot Unit.

Two incidents provoked wide condemnation and in many ways were a catalyst for the changes that were to be instituted in protest policing in the early 1990s.

On 26 March 1990 a march was organised by the UDF in Sebokeng, a black township in the Vaal district, to protest against the crisis in housing and education. Permission to hold the march in the adjacent central business district was applied for five days in advance, but denied. The crowd was singing protest songs, and seemed to have posed no threat to any non-participants or to the police. Nonetheless, the police fired into the crowd, apparently without any order to shoot having been given. Shooting lasted about 20 minutes during which 60 rounds of ammunition were fired. Five people were killed and 161 were injured. A commission of inquiry concluded that the force used was excessive, and that there was poor co-ordination between police commanders and rank-and-file officers. Police involved in the operation were deemed to have been undisciplined and inexperienced in protest policing; six policemen were subsequently charged with murder (Jeffery, 1991).

In a second incident, on 14 March 1991, 200 ANC supporters gathered in Daveyton township on the East Rand. They were protesting the lack of protection for residents under attack from members of Inkatha. According to members of the ANC, 'the police arrived on the scene, gave the group ten minutes to disperse and then, while the men were still discussing the issue, opened fire' (Jeffery, 1991: 38). The police claimed that the men were armed with petrol bombs, pangas (cane knives), and other weapons, that they were under attack and that they fired on the protestors in 'self-defence'. Twelve ANC supporters were killed, including a nine-year-old girl, and twenty-seven people injured (Jeffery, 1991).

Later that same year, for the first time in history, white right-wingers incurred the wrath of the Riot Police. On 9 August 1991, white right-wingers organised by the Afrikaner Weerstandsbeweging (AWB) threatened to disrupt a meeting in Ventersdorp where State President F.W. de Klerk was scheduled to speak. Two thousand AWB supporters armed with pistols and hunting rifles advanced on the hall where the meeting was to take place, ignored the police line outside the hall, and fired on two nearby minibuses. The police opened fire and killed one of the AWB protestors. A street battle ensued and forty-eight people were injured, six of them policemen. According to the AWB, the police acted without warning and had been given the order to 'shoot to kill'. The police did not deny that such an order was given, but stated that this took place only after three policemen had been shot by AWB supporters (Jeffery, 1991).

Following these events the government came to recognise the need for a radical change in the policing of public order. In November 1991 a new Strategic Plan for the SAP gave its endorsement to the principle of community policing, which had been the leading influence in policing in most western democracies since the 1980s but was entirely new to the South African police. The Strategic Plan acknowledged for the first time the necessity of a representative, depoliticised, demilitarised, service-oriented police force that would actively forge alliances with the community (Cawthra, 1993). There was common ground between the apartheid government and the ANC in the urgency they saw for restoration of public confidence in policing, with community involvement so that genuine partnerships could emerge between the police and the broad South African community that it should be their duty to serve – policing to be founded upon consensus, not coercion. The continuing death toll of protesters at the hands of the Riot Unit underlined the urgency of getting the reforms under way, and certainly for this unit in particular.

As part of the plan to reconstruct and reform the police force, it was decided to rename and reorganise the problematic Riot Unit. In its strategic planning for 1991 the SAP leadership had come to see that their traditionally confrontational, aggressive policing style against unrest had 'contaminated' the corporate image of the SAP and also 'reduced its capacity for crime prevention and control, because of the number of police officials required for dealing with unrest' (Rauch and Storey, 1998: 22). It was accordingly decided to create an easily identifiable, separate division in the SAP with a national command structure, the Internal Stability Division (ISD). The ISD was formed in 1991 and was made up of 40 locally based Internal Stability Units with over 7 000 members operating throughout the Republic (i.e. excluding the 'independent' homelands). One of the largest of the local ISD units was Unit 19 (which had continued to operate since the time of the Reaction Unit), the special national unit based in Pretoria, which had a complement of 1 200 officers. Another 32 similar units were established in the various homelands.

The ISD was ostensibly committed to less aggressive crowd control. It defined its primary role as

> the combating of riots ... and combating of violence and unrest in the Republic of South Africa. The division placed emphasis on preventive actions, such as patrols in areas where unrest and intimidation and other unrest related crimes prevail ... If there is not unrest in an area, the ISD is fully employed in the prevention of crime (quoted in Cilliers, 1995: 25).

Organised as a separate full-time paramilitary unit within the SAP, the ISD was, however, hardly less problematic than its predecessor. It was a massive unit, able to deploy 17 000 men at any particular time, with their own distinctive (and distinctly military) camouflage uniform, equipment, and, not least, their khaki-green Casspir and Nyala armoured vehicles – the notorious 'mello yellos', so omnipresent on the townships' dusty streets.

The training was slightly more sophisticated than the previous riot unit training and focused more directly on crowd control. Some soft skills were introduced into the training, which included negotiation skills and crowd psychology, yet still the main focus continued to be the use of force and mechanical application of the law (Rauch and Storey, 1998). While police seemed to have become a shade more tolerant of protest and demonstrations, there continued to be numerous incidents where police intervention in crowd situations resulted in death and serious injury.

Riot control training was still offered at the police college in Maloeskop in the Eastern Transvaal. ISD members were instructed in the legislation pertaining to crowd control, the handling of weapons, and 'crowd psychology' – which focused on de-individuation based on the writings of Le Bon on mob psychology (Jeffery, 1991). In theory the training emphasised minimum force followed by gradual escalation as the situation required, but this principle was undermined by the actual weaponry the police were still being issued with and by the continuing emphasis on the unpredictability of crowds. This type of training continued until the mid-1990s.

In September 1991 an historic event took place that radically redefined the mandate for policing, and public order policing especially. Together, the government and 27 political parties (most importantly the ANC and the IFP) signed a National Peace Accord (the first of many multi-party agreements), the thrust of which was to 'signify a common purpose to bring an end to political violence in the country and to set out the codes of conduct, procedures and mechanisms to achieve this goal' (Marais, 1994: 2). Police were henceforth accountable to local communities and obliged to consult with communities and political parties on the methods of policing they would employ. All police were expected to sign a Code of Conduct that committed them to acting impartially and with propriety (Jeffrey, 1997).

The National Peace Accord also made provisions for a commission of enquiry which, in terms of the Prevention of Public Violence and Intimidation Act of 1991, was given the brief to: (a) enquire into the phenomenon of public violence and intimidation in the Republic, and the nature and causes thereof; (b) enquire into the steps that should be taken in order to prevent public violence and intimidation; and (c) make recommendations to the State President regarding steps to prevent violence and intimidation. The Commission (headed by Supreme Court Judge Richard Goldstone) generated some 40 reports pertaining to ongoing violence: ongoing taxi conflict, train and hostel violence, violence on the East Rand, the violent conflict between the ANC and the IFP, particularly in Natal (Marais, 1993b), and more besides. A number of recommendations were also made for improving the relationship between the police and local communities. These included the following:

- ISD members should wear blue uniforms to promote the image of the ISD as a policing agency, not a military force.
- Ordinary police vehicles should be used, with armoured vehicles confined to high-risk situations or areas.
- Weapons and tactics should be appropriate to the principle of minimum force.
- The name of the ISD should be changed to accommodate its new image.

One of the principal incidents that the Commission investigated was the Boipatong massacre on 17 June 1992 when IFP-aligned hostel dwellers from KwaMadala Hostel attacked Boipatong township residents in a night raid. Residents were hacked, stabbed, shot, beaten and disembowelled; 46 died on one of the 'darkest days in South Africa's history' (South African Press Alliance, 7 August 1996), and the ANC suspended its negotiations with the government. Once again the police were implicated, with eyewitness claims that policemen had been present during the night attack (South African Press Alliance, 7 August 1996). Shortly afterwards President F.W. de Klerk visited the township and in the commotion that immediately followed, police fired on a fleeing crowd. According to journalist Allister Sparks, the ISD fired at point-blank range and without warning on an unarmed crowd. Two people were killed and twenty-nine seriously wounded (cited in Brogden and Shearing, 1993). The Goldstone Commission's report concluded that the police (the ISD) had been undisciplined, incompetent, lacking adequate command and control, had ineffective intelligence, and had extremely poor relations with the community (Waddington report cited in Brogden and Shearing, 1993). They were also very poorly informed about internationally accepted principles and techniques in crowd control. Most of the ISD members involved had previously been in the Riot Unit, and in the mobile units prior to that, and had received very little training in crowd management techniques during the course of these careers.[13]

On 6 December 1991, the Goldstone Commission announced the appointment of a committee to consider how demonstrations should be conducted and policed. The Commission recognised that 'unpredictable or undisciplined conduct by mass demonstrators or members of the police force create a very real potential for violence' (Goldstone Commission, 1991: 1). The committee would look into (a) the procedure which should be followed in order to arrange or organise mass demonstrations; (b) the procedure that should be followed by the organisers before, during and after mass demonstrations; (c) the norms of behaviour of the persons who participate in mass demonstrations; (d) the role and duty of the police and, if relevant, of other security forces, in relation to mass demonstrations; and (e) the adequacy of present legislation relating to mass demonstrations.

On 22 May 1992, it was announced that a multinational panel of experts had been appointed to advise the Commission's committee on the matters outlined above – especially as they related to mass demonstrations, marches and picketing. The panel recommended that bodies other than the police should be involved in public order policing. Marshals from the community (who had a very different culture from the police) should be involved along with police in the regulating of crowds. In this way, policing would also become the responsibility of demonstrators and the organisers of demonstrations; demonstrators themselves would participate in the planning of a policing strategy prior to a protest or demonstration. The panel proposed the establishment of 'triangles of safety' (now known as the Golden Triangle) that would be made up of local authority representatives, representatives of the demonstrators, and the police, all three thus jointly involved in the planning and evaluation of demonstrations and protests with the police no longer in sole control (Shearing, 1995).

In response to its 6 December 1991 invitation, the Commission received submissions from a wide range of organisations, including political parties, academics and the SAP. From these, along with input from panel members and other documentation, the panel compiled the report it delivered to the Commission on 9 July 1992 at a public hearing. The hearing lasted four days during which time members of the public and other organisations had further opportunity to respond. The most important participants were the SAP, the ANC, the IFP, the SACP and Cosatu.

The panel accepted the following principle as its point of departure:

> The right to demonstrate is as fundamental a right of democratic citizenship as the right to take part in political campaigns. Where the purpose of the demonstration is protest, the demonstration is at the core of free expression in a democracy. One of the central responsibilities of the police is to facilitate the right to demonstrate (Heymann, 1992: ix).

The Commission subsequently prepared a draft bill that captured the code of conduct as represented in the panel's report. On 28 January 1994, the Regulation of Gatherings Act 205 of 1993 was published in the Government Gazette. According to the Regulation of Gatherings Act and the 1996 Constitution of South Africa, each and every person has a right to freely express their views, to demonstrate and to protest, provided that their actions are peaceful. Section 16 of the Constitution entrenches the right to freedom of expression, and Section 17 provides that everyone has the right to assemble, picket, demonstrate, and present petitions in a peaceful and unarmed manner. The Act also stipulated that all assemblies, marches, gatherings, meetings, demonstrations must be considered lawful. No longer was there to be a distinction between legal and illegal gatherings and demonstrations – gatherings were now defined as either 'peaceful' or 'unrest' incidents, depending on their outcome.

The role of the police in accordance with this Act and with the Constitution is to protect the rights of all people affected by gatherings, both participants and non-participants. Another important aspect of the Act is that the convener of a gathering must notify a responsible officer appointed by the local authority that a gathering is to take place. Negotiations should then be instituted with all interested parties (an authorised member of the police, local authority representative and the convener) to ensure the peaceful progress of the gathering and the protection of participants and non-participants. The primary role of the police should, therefore, be that of negotiator rather than enforcer.

The Act, together with the provisions of the 1993 Interim Constitution, turned public order policing in South Africa as it had functioned in the apartheid years completely on its head. The newly renamed South African Police Service (see below) now had a legal responsibility to protect the rights of citizens when they engaged in peaceful protest activities. More specifically, the role of the police responsible for public order policing changed from repressing protest to managing protest, with fundamental implications for selection and training, operational procedures, and equipment.

But despite the Gatherings Act (which was not promulgated until 1995) and the Goldstone Commission Report, by 1994 the ISD was still viewed as extremely problematic. An opinion survey conducted in that year by the Human Science Research Council concluded that in the view of the public 'the ISD is beyond redemption, [and] a replacement must be created' (Cilliers, 1995: 25).

Democracy – and a new vision for public order policing
In April 1994, South Africa elected its first national democratic government and there began a far-reaching process of transformation in the South African police. The new Minister of Safety and Security, together with the National Commissioner, set in motion a series of internal changes, in line with the new democratic order, aimed at producing increased civilianisation, transparency, accountability and representivity. The military ranking system was abolished, legislation pertaining to police unionisation and labour relations was liberalised, affirmative action recruitment and career-path processes were set in motion, and, at a more symbolic level, the insignia of the police were changed. The new South African Police Service Act (68 of 1995) also renamed the force as the South African Police Service (SAPS) which was to be a single, united police service formed from an amalgamation of the old SAP, the homeland police forces and the railway police.

While there was reasonable clarity as to what the new police service would look like overall, the future of the ISD was a source of much contention. In the transition years of the 1990s, academics and the ANC had called for the disbanding of the problematic ISD. But then in the 1994 run-up to the first democratic elections the ISD was heavily deployed across the country to secure the environment for free and fair balloting. Perhaps the ISD knew that its days were numbered, since its conduct during these months was both professional and efficient. Maybe it was this 'good behaviour' that earned it a reprieve after the elections when the new ANC Minister of Safety and Security declared that a separate, specialised public order unit would be retained in the newly 'transformed' SAPS.

But there have also been other explanations for its retention. For David Storey, a member of the Technical Team on the Transformation of Public Order Policing (discussed below), the need for a separate public order unit was indisputable, and for eight separate reasons:[14] (a) the ready availability of firearms to virtually anyone presented a real threat to public order; (b) social conflict persisted due to antagonistic relations in industry, ethnic divisions, continued racial tensions, and continuing local turf wars between rival political organisations; (c) the high crime rate, particularly of violent crime, required special interventions by paramilitary units; (d) regular visible policing lacked capacity to carry out routine police work, let alone crowd management functions; (e) the huge socio-economic disparities fuelled constant discontent; (f) the legacy of paramilitary structures and tactics in all political organisations created the need for potential paramilitary intervention; (g) the huge numbers of people involved in protests and demonstrations required highly specialised policing; and (h) the volatility of protest action required a paramilitary response capacity.

In the case of KwaZulu-Natal, with its history of, arguably, the highest level of internal conflict and public disorder among the provinces, the need for a separate public order unit was regarded as even more self-evident. According to Director Wiggins, Commander of what was shortly to be established as the Public Order Police Unit in KwaZulu-Natal, there were in 1994, an average of 200 public order events each month in KwaZulu-Natal alone. This, in his view, called for a high level of readiness and 'a force which can act in unison at very short notice'.[15]

The decision to continue with a successor unit to the ISD was taken in 1995. Like the ISD, it would be a separate division in the police with its own distinctive identity.[16] In this 'new' incarnation the former ISD was subsumed into the Public Order Police Unit (POPU, later POP), but there was general consensus that radical changes would be needed to increase its effectiveness and improve its fragile relationship with the communities it serviced. In accordance with the South African Police Service Act (68 of 1995), the new national public order policing unit was established by the National Commissioner in September 1995.

POP, following the rest of the 'new' South African Police Service, was to be an integrated unit. In other words, just as all existing police agencies would form part of a single SAPS, all elements from these same agencies that had previously been involved in public order policing would be integrated into the single new national

POP unit. In November 1995, ISD was accordingly amalgamated with the Riot Control Units of the homeland police. What still lay ahead for POP would be a major transformation to rid it of its tarnished past and bring it into line with international standards and practice.

A report, drawn up in 1995 by the SAPS-initiated Technical Team on Public Order Policing, set out the guidelines for what public order policing should become: community based and accountable; integrated with mainstream policing; decentralised; demilitarised; transparent, representative, and professional; policy driven; mobile and multi-skilled. It was considered important for visible changes to be seen in uniforms and equipment and vehicles to eliminate the former military associations and appearance. There also had to be significant changes in the composition of the unit to make it more reflective of South African demographics of race and gender.

Following from the Technical Team report, new objectives were outlined in the Public Order Police Policy Document on Crowd Management (1996), notably:
- to establish standardised procedures to manage crowds in such a way that these conform to democratic values and accepted international standards;
- to instil an approach in POP of acting at all times in a professional, acceptable and effective manner and in a way which is community-oriented and accountable for every action.

For these to be achieved, the Policy Document outlined a new set of governing principles:
- The constitutional right of individuals and groups to voice their concerns/ grievances/opinions must be upheld at all times.
- The rights of citizens and the community to demonstrate peacefully without infringing on the rights of others must be acknowledged.
- In their actions, members of the unit must be fair, impartial, and firm.
- Responses and actions must be predictable and tolerant.
- There should be no loss of life.
- There should be no damage to property.
- There should be no injuries.
- All citizens should be satisfied with the conduct of the SAPS.
- All citizens present at a gathering are to feel safe and secure.

Very clearly, a major transformation process lay ahead. As we shall see, it would involve training, recruitment, policy and legislation, and also operational equipment. Its successes and failures over five years of reform until 2001 are the focus of this book.

The pace and outcome of police transformation is shaped by a number of internal organisational constraints. Public order policing is circumscribed by past politics and practices. Informally, police cultures are rooted in inherited assumptions about police work itself, and about the wider external environment in which the police operate (Della Porta, 1993). Histories, forms of knowledge, assumptions, and practices all make 'change in mind-set' an elusive and perplexing goal. All these confronted the new government of national unity in 1995 in the legacy it had inherited: a huge national Riot Unit, fragmented, over-centralised, unaccountable, ill-equipped and poorly trained for the new challenges it would be facing in a democratic South Africa.

4

Durban POP in 2001

SIX YEARS INTO the new political order, what was the face of public order policing in South Africa as it showed itself in Durban POP in 2001? Outlining the composition of the unit, its operational routines, and the background and motivation of the men and women who made up its workforce at this point in its transformational history, we shall begin to see the roots of what were to be both successes and failures in that transformation, embracing complex and often contradictory patterns of incentives and constraints, solidarities and cleavages.

Composition and structure

In its racial composition, Durban POP in the year 2001 was unquestionably a very different creature from its Riot Unit and ISD predecessors. In 1992, 80 per cent of the Durban ISD members were white – those in command positions uniformly so.[1] By 1998 the majority were African, clustered still in the lower ranks, but most with extended service in the police. They shared the daily work – and the occupational culture of the police – with their white colleagues.

In large part, the change in the racial composition came about through the amalgamation of the SAP with other police forces in the various apartheid homelands. In the case of the Durban unit, the amalgamation was with the former KwaZulu Police Force.[2] An additional factor, according to the 1997 Unit Commander, was that 'there were many white members who felt uncomfortable or threatened by the transformation process in the unit, and opted for retrenchment packages'.

Table 4.1 indicates the 1998 figures for each race group at each rank level of the unit. By 1998, the majority of unit members were Africans but whites continued to dominate at management and leadership levels. This only began to change a year or two later. By May 2000, both Senior Superintendents were Indians and the newly

Table 4.1: Durban POP rank totals by race (1998).

	Indian	White	African	Coloured	Total
Director	0	1	0	0	1
Snr Supt	1	1	0	0	2
Supt	2	5	0	0	7
Captain	35 (2*)	11 (1*)	6 (1*)	0	0 (4*)
Inspector	53 (1*)	15	37	1	53 (1*)
Sergeant	93	61 (4*)	305 (3*)	12 (1*)	93 (8*)
Constable	12	13	190	5	222
Total	196 (3*)	107 (5*)	538 (4*)	18 (1*)	859 (13*)

* female members

appointed Unit Commander was an African, the first such appointment for Durban POP. In January 2001, an African Senior Superintendent was appointed as one of the two Operational Commanders. All of these appointments represented important attempts on the part of police management nationally to transform the racial representation in the higher ranks.

Table 4.2 shows that by May 2000, Indians continued to be over-represented at the middle management level, and there remained, too, a very evident under-representation of African commissioned officers. As we shall see later, this was a source of considerable friction in the unit, African members welcomed the new Unit Commander, but they also wanted the proportion for Africans in commissioned officer ranks to be far higher, at 70 per cent. In 2000, black Durban POP members formed a group called the Empowerment Committee of Public Order Police specifically to take up the grievances of (mainly black) individual officers and to press for speedier affirmative action and transformation.

Table 4.2: Durban POP rank totals by race (2000).

	Indian	White	African	Coloured	Total
Director	0	0	1	0	1
Snr Supt	1	0	0	0	1
Supt	2	2	0	0	4
Captain	29 (2*)	8 (1*)	6 (1*)	0	43 (4*)
Inspector	82 (1*)	22 (3*)	54 (4*)	6	164 (8*)
Sergeant	173	37 (3*)	289 (3*)	1	500 (6*)
Constable	12 (1*)	4	86 (1*)	1	103 (2*)
Total	299 (3*)	73 (7*)	436 (9*)	8	816 (20*)

* female members

The African female Captain (Table 2) was the only female Platoon Commander in the unit and indeed in the entire country. In November 2000 she was promoted to Superintendent and appointed as Company Commander, which was a major advance for the unit in terms of both race and gender representation in the higher ranks. Less than 3 per cent of unit members overall were female, and most of these were non-commissioned officers.

In its organisational structure Durban POP retained the military-style configuration of its antecedents, and with it, at this basic level at any rate, a significant measure of its original paramilitary character. The Unit was divided into Platoons, each made up of four Sections, the lowest unit of organisation. Each Section had eight members and a Section Leader. A Platoon Commander (Captain ranking) and a Second-in-Charge headed each Platoon. Four Platoons made up a Company. A Company Commander (Superintendent ranking) and a Second-in-Charge headed each Company (Figure 4.1).

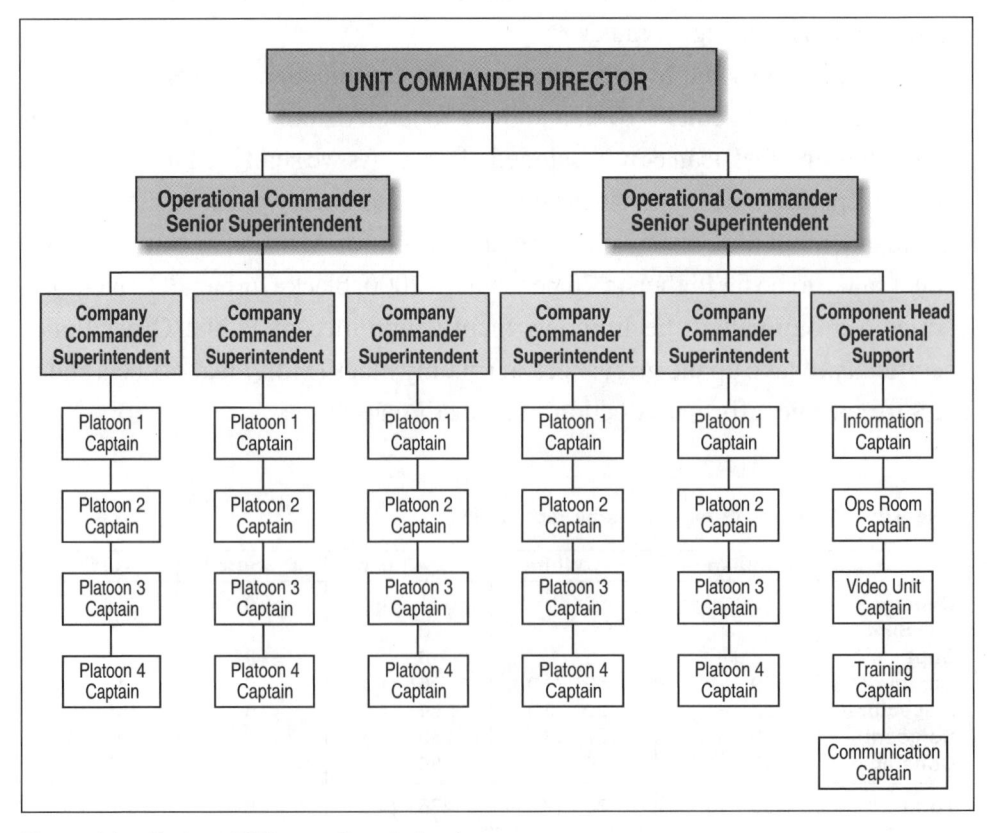

Figure 4.1: Durban POP operational structure.

One Durban POP company differed from the others in being comprised of four specialised platoons. These were:
- the RDP Platoon: established to safeguard workers and contractors involved in state RDP (Reconstruction and Development Programme) projects. For example, if a school was being built in a particular locality, the unit would make sure that unauthorised persons were kept out of the site and no materials were stolen. This platoon was also deployed to escort vehicles carrying large amounts of cash and had a special role in recovering weapons and stolen vehicles during crime prevention operations. The RDP platoon was composed almost wholly of white members.
- the Field Platoon: deployed mainly in peri-urban areas, their primary mandate was to recover firearms and stolen vehicles. They were known to have an extensive network of informers who assisted in their intelligence gathering. This platoon was composed entirely of African members.
- the Bike Platoon: deployed when the Company Commander or Operational Commander called for motorbike support at a crowd management or crime prevention operation. This platoon was also mainly white in composition. A few Coloured and Indian members were introduced to the platoon in 1998.
- the Reaction Platoon (or Reaction Unit): a reserve platoon meant to provide tactical support to other platoons operating in the field. The members of this platoon were regarded as elite operatives with special training in handling dangerous situations. This unit was likewise originally all-white, though some black members joined after 1999.

These four platoons were a source of much controversy in the Unit, both because of their racial composition and because of the perceived preferential treatment they received with respect to resources, shifts, and even pay. The RDP and Reaction Platoons also shared a reputation for being the most brutal platoons in the Unit,[3] prepared to do anything to achieve their goals, regardless of regulations.

POP nationally was a specialised unit within the SAPS. It had its own command structure at all levels – national, provincial and local. In terms of the South African Police Service Act of 1995, the SAPS Provincial Commissioner had to approve any deployment of the unit at provincial or area level. Area Commissioners of the regular visible police could request the support of POP but the Provincial Commissioner had to approve this. The National Commissioner had the authority to deploy the POP units to any area at any time as he/she deemed necessary to restore public order. Consequently the unit had to be highly mobile and able to respond at very short notice.

When and why members joined the unit
Although there was an influx of African members into the unit and an exodus of white members in the early 1990s, this abated in later years. Aside from some significant shifts in the higher ranks there was little movement in and out of the unit between 1996 and 2001. Most members had joined prior to the democratic transition and had been members of the ISD and even of the Riot Unit in the past. This long-term continuity of personnel had serious implications, I believe, for attempts at transformation of the unit.

A formal survey I conducted with Durban POP members in 1999 (described more fully in Chapter 5) established that three quarters of the officers in the unit had been in public order policing for more than five years. Of these, 16 per cent had been in the unit between ten and fifteen years and just under 3 per cent for more than twenty years. This meant that for the great majority of members their training had been in the old tactics of counter-insurgency and riot control and they were socialised into a sub-culture where excessive force and disregard of basic freedoms were considered normal and legitimate.

The length of time members had been in the unit varied somewhat according to race. More than half the white members (53 per cent) had been involved in public order policing for more than ten years. Almost all Indian members (87 per cent) had been in the unit for between five and ten years, but only 9 per cent had been doing this type of work for more than ten years. Some 24 per cent of African members had been involved in public order policing for more than ten years. A little under half of all members had been in the police for more than ten years.

Members of the unit joined the police for a multitude of reasons. Fielding (1988a) argues that the motivations people have for joining the police are important to understand since they impact directly on the degree to which new recruits adapt to and imbibe both formal and informal processes of police socialisation and on their identification of reference groups within the police. And there are a variety of motivations that dispose the police for the work they do in the course of their careers. As Reiner puts it:

> Police officers will remain motivated by a complex and varying mixture of a

search for interest, excitement, and a cup of tea; loyalty and esprit de corps, commitment to public service, concern with the plight of victims will all play their parts, as will wanting to get through as trouble free a shift as possible avoiding the rain and the cold, and yes, job security and a fair financial reward (in Critcher and Waddington, 1996: 263).

The reasons Durban POP members gave for joining the police differed markedly between the four ethnic groups represented in the unit (Figure 4.2). The majority of African members claimed they joined the police for altruistic reasons – to serve the

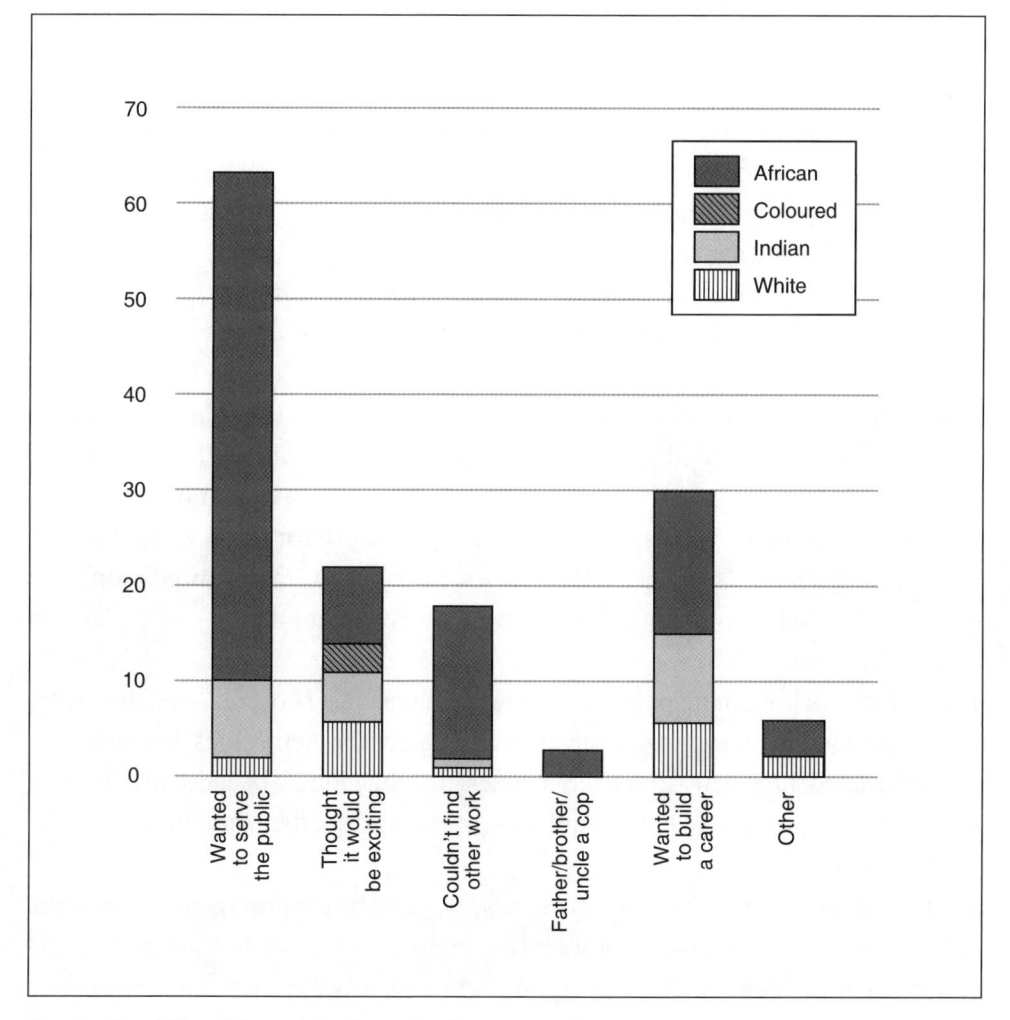

Figure 4.2: 'Why did you join the police?'

public – but there were also a significant number who said that they joined because they were unable to find other work, particularly those who signed up in the 1970s and 1980s. Even the recently appointed African Operational Commander of Durban POP stated that the labour market restrictions in the apartheid years were the decisive factor in his decision to join the police:

> To be honest, black policemen like myself joined the police because there were few job alternatives open to us. I joined in 1982 when really it was not a popular thing to do. I was ostracised by my community who hated the police. But, where else could I think of starting a career? Black police at the time knew that they would be acting against the community and not for it.[4]

Joining the police was one of very few alternatives to a strictly blue-collar job for South African blacks, which is why, despite the isolation from their own communities that black police experienced and the racist treatment they received in the police force, there 'appears to have been no shortage of recruits among black people' (Brogden and Shearing, 1993: 78).

Lack of job opportunities continued to be a motivating factor for African recruits even in the 1990s. Sergeant Miriam Ncobo stated that she

> joined the police in 1993. The reason I joined is because I couldn't find any other job and I needed money to further my studies. At first I wanted to become a teacher, but at that time all the teacher colleges were full and I did not get accepted. So, I stayed home doing nothing for three years after finishing school. Then I heard the police were trying to employ more people and I decided to join. I must say I am happy now that I did.[5]

Indian officers joined the police for three main reasons. Most claimed they were motivated by self-interest, wanting to build a career for themselves, but almost as many declared, like their African colleagues, that they joined because they wanted to help people. About one in five said they joined because they thought it would be an exciting job.

Whites seem to have been the ones most attracted by the promise of excitement, which is the motivation most commonly cited by police recruits around the world (Reiner, 1992a; Banton, 1964). Very few white members claimed to have joined the police out of a desire to serve the public.

Equally significant are the motivations POP members gave specifically for joining the public order units (POP or its predecessors the Riot Unit and the ISD). These too varied according to race (Figure 4.3) and they point up several interesting issues. More than a quarter of the respondents claimed that it had not in fact been their choice to join the unit. In the 1970s and 1980s, serving officers on station assignment and new recruits alike were simply transferred, or appointed, to the Mobile Unit, the Riot Unit, and later the Internal Stability Unit. This seems to have been the case particularly with Indian and white officers but a significant number of African officers, almost one in five, also said they had had no choice in the matter.

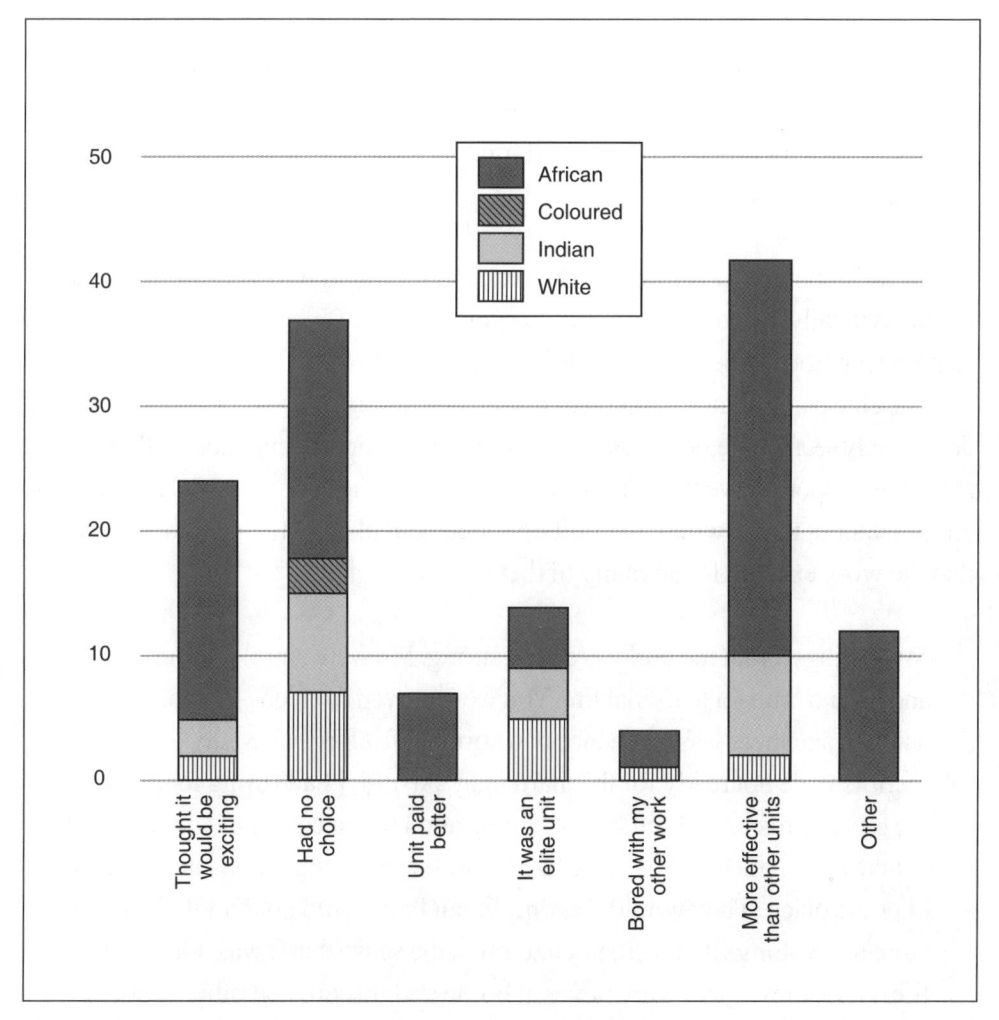

Figure 4.3: 'Why did you decide to join the Riot Unit/ISD/POP?'

Africans and Indians who joined the unit because they wanted to said it was because they considered it more 'effective' than other units. For white members it seems to have been more important that this was an 'elite' unit. Wanting to be part of an elite unit is typical of those who join specialised public order units; Jefferson, writing from a British perspective, claims that recruits into specialised paramilitary units tend to join because it is perceived as an avenue to 'highly valued police work' (1990: 114).

The third most frequent reason given by white members was that they thought it would be more exciting than working in the police station or doing regular beat work:

> I wanted to join the Reaction Unit. It was a unit engaged in high-risk and dangerous work, which is what I wanted. It also was a unit made up of disciplined members who are well trained and where there is no place for error.[6]

This is an archetypal sentiment from someone recruited into a paramilitary unit — where, typically, recruits are 'ambitious young male officers of four or five years' standing, anxious to be "active"' (Jefferson, 1990: 134).

The elite paramilitary standing of the unit and the exciting working environment do certainly seem, together, to have consolidated a distinct occupational ethos. White respondents spoke fervently of a solidarity kindled by the dangerous and even horrific circumstances under which the unit operated, and also by the personal sacrifices that the work exacted for so many of them:

> My feelings about the unit were very strong. We were simply doing our job and had no time for a normal life. You were moved from one violent place to another, and there was no chance of a normal life after that. Many of the new recruits were not ready for this hard man's world. I had strong feelings for the guys at this time. I felt bad for them, and I was a commander who tried to take care of them. They were like the military, seeing blood and sweat all over the place. They wouldn't admit it but they could not handle it. There were many things that were not natural in the sense that it was not a normal life. Also, these guys were never at home and this created other problems such as very high divorce rates in the unit . . . we stayed in awkward places

and had awkward hours. And there was no racism during that time. We slept together, we ate together, and we bathed together. We were all buddies. We had a relationship. Your buddies were your back-up and we all protected each other.[7]

The Senior Superintendent quoted here is reflecting on life in the unit in the 1980s. In his memory, this was life under combat conditions – where the unit became your home, and colleagues the family on whom you depended and with whom you shared your daily predicament. And, for all the security and reassurance provided by this surrogate family, there remains his persistent iteration that these were 'abnormal' conditions resulting, it would seem, in detrimental personal consequences.

Operational patterns
The primary function of the POP as outlined in the Technical Team Report on Public Order Policing (1995) was 'the management of events/incidents of public collective action and behaviour particularly where there is a potential for violent or disruptive conduct. Management includes preventive, protective, pro-active, reactive and restorative conduct'. The secondary functions mentioned in the Report included: the prevention of crime; rendering support on an ad hoc basis in respect of policing activities or tasks which require the specialised training, equipment and personnel of the unit; policing of and rendering support in natural and man-made disaster situations; support of the governmental development programmes. The intention, at least, was that the unit would be deployed to these secondary functions only if there were adequate resources (human and physical) to carry out its primary function in the first instance.

Although the Durban POP unit gave priority in its planning to its primary function, it engaged in a wide variety of activities overall. These ranged from strictly public order or crowd management operations (the policing of marches, demonstrations, sports events, political rallies, or anything else that could be considered as the management of crowds), to maintaining a presence in volatile areas that required 'stabilisation', to more mainstream policing, which included patrols and crime prevention.

Every week the unit drew up a plan of activities (specifically for crowd management events) based on requests from the public and from the SAPS Area Commissioner and in response to intelligence (police and military) pertaining to possible events and sites of public disorder. The following, by way of illustration, is a list of planned activities for the first week of March 1998, copied from a Planned Activities Report of the Provincial Operational Co-ordinating Committee (POCOC), and gives an idea of the crowd management events the unit dealt with week by week:

> 1998-03-01 Sunday: 9 am
> A meeting will be held at the Folweni garage in Umbumbulu where work opportunities in the greater area will be discussed. Problems can be expected, as the community is unhappy that the organisers are from the outside.
>
> 1998-03-01 Sunday: 10 am
> A meeting to be held at Nhlakanipho High School in KwaMashu. Report back from Education Department.
>
> 1998-03-01 Sunday: 10 am
> A meeting of Inkatha Freedom Party to be held at the Phikiswayo ground in Richmond Farm. The purpose of the meeting is to increase membership and to relaunch the branch as well as to combine five other branches into one branch. A large crowd is expected.
>
> 1998-03-01 Sunday: 10 am
> A meeting between the ANC chairperson and the community regarding the conflict between the community of Shonokona Squatter area and the councillor in the area. Meeting will take place at the Catholic Church.
>
> 1998-03-01 Sunday: 2 pm
> A community meeting will be held at Cato Crest, Cato Manor. The purpose of the meeting is to elect a committee that will be responsible for the allocation of houses in the area.
>
> 1998-03-02 Monday: 10 am
> Security guards employed by Rhino Security intend to march from

Pinetown Taxi Rank, via the central business district, to Rhino Security offices.

1998-03-02 Monday: 2 pm
A further meeting between the Dolphin Coast and the Stanger Taxi Association over the use of routes to be taken. Previous negotiations between the associations have so far been unsuccessful.

1998-03-02 Tuesday: time unknown
A meeting will be held at SAPS Chatsworth to resolve the conflict between Africans in the community and the Indians at Welbedacht. The tension developed after an Indian tavern owner allegedly shot a patron.

1998-03-03 Wednesday: 1 pm
The Natal African Teachers Union will hold a protest meeting outside the Durban City Hall to highlight the plea of the 5 000 teachers to be retrenched. No permission for this gathering has been obtained. It is unknown how many persons will attend.

1998-03-06 Saturday: time unknown
An IFP rally will be held at Menzi sports ground in M-section, Umlazi. Premier Ben Ngubane will be the guest speaker and IFP members from various surrounding areas will attend. Presently there are no indications of violence manifesting during or after the rally. Although no threats/problems are foreseen, confrontations between supporters of opposing political groups cannot be ruled out, especially en route to and from the rally.

1998-03-06 Saturday: 12 am
A mass meeting will be held outside the Workshop complex in Durban. The aim of the meeting is to promote peace, reconciliation and to fight crime which has plagued Durban and the surrounding areas. About 7 000 people are expected to attend.

1998-03-06 Saturday: time unknown
The funerals of the following gang members who were killed in Clermont will take place as follows . . . The above mentioned were members of the Abashana gang and the possible burning of stolen motor vehicles, discharging of firearms, revenge attacks, etc. cannot be ruled out from occurring at the funeral.

1998-03-07 Sunday: 11 am
A meeting and community feast will be held at Nkosi Ntinyane's kraal in Umbumbulu. About 5 000 people are expected to attend. The area is currently stable and there are no threats foreseen.

1988-03-07 Sunday: 10 am
The funeral of the late vice-chairman of the Chesterville Taxi Association will be held at Chesterville Cemetery. Prior to that a memorial service will be held at the Chesterville Hall. Possible revenge attacks cannot be ruled out as the situation remains tense.

The range includes large events like mass meetings, funerals, protests and demonstrations, but also smaller community gatherings. Even though there seemed to be little immediate threat of disorder at most of these events, the volatile political history of the province was clearly still a concern and provided a justification for the presence of the unit at seemingly inconsequential gatherings.

From a scrutiny of the Daily Events Planner of the unit and the Company Commanders' Monthly Reports it is possible to get a sense of the more general activities the unit undertook on a regular basis. The Information Management (Intelligence) Department of the unit compiled the Daily Events Planner; based on information and requests received and the Planned Activities Report, a list of activities was drawn up for the unit on Monday mornings. Below is a Daily Events Plan for the Durban POP unit for the week 6–11 February 2001.

Tues 6 February 09:00–17:00: Umbilo:[8] Crime Prevention Operation [Roadblocks and searches in the area at the request of the Umbilo Police Station Commissioner in response to high levels of theft, housebreaking and unlawful sale of liquor.]

Wed 7 February	09:00–17:00: Berea:[9] Crime Prevention Operation [Patrolling the area in response to the rising number of car thefts.] 00:00–04:00: Sydenham:[10] Crime Prevention Operation [Drug raids and patrols at the request of the local Station Commissioner.]
Thurs 8 February	08:00–15:00: Maydon Wharf:[11] Crime Prevention Operation [Searching port containers for illegal goods and persons.] 18:00–22:00: Sydenham: Crime Prevention Operation 14:00–18:00: Pinetown:[12] Crime Prevention Operation [Patrolling the area and creating a visible presence in response to high levels of car hijacking and theft from motor vehicles.] 10:00–24:00: Pinetown: Crime Prevention Operation
Fri 9 February	16:00–24:00: Central Durban: Road blocks and vehicle checks 16:00–21:00: Absa Stadium rugby match: Crowd Management Event 14:00–22:00: Pinetown: Crime Prevention Operation
Sat 10 February	10:00–18:00: Point:[13] Crime Prevention Operation [Drug raids, patrolling the streets looking for 'illegal' prostitution, monitoring street crime] 06:00–18:00: Pinetown: Crime Prevention Operation 18:00–06:00: Pinetown: Crime Prevention Operation
Sun 11 February	10:00–18:00: Point: Crime Prevention Operation 07:00–19:00: Absa Stadium benefit concert for ill national soccer player: Crowd Management Event 18:00–03:00: Pinetown: Crime Prevention Operation

These were not the only activities the unit was engaged in during the week cited here. There were also a number of other operations that remained ongoing and were intended to stabilise areas that had been categorised as 'unstable' or as 'volatile'. For a number of months previously, the unit had been involved in monitoring and patrolling taxi ranks, which had been the site of bloody armed conflict as quarrelling taxi associations fought over route allocations. Durban POP was also involved in an ongoing operation in KwaMashu, one of the biggest and most crime-ridden African townships. Durban POP had been deploying one company a day to KwaMashu for over a year, patrolling day and night. Objectives were to keep up a strong policing presence in the area, to conduct roadblocks and weapons and drug raids, and to assist the local police in any other crime prevention operations.

A third stabilising operation the unit was involved in at the time was maintaining a presence in certain of the hostels[14] in the Durban area. Since the early 1990s, the hostels had been sites of acute conflict between IFP and ANC supporters, with a high percentage of hostel inmates armed with weapons ranging from spears, to knives, to live ammunition. In one, Glebelands Hostel, 36 inmates were killed between January and May 1998 alone. Durban POP maintained a visible presence in three of the most volatile hostels. They conducted searches for illegal weapons and stolen goods, tried to prevent and curtail outbreaks of violence, and made attempts at mediating between conflicting parties.

None of these stabilisation duties seem obviously to fall within the primary crowd management brief.[15] They could be classified as crime prevention, the unit's secondary function, yet the distinction between crime prevention and crowd management is not always straightforward. High levels of crime and even fear of crime can create situations of public disorder that in turn produce a crisis where crowd management is required. As Inspector Prem from the Information Management Department of Durban POP explained:

> You can't really say that POP should stick strictly to their primary function. Crowd management situations can emerge at any time in the other work we do. Let us say for example that a taxi driver is killed in the middle of Warwick Circle in the centre of town. A crowd begins to form and people take sides. If POP is not there, there would be a real crowd situation and a problem with disorder. In the hostels as well we have to see the bigger picture. Someone from one of the political parties is attacked and maybe even killed by someone from another party in the hostel. If POP was not there to make arrests and deal with the situation immediately, you may find that members

of both parties come together and try to attack each other. This has happened before and it is a very dangerous situation. Have you seen how many weapons there are in the hostels?[16]

Over the years Durban POP expended more and more time and resources on its secondary functions. The Unit Commander estimated in 1998 that secondary functions took up 80 per cent of the unit's time. He noted three principal reasons. Firstly, in his own view, following the 1994 elections there was a complete breakdown in regular visible policing in the Durban area and consequently a dependency relationship had developed between the regular police and Durban POP. Secondly, citing Director Wiggins, Provincial Head of POP, he made the point that the regular visible police were generally not willing to engage in operations considered 'vaguely dangerous'; POP, on the other hand, was seen as the unit with the appropriate equipment, training and person-power for that kind of work. Thirdly, according to the POP National Head of Training, the involvement in secondary functions had its roots in the operations of the Internal Stability Unit in the early 1990s, at which period the ISU deliberately got involved in crime prevention work so that they could present themselves as 'indispensable', as insurance against being disbanded.

Involvement of paramilitary units such as POP in mainstream policing is not peculiar to South Africa. Kraska and Kappeler (1997) note that in the United States almost every police department has a paramilitary unit attached. These have become increasingly involved in mainstream policing, though their interventions are generally in situations that are potentially 'high risk', drug raids being the most obvious.

The extensive deployment of Durban POP in mainstream policing was not unproblematic. Whether there should be a large specialised unit dealing with public order policing is debatable in the first place and has been so within POP for many years. In 2000, POP initiated a project to train local visible police in crowd management techniques and legislation. The objective was eventually to devolve the task of managing non-volatile crowd management events to local police stations; POP would then be scaled down in size and activated only where there was potential for disorder and violence, or where assistance was requested by the local police. (What eventually happened was that POP was converted into the Area Crime Combating Unit, focusing on high-risk interventions in crime control.)

Debates aside, in 2001 Durban POP was still part of a centralised national paramilitary unit, though serious attempts had indeed been made to demilitarise and civilianise the unit. Camouflage uniforms were replaced in 1995 by the same blue uniform as other police members; aside from a red badge that POP members wore, they were indistinguishable from the regular police. POP vehicles were painted bright yellow and blue, or white with blue lettering, instead of their previous military khaki-green. The ranking system was changed to bring it into line with practice in countries like Britain and there was reduced emphasis on military discipline: lower ranks, for example, were no longer expected to salute commissioned officers on sight. The unit did, however, still retain its military structure and command system.

Six years into the process of its transformation, Durban POP presents us, then, with a body of (nearly all male) officers who for the most part had been involved in riot and crowd control police work for many years. Their long experience equipped these officers, for better or worse, with personal, but also in many respects shared, schemas for doing what counted as 'effective' policing. It set them up with a memory album of working careers in a unit bonded by high levels of solidarity and freighted with recollections of collective tribulations and traumas – although actual sharing of those memories was offset by notable cleavages in the unit along lines of racial categorisation and identification. In the chapters that follow, the implications for Durban POP of this shared history and its shared stories will be important for our narrative of the successes and failures of transformation in the unit.

5

Me and my Uzi
Stepping into Durban POP

> We invite residents of Hotel Criminology to leave the hotel room for a while. Go into the streets, into living rooms and corporate bedrooms, into juvenile lockups. Situate yourselves as close as you can to the perpetrators of crime and deviance, to the victims, to the agents of legal control; put yourselves, as best you can and for as long as you can, inside their lives, inside the lived moments of deviance and crime. You won't experience it nicely, and if the danger and hurt become too much, be glad of it. Because, as near as you will ever get, you have found your way inside the humanity of crime and deviance (Hamm and Ferrell, 1998, cited in Goldsmith, 2003: 124).

IT IS STILL not very usual for South African scholars to do participatory research with the police, so it was no surprise to find myself regularly fielding the same set of questions as I went about my research: How easy is it to access the police in South Africa? Aren't you afraid to go out on active operations with the police? Isn't it difficult for a white woman like you to be accepted in a police organisation comprised mainly of black men? How do the police understand your role as a researcher? How objective is your research if you have developed such close working relations with the police? What do the police think about what you write?

Certainly, these are important questions and they capture the fundamental challenges of doing research on, or in, the police. They are questions familiar to scholars of the police throughout the world. In this chapter I try to answer some of them and, so doing, to speak also to the moral difficulties that not infrequently confront police ethnographers. I focus on my own experiences of stepping into the world of the public order police and I look at the difficulties and the dilemmas that I faced there. Speaking for myself, I can report that ethnographic policing research was at the same time both daunting and exciting. I also doubt that I could ever really have understood the contradictions of change in a policing unit like Durban Public Order Police (POP) had I not been in the unit with the members, joining them in the range of activities they were engaged in. Rightly or wrongly, it is my own journey with the Durban POP that I have chosen to concentrate on, and that has left me with little opportunity in the present study to review the range of truly wonderful policing ethnographies that preceded and informed this one.

So I begin with the story of how I first gained access to the Durban POP.

Negotiating access to Durban POP
In the literature, police ethnographers often seem to gloss over the difficulties of getting access to the policing milieu. Sociologists and police don't in general have a reputation for getting on together and slanging matches are not unknown. As Greenhill puts it, 'Police often see sociological work as ill-informed, and sociologists tend not to take seriously what the police do' (1981: 103). As Maurice Punch observes, in a more ideal world there should be a positive and constructive engagement between the institutions concerned – police and the universities – that would allow 'academics to scrutinise their theories in the "real" world, and policemen [to] test their practical experience against intellectual generalisations' (1975: 84).

South Africa is a long way from being an ideal world and I felt as intimidated as any researcher at the prospect of venturing into the 'world of the police'. I distinctly remember wanting to back my car straight out again when I first passed through the gates of the Durban base of the POP unit on my introductory visit. I noted these feelings in the research diary in which I recorded my observations, conversations and reflections:

> 05/04/1997
> As I drove into the base I felt my stomach drop. What was I doing in a place that looked like a prison with lines of heavily armed vehicles (Nyalas and Casspirs) all around? Everywhere I looked I saw groups of strong-looking men with hand-guns, machine-guns and batons attached to their bodies. When I got out of the car I felt as if everyone

was asking each other what this small unfamiliar woman was doing in a place like this. I walked past the groups of men in uniform and shyly greeted them all. They returned my greeting and continued their activities as though I were not there. A smile came to my face as I entered the main building to introduce myself to the unit commander. This is going to be tough, I thought to myself, but it is going to be a challenge and I am going to enjoy it.

It is not unusual for ethnographers in the field to feel estranged from the research setting. Van Maanen goes as far as to suggest that

> to do fieldwork apparently requires some of the instincts of an exile, for the fieldworker typically arrives at the place of study without much of an introduction and knowing few people, if any. Fieldworkers, it seems, learn to move around strangers while holding themselves in readiness for episodes of embarrassment, affection, misfortune, partial or vague revelation, deceit, confusion, isolation, warmth, adventure, fear, concealment, pleasure, surprise, insult, and always possible deportation (1995: 2).

My own entry to the unit had, however, been eased by relationships I had already established with various members of the police. For two years prior to embarking on my formal research into the POP, I had worked with members of the SAPS and non-governmental organisations in a forum concerned with facilitating and building community policing in the province in which I then lived. While this work had not involved the POP, I at least had some familiarity with the broader police community. In addition, and perhaps more importantly, I had earlier in the year invited two members of the Durban POP to talk to my undergraduate class about paramilitary policing. Both of the officers who addressed my class were involved in training initiatives in the unit. One of them, Captain Mohamed, was the Head of Training for POP Durban. After the class I sat down and chatted with the two policemen about what was happening in the unit and how they had felt about talking to university students. A relationship of mutual interest and respect was established almost immediately.

A week later Captain Mohamed phoned me and asked if I would assist the unit by doing an evaluation of their new training programme. He wanted me to assess whether their new in-service training programme was helping to transform the operational conduct of the unit – from what had been an inflexible, militarised approach to a new minimum force policy employing more situationally appropriate tactics. No funding was in prospect, I knew nothing at all about the unit, but the invitation was intriguing and I agreed to do the research.

The relative ease with which I gained entry to the unit was also attributable to the broader political and organisational changes that were taking place at the time. State institutions that had previously been closed to public scrutiny were under a new obligation to be transparent and accountable. This opened new spaces for researchers and observers to 'investigate' previously protected organisations. Furthermore, the changes that were expected from public organisations generated a good deal of insecurity and uncertainty among their personnel, making them more inclined to welcome 'experts' supposedly able to give advice.

I laid down a few preconditions. First, Captain Mohamed and his training team would have to spend time explaining to me what the new training objectives were and how they related to the overall change programme within the unit. Second, I needed to have access to both trainers and trainees for the purpose of conducting interviews. Third, I had to be able to observe the training, both practical and theoretical, and if possible, accompany officers in training when they were deployed on operations. Finally, my research findings would be my own property, and the police would have to accept my autonomy as an independent researcher. These conditions were agreed to and in turn I had to accept that the police were not responsible for any harm that might result from my participating in field operations (though they would make every effort to ensure my safety). I was also asked to formally present my research findings to officers at the POP in-service training centre in Chatsworth on completion of the research. It was mutually agreed that the research project would last about two to three months, and that the time I spent at the college was subject to the convenience of the trainers and the members in training.

Both the police and I benefited from this arrangement. I got full access to the police training centre where I could develop a new area of research. The police, on the other hand, would receive an evaluation of their training programme. I also agreed to run sessions with the trainers discussing new trends in public order policing internationally. I provided trainers with any literature and information on public order policing and police training that I could find. Members of the unit were also free to come to my office at the university at convenient times and look for documentation that they thought would benefit them. Sometimes I felt as though my office at the University of Natal had been turned into a police reference facility. In time my amused colleagues grew quite accustomed to the sight of uniformed police officers strolling in and out of my office at all hours of the day.

Ultimately, the police hoped to benefit from the research by gaining insight as to possible ways of improving the training they were providing. The evolution of this mutual relationship proved to be invaluable both for the initial research and for my long-term engagement with the unit, and it counted for a great deal that I was able to offer useful information and knowledge to the police.

This is not to imply that access was completely smooth and unproblematic: Captain Mohamed was confident of the benefits of the research, but these feelings were not always shared by other trainers or by the unit members attending training at the college. Greenhill (1981) correctly notes that if sociologists hope to maintain access to autonomous organisations such as the police they need to be able to show that the research can potentially benefit the organisation and that individual members will also benefit from increased information and knowledge. While some of the Durban POP trainers enjoyed hearing what the research was revealing and liked to discuss the latest policing literature, there were others who remained sceptical about research in general. In many police settings the negative perception of sociologists and academics in general also has a lot to do with their reluctance (real or perceived) to spend enough time *with* the police in uncomfortable situations (Young, 1991).

The following exchange was recorded after a long discussion I had with the trainers at the college about international developments in public order policing. We had been talking about some of the key debates in the policing literature on paramilitary forms of policing:

> 11/06/1997
> While we were discussing some of the arguments that have been proposed as to whether there should or should not be a separate paramilitary unit in the police, I could see Sergeant Snel was becoming agitated. The following conversation transpired:
>
> *Sergeant Snel*: Monique, I don't mean to be rude, but this is all a load of junk. What do people who write books in universities know about the way the police should organise themselves? There would be chaos in this place if we didn't have a specialised unit like ours.

Sergeant Peters: Ja, man. These people just know about theory. Have they ever been out in a crowd and seen what chaos can take place? Sometimes I think academics must do what they are good at and we must do what we are good at.

While I had formal assurance of access from the highest-ranking officer at the Police College (Captain Mohamed), this did not automatically mean acceptance by other force members. And indeed, research access to different levels in the police organisation and to different police settings requires continual negotiation and renegotiation. Strangely, it was often those in lower ranks who were resistant to being observed and 'interrogated'. In hierarchical organisations like the police, members may feel that they have been ordered to co-operate with researchers and don't therefore see themselves as voluntary participants (Ericson, 1982). When I detected reluctance or resistance on the part of lower-ranking officers I checked whether or not they felt comfortable about participating. If they did not, and were still uncomfortable after I had told them more about what I was trying to do, I made it clear that they were in no way obliged to participate in individual interviews or discussions. For the most part, however, officers were willing to participate and share their views, feelings and experiences. Many in fact welcomed the presence of someone interested in what they had to say. But throughout the research I had to find ways to make sure rank-and-file police didn't think that I was working on behalf of police management. I had to state this again and again when I went out with police on operations, when conducting interviews, and even when administering surveys. I also encouraged unit members to ask me questions about what I was doing.[1]

My time at the college provided me with an invaluable entry to the POP Unit. However, when I decided to extend my research beyond the college and to issues broader than those of training and transformation, a whole new phase of negotiation had to take place. To begin with, I had to get official permission to conduct the research from senior officers in the unit. I was also aware that this opening up of the police to outside researchers was something very new and that senior officers would be suspicious of any research initiative. So I made sure to provide ample information on the objectives of the research, how it would be carried out, and what I intended to do with the findings.

I described earlier my trepidation on first arriving at the Durban unit to meet the

Unit Commander, Director Coetzee. I was fortunate in that Captain Mohamed had already spoken about me to Director Coetzee and told him how useful my interaction with the training college had been. In the event, I was warmly welcomed by the Unit Commander who straight away wanted to hear about my research at the college. The meeting was initially scheduled to last half an hour; we ended up spending three hours talking about my research findings and his own hopes and frustrations in the unit. I knew that, whatever my own time pressures, I must spend as long as it took gaining his trust if I was to be granted wider access to the unit; as it turned out, I was taken by surprise at the warmth of the welcome I got. Maybe, as Brewer suggests, 'the ethos with which the police authorities are imbued . . . has led to a recognition that social research can bring valuable results, so they have opened up their leviathan to strangers and specially commissioned specific pieces of research' (1991: 16).

In South Africa, not only has there been, since the early 1990s, a move toward greater professionalism in the police, there is also, especially since 1994, a new ethos that stresses transparency and openness. The police have an obligation to open the organisation to outside scrutiny and oversight and this includes giving access to outside researchers. This did not mean, however, that access was unconditional. Director Coetzee expressed some of his concerns about outsiders like myself conducting research in the unit. He was afraid that I would publicise negative research findings about the unit and I had to assure him that this was not my intention and that my research would be used for purely academic purposes. I also undertook to give regular feedback to him and other interested police officials about the research findings. While this did not imply that I would modify my findings or analysis, I understood their need to check the accuracy of my reporting and interpretations. I had to promise that I would at no point release, to any members of the press or to anyone who might harm the unit, information discussed in confidence. I also had to protect the interests of rank-and-file members of the unit. This meant that my observations and conversation with rank-and-file members would not be reported to authorities in the unit – an undertaking that at times compromised both my personal and political ethics, as I discuss later.

At the end of our first meeting Director Coetzee informed me that I was free to observe and participate in any way I needed in the unit and he promised to facilitate my research in any way possible. Director Coetzee took early retirement from the unit towards the end of 1999, but until that time we spoke regularly, usually informally, and each time I completed a report or a paper about the unit I gave him a copy and welcomed any feedback from him. As a symbol of my appreciation for the access I was being given I also drew up a confidential report for the Director which explored all aspects of the unit – the positive developments and the limitations. I also offered tentative recommendations for dealing with some of the existing problems.[2]

The SAPS is a centralised organisation and I knew that permission to do research in the unit also had to be obtained from higher authorities. In the first instance this meant requesting permission from the Provincial Head of Public Order Policing, Director Wiggins, a decidedly different prospect from my encounter with the mild-mannered Director Coetzee. Director Wiggins had spent almost his entire life in the police and claimed to be the longest-serving policeman in the SAPS involved with public order policing. His inclination was to open negotiations through banter and jokes and I worried that I would never get him to take me seriously. I decided that the best approach was to join in the banter while at the same time being at pains to establish that I did have a degree of insight into the unit and some authority to speak on matters of public order policing more generally. And within an hour at that first meeting we had found a shared wavelength, discussing the history and future of the unit. I told him about the research I had been doing at the college, and by the end of the meeting had his permission to participate in the activities of the unit and conduct any interviews I needed.

Engaging with Director Wiggins wasn't always easy. Often I felt I was simply being brushed aside, perhaps because of my gender, yet in time a more informal dimension to our relationship evolved and we would chat about our families, our travel, and broader political developments. Over the years I came to know him well and we developed a respectful yet congenial connection. In 1999 he invited me to participate in a Provincial Transformation Team Forum he had established, and when international guests and observers came to visit the unit he made a point of inviting me to participate in discussions and activities with his guests.

Captain Mohamed and I also developed a relationship that combined professionalism and friendship. In November 1999, for example, I was invited to his wedding, and from time to time we would meet for a chat over lunch or a drink. My research was certainly helped along by the mutual familiarity and trust that this kind of informality engendered.

This more friendly level of relationship even extended to officers I initially thought would be especially sceptical about my research. When Director Coetzee resigned he was replaced temporarily as acting Unit Commander by Senior Superintendent

Meiring, a long-serving Afrikaans-speaking officer whose entire working life had been spent in the ethos of apartheid policing, and with no experience of ever meeting with academics or international 'experts'. His appointment certainly seemed a reason to worry that my access to the unit would be cut. Yet here too, soon enough, we established a good footing, and I found myself chatting with him for long hours in relaxed and, for me, illuminating discussions about his personal history and the history of the unit. He shared with me his involvement in apartheid policing; I told him about my past as an anti-apartheid activist often at odds with the police.

The most difficult encounter was with the POP Head Office in Pretoria. I knew that Head Office permission was indispensable both for long-term access and for my work to be recognised by the unit, so at an early stage in my research I travelled to Pretoria to meet with the Head of Training and the National Commissioner of Public Order Policing. I decided that my best strategy would be not just to set out the principles and objectives of my research but to show also that I had knowledge and understanding of the unit and of public order policing in general, so I made sure to arrive at Head Office armed with copies of numerous papers and articles I had written and I set aside plenty of time for what I knew could turn out to be protracted negotiations.

When I got there, Head Office officials immediately wanted to know if I had permission from the SAPS Head of Research. No, I didn't, so that meant phoning the research department at very short notice to ask for a meeting – and in the event this went well enough; in fact the research office positively welcomed my request, there being at the time no other academic researcher in South Africa with a specialist interest in public order policing. So far, so good, but back in the corridors of Head Office with my consent from the Research Department, I was stricken by a sense of being lost and utterly out of place in what felt like a very alien and unwelcoming milieu. Some Head Office officers continued to be very suspicious of my project and I was grilled all over again. Access, I was told, needed permission from the National Commissioner and he was a very busy man. But by now I had persuaded myself I was going to sit it out and wait for as long as it took, not leaving the building until National Commissioner Cronje agreed to see me.

In the end that worked and I got my meeting, though feeling thoroughly intimidated by the time Commissioner Cronje ushered me into his office, and wholly at a loss to know any longer what I could offer him or the unit in return for research access. But once again my fears turned out to be unfounded:

05/02/1998
Commissioner Cronje: Monique, you don't know me but I already know you.

I was very confused and had no idea where I could have possibly met him before.

Commissioner Cronje: I have been curious to meet you. You see, I have already read some of the stuff you have written and have found it most useful. In fact, I used one of your articles in a meeting recently.

He went to his desk and pulled out a copy of an article I had written for the publication *Crime and Conflict*, entitled 'The case for paramilitary policing', and written really as a polemic for a research and academic audience.

I was completely taken aback that the Commissioner was reading such publications and that he should even remember who the author was. It was a huge relief to know that I was valued and already seen as having insight and understanding.

In no time, the meeting became an easy conversation about the unit and about my work, and the Commissioner's blessing was readily forthcoming. He asked only that I keep him informed of my research and communicate my findings from time to time; and from then on I made a point of sending him a copy of all the reports, conference papers and publications I had written, inviting and welcoming any feedback from him. And in subsequent months this sharing of information proved to be very important in the good relations I was able to maintain with the Commissioner. I had helpful responses from him and he actively sought out my opinions.

The generally positive relationships I developed with high-ranking officers didn't automatically extend throughout the unit. There were certainly times when members at lower ranks resisted my research approaches and made access difficult, though never impossible. This was perhaps because they felt that divulging information that might be regarded by higher-ranking officers as sensitive or potentially damaging to the unit could lead to some form of retribution. So I in turn had to learn to adapt.

Perhaps my trickiest moment was when I tried to administer a survey to a recalcitrant group of (mainly white) specialists. They made no bones about their disdain for researchers:

> 21/08/199
> What a scene! I went to do the long-awaited survey with the RDP Platoon. I knew this was an important but tough one to do. Most of the members in this platoon are white and from the old school of paramilitary policing. I walked into the seminar room and was confronted by 30 large, smoking, obnoxious, plain-clothes policemen. They had their firearms on the table in front of them and they were intimidating to look at. When Captain Padayachee introduced me and explained what I had to come to do, members told him that they refused to answer any questions or fill out any surveys. They just laughed and carried on smoking. I don't know where my bravery came from, but I thought, 'I can deal with these guys, leave it to me'. I felt that I had learned to speak the police language and to adapt to the different types of responses that I received. I also realised as a (white) woman, and not part of the police institution, I would be received slightly more openly than someone from within the police, or a male who might be seen as more threatening. I decided to joke around with them for a bit and let them have their fun. I then explained what I was doing, was firm but sympathetic, and had them all answering away in no time. By the end of the session, twelve of the members present volunteered to have individual interviews with me at a later point. I have to say though that for a moment I just wanted to walk out and abandon the exercise.

Open antagonism was not something I often encountered, but there were other access points that had to be negotiated, and sometimes abandoned. While most members of the unit got used to having me around and going along with them on field operations, some of the commanders were less comfortable with my presence while they were in charge. A few felt compromised by questions about my safety and others were uncomfortable being observed by me. When I sensed this kind of hesitation I would opt out of participating in the operation. I did find, however, that as commanders became more familiar with me and the work I was doing they would eventually invite me to join them in the field. Some even requested my presence on operations that they thought I would find interesting.

In short, access proved not to be terribly difficult but there was a constant need to renegotiate it and considerable effort and time had to be devoted to maintaining positive and collaborative working relationships at all levels. I had to take care constantly that both the police and I benefited from my access to the unit. And I had to make sure, too, that unit members did not feel compromised by my presence and my research.

Immersing myself in Durban POP

In the early stages of my research I hesitated to call myself an ethnographer, given my lack of formal training in the trade. I have since grown bolder about using this label once I realised that my lack of training is probably the norm. Van Maanen stresses that most ethnographers have not been formally trained. Speaking for himself, and most other ethnographers, he contends that 'our appreciation and understanding of ethnography comes like a mist that creeps slowly over us while in the library and lingers with us while in the field' (1995: ix). The approach used in this study is what I regard as ethnographic: one entailing 'a gradual and progressive contact with respondents which is sustained over a long period, allowing rapport to be established slowly with respondents over time, and for researchers to participate in the full range of experiences involved in the topic' (Brewer, 1991: 18).

The primary ethnographic method I employed was participant observation (also known as 'getting the seat of your pants dirty'). What the participant observer hopes to do is to immerse herself in a host society (like a police service) and try as far as possible to see, feel, and even act as a member of that 'society' (Walker, 1985). This involves a process of 'indwelling', of suspending one's own ways of viewing the world in order to understand the world of others (Maykut and Morehouse, 1994). In the world of the police this indwelling has the potential to uncover the 'unspoken agenda' that determines many aspects of police practice (Young, 1991). In turn this allows the researcher to explore the ways in which culture (deep-seated assumptions and beliefs) is self-sustaining even in the face of calls for change, questions that lay at the heart of my investigation.

Participant observation has other advantages too. It opens the space for other methods such as interviews, because familiarity and mutual understanding is developed in the process of researcher indwelling (Cain, 1973; Ericson 1982). Added to this, observation helps the researcher to know what questions to ask, what direction the research should take, who the key role players are, and so on. Without having participated in the everyday life of Durban POP, I would never have understood either the informal or the formal interactions that took place. I would have developed only superficial relations with the police that would have rendered more formal interviews bald and possibly invalid. As it was, through my observation and participation I was able to enter the life-space of the unit and develop substantive relationships with POP members of all ranks.

I cannot begin to say how many hours I spent hanging about with Durban POP over the three-year stretch of the research process. I began by sitting in on classes and training sessions at the police college where I would observe and take notes on the content of the teaching, and on interactions among the 'students' and between 'students' and their trainers. I joined platoons that were studying at the college when they were called into the field. There were a number of activities I observed these platoons carrying out during these times: managing crowds of students protesting outside the Department of Education offices; cordoning off a police station where black police were protesting the appointment of an Indian police officer; even policing a group of policemen and women who had downed tools because of the slow pace of affirmative action in the SAPS. During these events I observed the interaction between the unit and the communities they were policing; I also observed the relationships between those in command and the rank-and-file. I looked to see what procedures were being followed and to what extent members were applying what they learned in training when 'in the field'.

While I was doing research at the college I got invited to passing-out parades, simulation exercises, and also social events that took place outside of working hours. During these times I was able to observe and record the informal relationships in the unit: how, for example, unit members from different race and religious groups related to each other, how they spoke about the unit informally, how they liked to spend their leisure time. In the beginning I felt like someone who had to be minded, but after a while I seemed to be almost invisible to the college trainers as they grew more accustomed to my presence. Some of them were self-conscious about being observed and I usually avoided intruding on their classes.

My engagement with the unit deepened as I increasingly steered away from my initial focus on the college to a concern with the unit more broadly. I established an arrangement with the Head of Public Relations, Captain Dada, for participation in daily operations. I would call Captain Dada in the morning and check what operations were taking place and whether arrangements could be made for me to join the unit in whatever activity they were engaged in. Captain Dada would also call me if an operation was coming up that he thought would be of interest to me and where the officer in command was comfortable with my 'going along'. I generally got to the base before the platoon or section was briefed by the commanding officer. After the briefing I would usually travel in one of the police vehicles to the scene of the event, doing my best to preserve my observer-as-participant role and be as unobtrusive as possible.

After an operation I would attend the debriefing, if there was one. This would also give me the chance to chat informally to commanders and rank-and-file members about how they had felt about the operation, if there was anything that they felt could have been done differently, and so on. Sometimes the ranking officers would ask me to comment on what I had thought of the operation and whether there were any problems in their approach that I had noted. In the beginning I was uncomfortable about these evaluative questions but soon came to realise that these officers did not feel threatened by my observations and appreciated my insights.

From time to time I would be asked to be rather more participant than observer and actually assist with tasks the unit was engaged in. On one occasion, accompanying the unit on a raid of a high school (to look for weapons and drugs), I was asked to check which classrooms had not yet been searched and alert the unit. In situations like these I was sometimes even taken for a plain-clothes member of the police. I would be asked by members of the public (like the teachers), or indeed police from other specialised units, what my rank was or which unit I was working with.

There were also times when I was thrust quite drastically into the participant role to a degree that was certainly compromising to me and potentially to the unit as well. In May 2000, the administration of the University of Durban-Westville requested Durban POP to come onto campus because students were on boycott and minor incidents of violence had been reported. Student/administration tensions were running high and the administration was concerned that conflict would erupt on the campus. Durban POP was called upon to monitor the situation and remain on call to manage crowds should they materialise, and if necessary make arrests. A series of meetings was convened between the administration and the police to consider how best to handle the situation. The police Commander in charge of the operation invited me to attend these meetings. When I expressed my hesitation – since I was not a member of the unit and therefore should not be party to the discussions – the Commander insisted that he would like to have me there and did not think it would be a problem. Once in the meeting, however, I was flabbergasted to find myself being introduced, by the Commander himself, as an undercover agent for the unit. This put me in an intolerable predicament that I was also completely unprepared for, nothing of the kind having been so much as hinted at, let alone agreed. Nor was it an easy matter to step away from, since the university administration continued to call on me for advice and information and at one point I was even asked to attend a graduation ceremony as an undercover agent in case a public order problem developed. I took up the issue with the Commander concerned and subsequently had to make a point of avoiding all contact with the university administration.

There were also times when I felt decidedly unsafe despite the protective attitude of most of the police toward me. During one of my participatory encounters I felt so afraid that I seriously questioned my own wisdom and sanity in getting so deeply involved with the unit. The following excerpt from my research diary describes this event. I had joined one of the platoons on an all-night shift in KwaMashu:

> 16/05/2000
> The guys from the platoon arrived at my house at 6 pm to pick me up for the night shift. There were two white Inspectors and one white Sergeant in the vehicle . . . They were armed with rifles, machine-guns and side-arms and I knew I was in for a hectic night ahead. One of the Inspectors informed me that I would see many things in the course of the shift that would disturb me and that I would probably think that their conduct was 'out of order'. I was told that what I saw and heard should not 'leave the vehicle'; I was not to speak to anyone at the Unit about my observations, or the press. I was also told to get rid of any cameras or tape recorders if I had them. I said that I did not have either of these.
>
> A second Inspector then explained to me what they were doing in KwaMashu township. The platoon had been in the township for the past seven months, and hoped to intervene in any way possible to fight the high levels of crime in the area. I started to worry a bit about my acumen in joining these guys on a night mission. I knew this

particular platoon had a reputation of being both ruthless and reckless ... The driver was driving at about 200 km/h. I felt completely unsafe. As we entered the township we were confronted by a sea of lights coming from the matchbox houses in amongst the darkness that characterises the African townships where there are almost no streetlights. Very few people were on the streets; most people were in their tiny houses or shacks. The township reeked of poverty – there were no proper roads, and there was a heavy smell from the lack of ablution facilities in the informal settlement areas. I was told that KwaMashu was a very unsafe area – shootings take place every night and often the police are the target ... They did not seem in the least bit fazed by this. On the contrary, they were excited and ready and waiting for action – they feared nothing.

We drove into an empty enclosed room (garage) to wait there for the rest of the platoon. The members got out of the car and explained to me how the night ahead was likely to pan out.

Inspector Botha: Monique, I have to be honest with you, white women are a target in this area.
Monique: What do you mean?
Inspector Botha: They will see you and think you are a police person. They know that it is easy to overcome a female and steal her weapon. You are also a rape candidate.

I felt my heart beating very fast. I honestly wanted to go home at that moment but knew that I could not turn back. I had a 12-hour shift ahead of me.

Monique: What information would you like to give me to protect myself?
Inspector Botha: Firstly, I want you to put on this bullet-proof vest. It will be uncomfortable. It wasn't made for breasts.
Monique: How effective are these bullet-proof jackets? Obviously they don't protect your head which could be shot at.
Inspector Botha: To be honest Monique, they are a bit useless. A

bullet can penetrate at close distance. Most police who have been killed in the area have been wearing bullet-proof vests. But it is all we have for your protection. I also want to show you how to use an Uzi machine-gun just in case you need it. If someone tries to shoot you, you just shoot back. It is a very easy weapon to use.

I was then shown how to use the Uzi. I became more fearful as the minutes went past. I had no desire to use a gun, and knew that I would be petrified to shoot anyone even if I was under attack. I told them this.

Inspector Botha: Well, you wanted to see what it is like out here. It is no joke in the field. We will try to protect you as best we can. Just stay close to me at all times. If there is a shootout, go and hide behind a bush or behind a shack. The informer will be with us. Just go with him. He will know where it is safe.

The rest of the platoon arrived and I was introduced to all the members. I sort of hoped that something would happen and we would have to go back home. But there was no way these guys were going to let go of a night of action. I took a deep breath, had a cigarette, and braced myself for the night ahead . . . We got back into the vehicle and 'went looking for action' . . . The police radio system was reporting that there was a stolen vehicle in the area that had been used for several hijackings. The driver stepped up the speed, and said 'let's go get them'. We drove through the darkness of the townships with the lights of the vehicle turned off (to surprise criminals, I was told). Both police in the front of the vehicle had their pistols pointed outside open windows . . . Another report came through on the radio. There was a kangaroo court in process in one of the informal settlement areas. We sped on through a maze of houses and back alleys. There are no street names in these areas, yet these cops knew exactly where we were going. They pulled up in a dark alleyway, and jumped out of the vehicle. The inspector told me to get out of the car and come with them. They rushed ahead and I sort of ran after them feeling completely unprotected. The next message arrived. There had been an armed robbery at a house nearby and we sped off again on our next mission . . . I was dying to use the toilet. I asked one of the women from the house where the robbery had taken place if I could use her bathroom. She took me to an outhouse at the back of the house. It was freezing and the door did not close properly. I had no option, so I used the toilet . . . When I came out of the toilet, I noticed that the police were very impressed that I went to the toilet at the back of the house. Through my 'tenacity', I had scored points with them. They could see that I had some familiarity with township life and that I could adapt fairly easily to new environments . . . It was by now 11 pm. They decided to go down to a petrol station to get some coffee and something to eat. The following conversation took place on the way:

Sergeant Marais: It is fucking quiet out here tonight. Monique, it looks like you have jinxed us. There is nothing exciting taking place.
Monique: What do you hope to take place?
Sergeant Marais: A bit of shooting at least. That is what we live for. Tonight has just been child's play while we are waiting for more action.

While patrolling the road, the police spotted four guys on the pavement. They pulled the van to a stop and jumped out. I followed. They searched the four guys and found nine Mandrax pills. They hit the four young men and asked them where they had got the pills. They did not say. They got hit again. They pointed to the house behind which was in complete darkness. The police looked at the house and debated for a few seconds whether to penetrate or not. They decided to go ahead. They broke the fence and crawled through the hole. I was told to follow . . . A man and his girlfriend were found sleeping in the back of the house . . . They started to question the woman. They asked her about the drugs. She said she knew nothing. They turned to me and shouted:

Inspector Botha: Monique, search this women and see that she doesn't have anything between her legs.

What could I do? I took the woman to a separate room and searched her half-heartedly. I couldn't bear to humiliate her by searching between the legs. I told her it was fine and encouraged her to go back outside . . . We drove into an unlit area where an informer had arranged to meet us. I said a silent prayer to myself that the informer would be gone and we would not have to go into the area. No such luck. There he was hiding behind a wall. He got into the car and we then went to meet the other members of the platoon who had followed us in their cars. The informer said that he knew of two houses where there were guns. He would take us to them. He directed the police and we landed up on a dirt road in the middle of an informal settlement. We took some more winding roads and were surrounded by darkness and hundreds of little houses and shacks. It was deadly quiet. The vehicle lights were off and guns were pointed out of the windows. I swallowed hard to try to get rid of the fear I was feeling. I knew that I could not remain alone in the vehicle because this was even more dangerous than going with the guys into the field. The informer told us to stop the car. We were in the middle of nowhere. He pointed to a house in the distance. There was no road, but rather a narrow footpath with shrubs on either side. I forced myself to get out of the car and to remain calm. I was given a two-way radio to hold and a flashlight. We crept through the dark along the path. We had to step over a stream of water. Two gunshots went off and we all crouched. I thought to myself, 'If I die of a gun wound it will be over quickly.' After a few minutes the police told us to get up and we continued walking. We got to the identified house. We were told to stay low . . . I thought I would die of fright as we walked through this unknown territory in the dark.

These were not situations I backed away from. Encounters like this were clearly an important component of the work and experience of members in the unit – experiences and contexts that impacted deeply on the way they viewed their work, given the dangers they confronted daily. But certainly there were times when I found this participation extremely draining, and would have much preferred staying in my office writing or talking to colleagues. On days like this I had to really push myself to drive out to the unit, knowing how important commitment and staying power were for maintaining my status with the unit. Yet once at the base, and participating or observing, I often found myself driven by the excitement of the experience.

There were more than a few things that worried me about that night out in KwaMashu, quite apart from the danger I encountered. I felt morally compromised in knowing that many of the responses of the platoon were brutal and completely disregarded the human rights framework that was supposed to guide police behaviour. And the very thought of holding a machine-gun, even though I could not imagine using it, raised a host of issues about research ethics. Nor was I at all sure how I would respond if I really were in a situation where my life was threatened. It brought home to me how fuzzy the boundaries of engagement were, given the possible consequences of placing myself as a researcher in such a dangerous environment.

Like most researchers, I would generally choose not to get involved in dangerous fields (Lee, 1995), but it would have been unrealistic to imagine this would always be possible if I chose to study a paramilitary police unit whose explicit brief was to impose 'order' in situations by definition 'disorderly'. I do not believe participant observers can always dissociate themselves from acts of violence, even when they clearly regard such acts as unjustifiable and even iniquitous. Rodgers confronted a similar dilemma in his research on gangs in Nicaragua. He joined a Nicaraguan *pandilla* (criminal youth gang) and 'actively and directly participated in a number of violent and illegal activities such as gang wars, thefts, fights, beatings and conflicts with the police' (Rodgers, 2001: 12). Rodgers believed that this involvement was necessary to consolidate his relationship with gang members and to show that he identified with the *barrio* and was willing to 'expose [himself] to danger in order to defend it' (2001: 11). A similar conclusion was arrived at by Winslow et al. in their ethnographic study of bouncers in pubs, clubs and bars. The chief researcher observed and even participated in acts of violence, which, he claims, was necessary to be able to conduct the research as a covert ethnographer. Winslow et al. make the point that they

> detested the violence [they] observed, and while there were adrenalising moments, [they] would have gladly traded them for an early night in front of

the TV and the prospect of analysing some questionnaires the next morning. Ethnographers of violence, however, do not allow for such luxuries, for the reflexivity that lies at the core of the process produces bruises that neither valorise nor ennoble the participants (2001: 537).

Winslow et al. argue that such involvement did, of course, raise ethical questions. They argue that these were not ignored but 'placed secondary to the pragmatics of getting a job as a bouncer and keeping it' (2001: 543). Researching 'violent groups', they claim, is often unpredictable, and ethnographers are forced to change roles and renegotiate interactions, often on the terms of the researched group – though not all ethnographers would agree with their decision to put research pragmatics above ethical and moral considerations.

Those very police officers who engage in acts of violence (not unusual in a police organisation) are often the same people who are struggling with personal and organisational transformation. In my own case, they were the same people who had allowed me to participate in the daily (sometimes out of the ordinary) activities of the unit. Being in the field observing (and indirectly participating in) acts of violence was my opportunity to understand a deeply ingrained element of the organisational culture of the Durban POP, which I could not adequately have captured through the more indirect tools of interviewing or survey questionnaires.

Participant observation, even in exciting contexts like paramilitary police units, is by no means always exhilarating or glamorous. To maintain existing relationships and develop new ones I had to spend a lot of time just 'hanging around' the unit. This meant endless hours in police offices talking about anything from how the unit was functioning, to family crises, to politics, to new personal business ventures. These informal interactions were important not only for building trust and familiarity but also for coming to grips with the everyday and more mundane thought processes of the police and their everyday interactions with one another. It also involved playing a number of different roles simultaneously – researcher, friend, adviser, expert. I had to be wary of saying anything that could be viewed as partisan or that could in any way compromise the status or security of members of the unit or the unit itself.[3] I also made it a very important point to attend events that took place outside of the working hours of the unit, like parades and social gatherings happening at weekends or in the evenings.

But it was also through the more 'protected' activity of attending and participating in formalised meetings and workshops that I functioned as a participant-as-observer. Here I engaged, almost as an equal, with higher-ranking police management about the present nature of the unit, its future plans and objectives, and the mechanisms for achieving these objectives. Attendance at these forums provided me with a space to share my observations with senior officers for the potential benefit of the unit, giving me some reassurance that the relationship was indeed one of mutual benefit rather than of my simply 'sucking information'. It also kept me in touch with organisational developments in policy, forward planning and general evaluation, giving me a yardstick to measure how far the unit had come in its change process, and how far there still was to go.

As important as observing and participating was the exercise of writing a diary or taking field notes, since the field researcher's time in any setting is always transient (Emerson et al., 1995). After each interaction with the police (whether in operations, hanging around, conducting surveys or interviews, or attending meetings) I would head for a computer to capture as best I could what I had seen, heard, inferred or remembered. I would record in some detail the activities that took place and the circumstances of those activities. I would record police interactions with myself, with other force members, or with the public. I recorded how unit members said things and what they expressed. I specifically recorded anything that indicated the meaning the police themselves gave to an event or situation. And I recorded my own immediate feelings and responses. Writing up my field notes also had another dimension that was important for me – as an opportunity to reflect on what I had seen and make connections with previous observations and with theoretical concerns.

I generally did not write field notes while actually in the field. I judged that this would have seemed intrusive and was too likely to upset the informality of many of the interactions; I didn't want police members to feel they were being evaluated and monitored. I preferred to be a part of the setting rather than apart from it. Nevertheless I did sometimes take surreptitious notes when I thought it would go unnoticed or when I was desperate to record something that was happening. I took notes while I waited for members to complete the survey questionnaire because they were too busy to notice me doing this. I also took field notes when participating in meetings or workshops since in such circumstances it looked as if I was merely taking notes of the proceedings. But for the most part, I would go to my office to write field notes after each significant interaction.[4]

I also made use of more formal interviews to 'cross check the hypotheses generated by observation and perhaps to provide a better understanding of the context' (Walker, 1985: 6). I wanted to discover individuals' feelings and perceptions of their jobs and their responses to the transformation process. I also wanted to probe further some of my field observations as well as generalities that came out of a survey I conducted in 1999 (discussed later in this chapter). These interviews had a wide utility for me. They were a means to probe prevailing stereotypes regarding race and gender and the nature of crowds. They gave me access to individual accounts of relationships amongst rank-and-file members and between rank-and-file and management. They allowed me, too, to 'tap into' those unit members who felt uncomfortable discussing issues with me in the presence of their colleagues. These in-depth interviews enabled me to have conversations with individual officers where they could communicate on their own terms. In total I interviewed 50 members of the unit in Durban and at POP Head Office. I interviewed members across rank and race. I also conducted one focus group with police at POP Head Office who worked in the department that dealt with incident reporting.

The more formal interviews were tape-recorded but all other events and conversations were recorded as reconstructions after the fact. While in the field I confined myself to jotting down keywords and statements to remind myself what was said and how it was said and I would make mental notes of what had to be recorded. The field notes are, I believe, as close as possible literal accounts of what was done and said subject to the imperfections of memory.

White, and a woman
The process of 'doing ethnography' as well as the outcomes of such research are in many ways dependent on the personal 'identifiers' (for lack of a better word) of the researcher: race, gender, class, nationality and the like. How the researcher personally constructs his or her identity, and the social constructs that frame such identities in any given society, are likely to shape the relationships that are formed in the field and the kinds of information that are made available as a result. The personality of the researcher also has a considerable bearing on the stories that are told (or hidden) and the exposure she will be afforded to the everyday lives of those he or she is studying. I think it is useful to offer some reflections on what it meant to be a white woman in an organisation dominated by black men. But I would like the reader to note, too, that in many ways it was the 'personality' that I projected which fashioned my research experience in the Durban Public Order Police unit.

In my fieldwork with Durban POP I found that being a woman was more of an advantage than a disadvantage. Although the unit was dominated by men, I was always treated with the utmost respect. There were very few instances when I experienced any form of sexual harassment or where male officers tried to make a pass at me, though there were flirtatious undertones to some of the relationships I established with male members of the unit. To be honest, I believe that these undertones may have played a minor role in facilitating research with male officers who would otherwise have balked at being 'observed and interrogated'. Complex and closed research settings require a variety of techniques to build relationships and get at information; flirtation was occasionally a good way to lighten up the interactions and get people to talk, but it always remained entirely innocuous. Not all woman researchers in police organisations are as fortunate. Marie-Louise Glebeek, who did an ethnographic study of Guatemala's Civil Police Force, records that the more familiar she became with male members of the unit, the more sexual advances were made toward her (Huggins and Glebeek, 2003).

My 'success' as an ethnographer had, without doubt, a good deal to do with the persona I seem to have projected while I was in the unit: matter-of-fact, bold, but also engaged and interested; game for almost anything, yet safe to engage with because I was an outsider and had no vested interest in the internal politics of the unit. Also, being a woman seemed to 'innately' mean that I was trustworthy and understanding. Members would talk to me about both their work and their personal dilemmas with very little hesitation. I would listen, share my own experiences with as much openness as I felt was necessary, and never break confidences. I also, of course, had a past of my own. I did not speak about my past as an anti-apartheid activist, but if asked about my history I would be open about it. This may have been disturbing information for some members but if so they kept quiet about it. More often my own history evoked interest, particularly from black members.

Women in the police often have to prove themselves over and over again as competent and intrepid while still projecting a feminine disposition (Brown, 1997; 2000; Martin, 1996). This is an extremely difficult balancing act. There were a few occasions when I was tested by male members who wanted to see whether or not I really had 'guts' to be out in the field with them. One was the incident I have already alluded to when I announced to the men with me in the armoured vehicle that I had to go to the toilet. They looked at each other and laughed, and one of them said I would just have to ask the township householders if I could use their outhouse. The toilet was outside in the darkness at the back of the house with a dog chained to a pole next to it. Feeling not a little apprehensive I used the toilet, thanked the members of the household and climbed back into the vehicle. The men in the vehicle were most impressed. I was told that even the policewomen who occasionally joined their section on township operations would not use outhouse toilets during the night. They would wait for the shift to finish and go to a toilet in the police station or a nearby shopping centre. So simply going to the toilet under 'difficult circumstances' proved that I was one of the boys. Behaviour toward me changed perceptibly after this incident and I found myself that much more accepted as a 'team' member.

Being 'white'[5] was more complicated in some ways than being a woman. The fact that I am identified as white (by supposed physical characteristics, historically privileged access to life chances in South Africa, manner of speech, apartheid race classification, etc.) probably made my access to the high-ranking officers of the unit far easier than would have been the case had I been otherwise classified. When I began my research, the highest-ranking officers (at local, provincial and national levels of the unit) were all white. Though they were curious about my research – and probably sceptical about its value – they displayed very little concern about my intentions or my integrity.

I can only guess that with the historically racist legacy of the SAP (carrying through to the new, reconstituted SAPS) my entry at this level would have been far more difficult were I a black person. At the lower rank levels being white gave me some sort of point of identification for the white members of the unit who, I think, would otherwise have refused me any access to the sub-culture they inhabited in the unit. They in many ways identified themselves primarily as white and were the least approachable members of the unit in my research overtures to them. Had I been a black woman, my access to this group would have been even more limited. Martha Huggins came to a similar conclusion after conducting interviews with Brazilian police who had been torturers or assassins during Brazil's 21 years of military dictatorship. She maintains that being a 'Caucasoid' researcher 'in a socio-cultural system that values light skin and associated physical characteristics above darker ones may have reinforced [her] presumed higher status relative to that of the interviewees' (Huggins and Glebeek, 2003: 373).

Indian unit members responded positively to my presence in the unit. On reflection, I think this may have been because my initial introductions to the unit (by the then white Unit Commander) were to middle and high-ranking members, many of whom were Indian. Also, Captain Mohamed, the person who really brought me into the unit, was 'Indian'. I spent a great deal of time with Captain Mohamed and through him, I became very familiar with other Indian members in the unit. Nearly all the middle managers in the unit were Indian and they displayed almost no resistance to my participating in their platoon activities and conducting interviews. In fact, I felt at times that I tended to spend more time with Indian members than with other race groups in the unit. I worried that African members might have noted this and perhaps have been less forthcoming with me as a result. While I experienced little resistance from African members of the unit when accompanying platoons on their operations, I did feel that they engaged with me less openly in formal interviews than members of other racial groups did. But perhaps this was a legacy of their own history of being silenced in the police force, and possibly they had learned to be cautious about what they said and to whom. I will never know if the silences were a reflection of that history or of my own personal demeanour.

Profiles and perceptions – the 1999 survey

An ethnographic research approach does not mean that quantitative methods and data are discounted. I realised early on that quantitative methods could uncover interesting 'framing' information, particularly regarding the attitudes of rank-and-file members to their involvement in public order policing, the internal dynamics of the organisation, and the changes that had taken place since state democratisation. Quantitative data could also provide important basic information about who the members of the unit were in terms of length of service, their reasons for joining, and their basic assumptions about their work and their environment.

I had already been doing participant observation and intensive interviews in the unit for about a year when I decided to conduct a survey with a representative sample of rank-and-file members of the POP unit in Durban. The survey was carried out between April and November 1999 and its findings are discussed in subsequent chapters of this book.

A purposive sample was used, stratified according to proportional ratios based on race and rank. Time spent doing participant observation in the unit revealed to me the importance of race in members' identities and experience. It became clear that race was a significant identifier in the unit and seemed to affect attitudes, behaviour and perceptions in all aspects of unit members' working lives. In analysing the survey data race was accordingly chosen as a key independent variable.

The questionnaires were self-administered to give me the opportunity to explain the purpose of the survey, the construction of the questions, and how to answer the questions. The surveys were translated into Zulu so respondents could have the choice of answering in Zulu or in English. This was necessary because while all members spoke English fluently (including those whose home language was Afrikaans), there were some African members who were far more comfortable in Zulu and found reading in English difficult and time-consuming.

I mistakenly assumed before embarking on the survey that it would be an easy task. In fact, it proved very difficult to bring together large numbers of unit members at one time since they were always on call, and at times when frequent crowd management events were taking place (such as during major international conventions or during the elections) officers were usually out on operations. I had to return repeatedly to administer the survey because Platoon Commanders could only volunteer eight or ten members at a time. When, where and how the survey was administered was at the discretion of Platoon Commanders.

Accountable research

If, as Greenhill (1981) suggests, proper access and 'fair research' on the police includes being able to give something back (especially knowledge) then it seems to me that participatory research is an essential route to follow. Holdaway (1983) insists likewise that using proper feedback mechanisms and being sure to involve the police in commenting on and evaluating his research work was critical for the validity of the research. These are perspectives I endorse, and so it was very important for me to share the findings of my research with the police at regular intervals and get their feedback. As far as possible I would give reports and papers I had written to officers with whom I was in regular contact and had good relations. They would read what I had written and we would then make a time to discuss my findings and their comments. Benefit from these meetings flowed in both directions: a return of new knowledge to the police, and for me another route to understanding their point of view. Validating my work this way certainly assisted me in establishing mutual and candid relations with the police, while at the same time enhancing, I believe, the legitimacy and utility of the research.

In the past, the police in South Africa were very likely to be excluded from such exchanges of knowledge, especially by more left-wing researchers.[6] It is for this reason that I considered the police to be in effect a 'disempowered' community, particularly the rank-and-file, and felt that democratising the research should be an important element of the process. Muller and Cloete (1987) argue that groups outside the academic community have commonly been excluded from the generation and validation of research, and they press the case for academic researchers instead to engage positively with the knowledge of local communities and by so doing empower them. This is what I sought to do with the police, considering them to be a 'community' in their own right.

While for the most part it was the higher ranking officials that I shared research findings with and got feedback from, I also made my writings and reports available to rank-and-file members at the unit by leaving copies with police administrators. I mailed papers I had written to some of the police I interviewed when they asked to read my work. Most appreciated my inclusion of them in the research process, and I would spend hours discussing their point of view once they had read my work. We did not always agree on the 'facts of the matter' or on interpretations and, while their points of view were always taken into consideration, I asserted my academic 'right' to reach differing conclusions.

Broadly speaking, I found acceptance from the police that my findings and interpretations would differ from theirs and that as an academic researcher I had to situate the texts within a wider socio-political context and also draw on more extended concepts and theories. For while the texts and testimonies I recorded gave me the starting point for the research, they still had to be read, as Bozzoli remarks, 'with a critical eye and with enough knowledge of the context to make it possible to shift the gold of true evidence from the bulk of ideology, poor memory, and wilful misleading that occurs' (1991: 489).

The research presented here can also be seen more broadly as focusing on organisational development and policy making. Cunningham (1993) makes the point that those who research organisations should aim to help them improve and change – making such research more than simply an end in itself. Research like this is sometimes referred to as 'action research' – a term indicating a spectrum of activities that focus on research, planning, theorising, learning and development, or, in Cunningham's words, 'a continuous process of research and learning in the researcher's long-term relationship with the problem' (1993: 4). Although I would hesitate to describe my own research as action research, it does have a longer-term goal of seeking to understand the problems of change in police organisations. Such research (and its findings) requires the support and co-operation of those studied, which in turn opens the research to a wider variety of relevant data.

Putting yourself on the line – publicising the research

Perhaps the greatest difficulty in researching the police is making one's findings public. As Holdaway (1983) has observed, this is often the most compromising aspect of research work in the police. You develop relationships with police members in a difficult environment, and then you are faced with the dilemma of not wanting to break levels of trust by exposing negative or detrimental things about the police organisation. Young makes a similar point about the moral and political implications of publishing research on the police – loyalties to the police may develop and writing anything at all can be extremely difficult: 'the insider finds it hard to bite that hand that feeds' (1991: 10). It is especially difficult when research comes to be seen by the police as espionage.

There is no doubt that a tricky path has to be negotiated when publishing or reporting research on the police. Researchers have to use possibly compromising information while at the same time guarding against breaking confidences or bringing harm or disrepute to the individual police and the organisation itself. So there will be observations that were made and conversations that were recorded that do not form part of writing up of the research. To break confidences and disregard the consequences of publication would be to destroy established relationships and de-legitimise the research in the eyes of the police, its subjects. What can diminish these pitfalls will be, I suggest, a diligently participatory research approach and an evident commitment on the part of the researcher to the ongoing development of the police organisation itself.

Police ethnographies that involve spending extended time with the police in a variety of circumstances often give rise to ethical dilemmas for the researcher. This is especially the case when researchers such as myself observe members of the police engaging in acts which can be defined as excessively forceful, abusive of human rights, or even illegal (Westmarland, 2001). Such information (where participants commit serious transgressions) is what Thomas and Marquart call 'dirty information' (1987: 81). Deciding what to do about it can be a tough call, as Westmarland has noted: 'ethnographers potentially tread a thin line between going along with police behaviour – colluding through inaction when unnecessary force is used – and "blowing the whistle"' (2001: 527). Revealing 'dirty information' can have serious repercussions, including professional discredit, social stigma, lawsuits, criminal charges and even the death of informants (Thomas and Marquart, 1987: 81). Ethical codes do not always provide the answers to morally compromising situations (Punch, 1986).

Like Reiner (2000) and Van Maanen (1982), I felt that my primary concerns were to safeguard access to the police organisation and to protect the confidentiality of the individual police officers who provided me with information, either in conversations with me or through my presence in their everyday interactions. At no point, therefore, did I report to authorities in the police the 'wayward' conduct of individual police officers. Although some of my observations of this kind of behaviour are recorded in this book, the intention has been to try to understand this troubling behaviour in its context, not to bring the organisation or its members into disrepute.

In publicising this research I have done my best to assure the confidentiality and anonymity of all members of Durban POP as well as other respondents. All names used are fictional and some dates have been changed in reporting observations that are controversial and compromising.

6

Half-measures?
Training, Policy and Recruitment

THE POLITICAL ANALYST Hein Marais argued in 1998 that South Africa's transition to democracy should be understood 'less as a miraculous historical rupture than as the (yet inconclusive) outcome of a concerted and far-reaching attempt to resolve an ensemble of political, ideological and economic contradictions . . .' (1998: 2). In this scenario there was never any real possibility of replacing the old with the new; the outcome of transition would always be an assimilation of the two. The old institutions would indeed be reshaped, but it would be a mistake to expect to see them simply swept aside.

As it affected the police, the political transition created a climate that both aided and impeded their transformation; new legislation intended to reshape the public service as a whole provided the overarching policy framework to guide that transformation. This conjunction of political and legislative determinants generates the complexities and contradictions of police transformation in South Africa.

'Transforming' South Africa's public service – accepting compromise
Early in their negotiations with the NP, the ANC[1] recognised that political consensus would have to be reached for a lasting and positive outcome. A number of compromises were arrived at, most notably what came to be known as the 'sunset clause'. This provided for an initial period of compulsory power sharing, and in particular an undertaking by the ANC not to purge the security forces and civil service of counter-revolutionary elements. In the (ANC-led) government of national unity that, in terms of the negotiated settlement, ruled from 1994 to 1999, the ANC accordingly agreed to 'refrain from purging the civil service, thus leaving intact much of the institutional culture and personnel of the old order' (Marais, 1998: 92).

The sunset clauses meant that government sectors and departments continued to operate according to many of the old apartheid determinants: the racial and ethnic mindsets; corruption and mismanagement of resources; poor and outdated management practices; a bureaucratic regulatory culture; lack of transparency and accountability; and poorly trained staff (McLennan, 1997). Nowhere did the burden of this legacy weigh more heavily than on the reformation of South African policing.

Two key documents provided an early framework for the transformation of the public service – the Reconstruction and Development Programme (RDP) unveiled by the ANC in 1994, and the 1996 Constitution (built upon its predecessor, the Interim Constitution of 1993). The RDP outlined four sub-programmes in its blueprint for political and economic transformation: meeting basic needs; developing human resources; building the economy; and democratising the state. The RDP document noted that 'democratisation require[d] modernising the structures and functioning of government in pursuit of the objectives of efficient, effective, responsive, transparent and accountable government' (cited in Patel, 2000: 186), and thus placed the transformation of the public service high on the political and social agenda.[2]

The 1996 Constitution also underlined the need for a transformed public service in guaranteeing 'the right to collective bargaining, to strike, to freedom of expression, speech and assembly, to privacy, equality before the law, access to information and to sexual orientation'. As McLennan notes, the Constitution sets out a clear framework for a restructured public service, recognising the key role this must play in addressing the ravages of the country's past: the public service should be 'non-partisan, career-oriented, and guided by fair and equitable principles. It should promote an efficient public service broadly representative of South African communities. Public servants should serve in an unbiased and impartial manner and loyally execute the policies of government' (1997: 109).

Both the legislative and the political environment were geared for transformation of the public service. Whatever the best word for the process that was embarked upon, reform or transformation, changes had to happen – and, however constrained by political settlements and the organisational legacy of the public service, they had to reflect the principles enshrined in the Constitution and the RDP, as well as the goals of democratic governance in its broadest sense.

The first national elections in 1994 were followed by an immediate spate of policy documents, one of which, the 1995 White Paper on the Transformation of the Public Service, provided both a mission and a vision for the entire public service, borrowing heavily from international trends in public service management.

The White Paper begins by stating:

> In forging ahead with the process of reconciliation, reconstruction and development, the South African public service will have a major role to play as the executive arm of government. To fulfil this role effectively, the service will need to be transformed into a coherent, representative, competent and democratic instrument for implementing government polices and meeting the needs of all South Africans.

Outlining the new mission for the public service, it directs that the public service should:
- become genuinely **representative** of South African demography, crucial for the legitimacy of the public service and essential for equitable service delivery.
- **transform the attitudes and behaviour** of public servants toward a democratic ethos underpinned by a commitment to human rights.
- promote **commitment to the constitution and national interests** rather than to partisan allegiances.
- respond **flexibly, creatively and responsively** to the change process and the needs of the public. This would require organisational decentralisation.
- promote **human resource development** for effective change and institution building.
- encourage the evolution of accountability and transparency.
- upgrade standards of **efficiency and effectiveness**.
- create an **enabling environment** for economic growth within the country.

The White Paper sets out clear parameters for change in government departments such as the police. But rather than creating new structures and institutions, the transformation process that the White Paper and the Constitution together set in motion took as its starting point the existing structures of the public service. The implications of this are explored by Wooldridge and Cranko who argue that the premise for change was to 'rationalise old structures into new ones'. Not much account was taken of the organisation's external context or its internal context of culture and capacity; 'the process of public sector change [consequently became] a technocratic process cast in terms of existing frameworks, institutional practices and procedures. Existing frameworks and vested interests [dictated] the pace and nature of change' (Wooldridge and Cranko, 1997: 337, 341). The Public Order Police unit (indeed the police in general) was no exception and it is therefore not surprising that the methods developed for bringing about change in POP were conventional and somewhat perfunctory.

Public order policing and public service transformation
The new political and legislative framework had important implications for policing in general, but especially for public order policing. The NP government as well as the ANC recognised early in the negotiation process that there could be no democratisation without the support, and the transformation, of the police. For

> few issues [were] more central to the future of the country's attempt at democratic compromise than the maintenance of public order . . . Restoring civil order and personal security for all South Africans [was] thus very important to a successful transition, and a credible, competent and accountable police force, enjoying broad public legitimacy, [was] a prerequisite for a durable democracy (Shaw, 1994: 1).

Police management realised as early as 1991 that reform of the SAP was unavoidable. Changes in the political arena forced police management to restate their allegiances and, consequently, 'during the negotiation process, both security arms [the police and the military] sought to cement their future by placing a distance between themselves and the NP, insisting that they would serve any elected government' (Friedman, 1996: 54) – a shift that Friedman finds hardly surprising for police management when both their own careers and the future success of South Africa's transition depended on their support for the new political dispensation.

The need to transform public order policing in the course of transition to democracy is not peculiar to the South African case. Parallels can be cited from Europe, where Della Porta argues that state democratisation sets the stakes especially high for the forces involved in public order policing since 'direct interventions by the police to restore public order . . . put the police on the front pages of the press, and increase the likelihood of public criticism' (1995a: 1). The way police deal with public protest is accordingly a key indicator of state democratisation.

The legislative framework contained in the Constitution and the new public sector policy documents set the tone for the type of policing that was required in a democratic

South Africa. The 1996 Constitution makes safety and security basic rights for every South African. It is also the only constitution in the world that prescribes community policing as a requisite style of policing for state police, in line with a political philosophy which lays emphasis on bilateral/trilateral agreements, community participation and community consultation in public service institutions (Adler, 2000). Public sector legislation more broadly compels the police to provide an equitable, non-partisan, effective and efficient service.

In 1995, a new South African Police Service Act was promulgated that reflected the spirit and concerns of both the Constitution and the new public sector policy documents. In its preamble, the Act states that a single police service would be formed to ensure the safety and security of all persons in the national territory of South Africa. This police service, the Act stipulates, should strive to uphold and safeguard the fundamental rights as guaranteed in the Constitution. The Act also highlights the importance of community co-operation and civilian oversight.

Although it was indeed the entire newly amalgamated police service that was about to embark on a comprehensive process of change, the need to transform the wing that had been responsible for public order policing was especially urgent. Not only had these units been responsible for some of the most brutal police actions during the apartheid years (and even during the transformation period), they were also the most public and visible units of the police. A number of challenges confronted public order policing. The newly established POP unit (Chapter 3) had to reflect commitment to the right to freedom of expression and to peaceful demonstration and protest. This, along with the parallel philosophy of community policing, would involve an almost wholly new conception of tolerance on the part of the police and an very unfamiliar emphasis on community participation, consultation, negotiation, problem solving, all hand in hand with use of minimum force (Heymann, 1992; Heuns et al., 1998). Structurally too, the make-up of the POP unit had to become representative of the communities it served and less military in appearance and organisation.

There were, however, evident limits to how far the change process was likely to be taken in the police. As Wooldridge and Cranko point out in relation to public service transformation more generally, change was limited to the revamping of existing structures: the sunset clauses made fundamental change unlikely from the outset. At a conference in 1992 on the prospects for democratised policing ANC representative Penuel Maduna noted this when he warned:

> The political and economic reality confronting us is that there is no question of the apartheid oriented, non-representative South African Police force, which is rooted in the gross denial of human rights to the oppressed black masses, being dismantled and replaced with a new force. At the same time, we cannot take over the SAP as it is, with its wrong orientation, tendencies and value systems . . . Trapped as we are between Scylla and Charybdis, as it were, we are constrained to talk about the need to transform the existing forces and instruments of the law . . . and infuse them with new, humane and democratic values and personnel . . . The alternative of us throwing them out lock, stock and barrel is just not feasible (cited in Cawthra, 1993: 176).

In sum, while change had to take place in public order policing, there were two important constraints that were shared with the rest of the public service. The personnel remained largely intact, and the managerial mindset for change was essentially technocratic. It was relatively easy to make visible changes in vehicles and equipment to diminish the military appearance of the unit, but changing patterns of behaviour and ways of thinking was a challenge of a different order. To transform performance and attitude, two avenues were identified by police management and their international advisers: training and policy development. Both, as we shall see, embodied traditional responses, and both entailed their own limitations.

New policy for a new vision
As early as 1992, Judge Goldstone had established a panel of international experts to make recommendations for procedures and rules pertaining to mass demonstrations, marches and picketing. The panel produced a document – edited, and subsequently published in book form by Phillip Heymann, a criminologist at the Harvard Law School – which laid out the principles and made practical recommendations for ensuring protected and peaceful demonstrations in South Africa. This would involve significant changes in South African practice to bring public order policing more in line with practices in Western Europe and North America (Heymann, 1992).

The recommendations of the international panel became a key reference point when the new ANC-led government decided to continue with a separate public order police unit. The Public Order Police Policy Document on Crowd Management, produced by the Technical Team on Public Order Policing to establish new objectives and principles and guidelines (see Chapter 4), noted:

As a result of the vast socio-political changes that have occurred in South Africa over the past few years, new approaches, tactics and techniques must develop to align the management of crowds with the democratic values of transparency and accountability. Police actions must also be reconciled with the Bill of Human Rights and the statutory provisions pertaining to crowd management (1996: 1).

Particular stress was laid on pre-planning, negotiation and consultation with public representatives, a gradual build-up of defensive and offensive measures in line with demonstrated need, constant communication with key players, and, finally, debriefing (both with key players, and within the unit itself).

Senior police in the POP unit, as well as trainers, believed that the Policy Document was crucial to bringing about what they termed 'mind change' and would generate new understandings of how crowd management should be conducted and new rationales to guide action. In the words of Captain Mohamed, Head of Training of Durban POP:

> With the advent of democracy we now have new values and regulations. Police are trained to work according to laws and policies, and when these change, police change too.[3]

These views are not surprising. As Jefferson (1990) has noted in his study of public order policing in Britain, most police supervisors and managers have an idealised respect for policy. Indeed, he argues, the whole police managerial enterprise is directed to and by policy.

While it is well and good to devise new policy, it remains to be established whether rank-and-file are aware of that policy, how they receive and understand it, and whether they carry it out day-to-day. Equally, does new policy kick in at command and supervision level in the way operations are planned and directed?

For the most part, members of the Durban POP received the Policy Document positively. They recognised the value of guidelines and instructions in a period that they experienced as 'in flux' and uncertain. They acknowledged that styles of policing public order had to change to conform to the new political dispensation and in line with the new Constitution and Bill of Rights. One of the Inspectors in the unit reflected this general feeling:

> The document has been important. In the past we had a lot of intolerance in public order policing. With the new document we have learned that you can't just charge at people for no major reason. The policy document helps the police and the crowd to know how crowds should be treated.[4]

Behaviour clearly had to change, but it also had to be guided. His views were echoed by one of the platoon commanders:

> The Policy Document has had a big effect. Previously we had no legislation or guidelines to prescribe how we behaved. New legislation now prescribes our behaviour. We have to comply with the new legislation or face the consequences.[5]

Durban POP members may have been persuaded of the importance of the Policy Document but this did not necessarily mean that they were knowledgeable about its content. In my 1999 survey of 143 members of the unit, most respondents said they had seen the document, though a sizeable number said they had not. Nor would distribution alone mean that everyone had read or absorbed it, and there was scepticism on both these counts (Figure 6.1; Figure 6.2). The less than complete familiarity with the Policy Document suggests that more discussion could certainly have taken place. Only a minority of respondents (Figure 6.3) were satisfied there had been adequate debate about the document's implications.

According to the Head of Training at POP Headquarters, although the intention had been that the Policy Document would be disseminated and discussed both in in-service training and in field platoons, in the event most members got the document only while they were in training and it was not actively distributed by section leaders and Platoon Commanders nor systematically discussed by operational members – as one Platoon Commander acknowledged to me:

> The members tell you, 'Captain, we didn't even know about that thing. We didn't even open it'. But they listen when you tell them about it. But sometimes, even I don't have time for that . . . You cannot instruct people to read. You have to go inside their spirits and inside their minds.[6]

And indeed, simply giving someone a document to read is not going to lead automatically to a change in attitude or values.

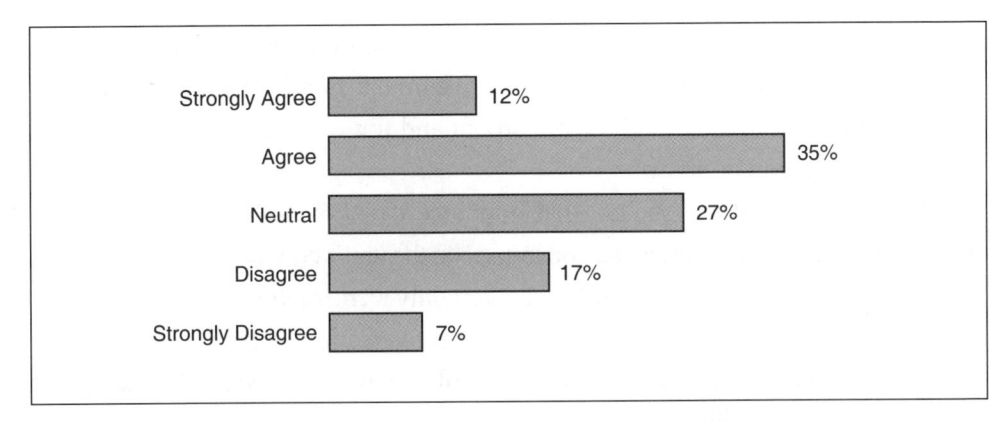

Figure 6.1: 'Most members of the unit have read the Policy Document.'

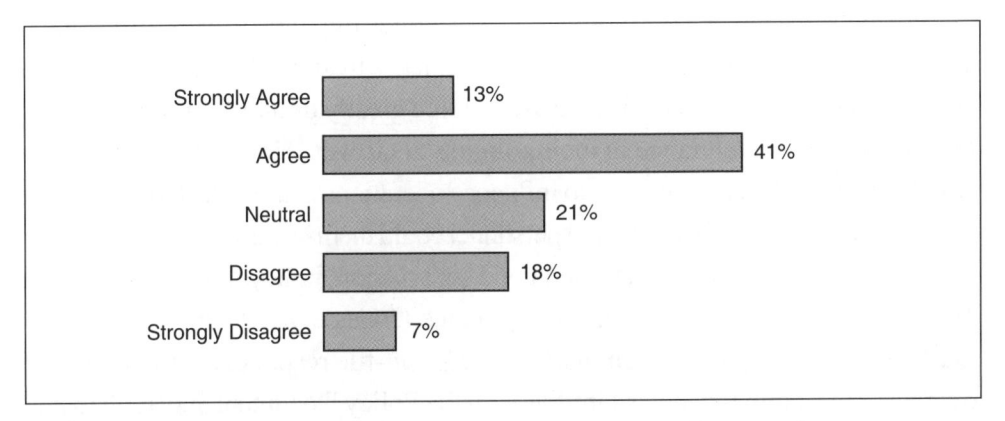

- Strongly Agree: 12%
- Agree: 35%
- Neutral: 27%
- Disagree: 17%
- Strongly Disagree: 7%

Figure 6.2: 'Most members are aware of the goals of the Policy Document.'

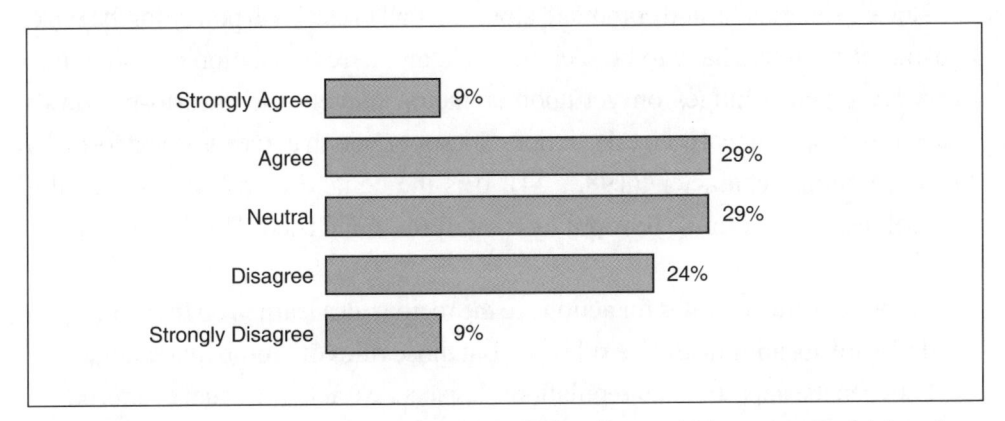

- Strongly Agree: 13%
- Agree: 41%
- Neutral: 21%
- Disagree: 18%
- Strongly Disagree: 7%

Figure 6.3: 'We have adequately discussed the Policy Document in our section/platoon.'

- Strongly Agree: 9%
- Agree: 29%
- Neutral: 29%
- Disagree: 24%
- Strongly Disagree: 9%

So while the Policy Document existed, and members were aware of it, the document alone was unlikely to be an effective transformative tool. Less than half the members had, in fact, read the document and few seemed to think there was much urgency about doing so.

But neither should we conclude that ignorance at rank-and-file level of the details meant that the Policy Document had no impact on the unit's conduct and performance. At supervisor and command levels, officers certainly were mindful of its implications. One of the trainers commented in an informal conversation with me that command personnel had been left in no doubt that the Policy Document was to be their point of reference and that failure to heed it would have serious consequences. Nevertheless the possibility always remained that compliance would be confined to the letter rather than the true spirit of the new policy.

Whatever the underlying motivation, new policy did impact on the procedures and methods used by the unit in crowd management situations. As we shall see in the next chapter, from 1995 onward, the use of force greatly diminished and members displayed far more tolerance in their policing of crowds. However, the extent to which the Policy Document came to influence operations in the field depended very much on how confidently command personnel could themselves implement the new approaches. Without clear orders and good supervision, policy directives alone do not simply transform themselves into practice (Jones et al., 1996). In my 1999 Durban POP survey, only about half the rank-and-file respondents thought their own Platoon Commander was familiar with the Policy Document and applied it in his/her command and there was almost as much scepticism about section leaders in this regard.

Nor are supervision and command alone enough to establish policy for the rank-and-file. Procedures have to be seen to work, and here translation of policy into everyday practice hinges on yet another factor, namely the hard-to-pin-down gradations of operational police discretion. Ericson argues that rules as stated formally 'have a fictional character' (1982: 44). It is the context of rules, not the rules themselves, that determine how policy is interpreted and used. This is because

> the police officer's rules for action are the recipe rules learned on the job . . . They are not administrative rules . . . but those rules of thumb that mediate between the departmental regulations, legal codes, and the actual events he witnesses on the streets (1982: 25).

Similarly, Holdaway argues that

> formal organisational rules, enshrined in law, policy or some other prescriptive managerial instrument, are changed as they are used within the context of policing the streets. A clear objective can be written into any prescriptive directive but it is not safe to assume that the same clarity of purpose will be affirmed by those who implement it (1994: 70).

Change in organisations cannot be accomplished one-dimensionally since, Holdaway argues, there are always assumptions lodged in the minds of those who implement policies in their daily work. These assumptions will shape the way policies are translated into daily policing practice.

Holdaway's cautions were echoed by one of the Durban POP platoon commanders:

> You definitely cannot change police through reading a policy document. There is nothing like that happening. You have to be physically involved and work hands-on with the members in a new style, and also ask members how they are feeling about these things. But the commander must be there at all times ... You need to make them involved physically, show them how to respond and what to do.[7]

The degree to which policy is taken heed of depends on the extent to which it can be applied to the situations and circumstances policemen and policewomen confront in their daily work. And here there were two problems with the reception of the Policy Document in the POP unit. In the first place, the document was solely concerned with crowd management, the primary function of POP; yet, as we saw in the previous chapter, most of the unit's activities focused on its secondary functions, leaving them with no real policy guidance for the work that they did most of the time. A second sticking point was the actual provenance, real or perceived, of the Policy Document: particularly at management level, POP officers were suspicious of policy devised by 'experts' invoking international trends in liberal democracies rather than what the officers saw as the volatile and unpredictable context of public order policing in South Africa, and KwaZulu-Natal in particular. This concern was voiced by station commissioners at a workshop for training high-ranking regular police in crowd management skills. I attended this workshop as an observer and recorded the following incident in my research diary:

> 19/04/2000
> I could see some of the station commissioners were shaking their heads as the trainers introduced them to the procedures outlined in the policy document. One female Station Commissioner from Empangeni,[8] in particular, looked very agitated. She eventually stood up and said: 'Crowds in Zululand are spontaneous and are not willing to negotiate. Often, crowds of people end up killing each other. The only thing we as police can do is use maximum force. So, where is the use of the policy document here?'

In fact the policy document nowhere states that force should never be used. What it does insist on is that maximum force should be a very last option when all other attempts have failed and that any force used should be proportional to the threat of violence on the part of the crowd. The Station Commissioner from Empangeni may have had an incomplete grasp of the Policy Document but she was also giving expression to a commonly held belief that in volatile situations it is better to use force first and talk later.

So we have to recognise that a range of factors determine whether or not policy directives can produce change: the competence, skill, knowledge and commitment of supervisors and commanders; the day-to-day street experiences of police members; the demands of the job; and existing attitudes and assumptions held by policemen and policewomen (particularly the rank-and-file) about their role and about the nature of policing. At a more basic level, the effectiveness of policy as a transformative tool depends on whether, in the first instance, police officers know and accept the objectives and directives of new policy. Also, they may outwardly conform to new policies and implement new procedures and methods simply to avoid the consequences of non-compliance. Basic assumptions do not alter just because you hear about new laws and new policies; 'mind change', a common phrase among Durban POP managers, requires positive experience of actual outcomes.

Training – the magic wand?

With the political transition, training came to be seen everywhere as the key to development of human resources, especially in the public service. According to the White Paper on the Transformation of the Public Service (1995), training contributes to strategic transformation in a number of ways: it equips public servants with the skills and knowledge to carry out jobs effectively and in line with new visions and missions; it increases representivity by equipping persons new to the civil service; it is key to the development of a new work ethic and professionalism and as a mechanism for reorienting values; and it helps public servants develop understanding of the communities that they serve and response to the needs of those communities.

While the training of new recruits to the SAPS had been revised, there was on the whole no systematic re-training for existing members. The Public Order unit was, however, a notable exception since here re-training was given high priority. Following the publication of the Technical Team Report on Public Order Policing in 1995 with its 'new vision' for public order policing, a completely revised training programme for the POP unit was designed with a lot of time, energy and money invested in its development. Approximately R46 million was spent on the re-training of all POP members at every level, with funding mostly provided by the Belgian government whose police directed the re-training programme.

The aim of the training was to supply new skills and knowledge that would relegate to history the discredited methods of the old order and set in place a fresh set of expectations: interventions would henceforth be well planned, properly equipped, held in check by the provisions of the law, and guided by priorities of prevention and consensuality. All existing members of POP were expected to undergo re-training within a five-year period;[9] all new recruits were expected to undergo extensive initiation training before being able to work in the unit. The training programmes were developed by senior POP trainers in conjunction with police trainers from Canada, the United States, Britain, the Netherlands and Zimbabwe, but the main contributor to the training programme was the Belgian Gendarmerie whose model of crowd management training is now closely followed in South Africa. Policing experts from five European countries conducted bi-annual evaluations of the training programmes over a period of five years.

There were a number of different levels to this new training. First, there was an Operational Commander Course, aimed at those responsible for the planning of operations including Company Commanders, Unit Commanders, and provincial and national heads of the unit. This course focused on operational planning and negotiating skills. Next came an initiation course targeted at rank-and-file members of the unit and aimed at standardising knowledge and skills relating to crowd management. In this course officers studied the new legislation pertaining to crowd management – the policy document and the Regulation of Gatherings Act – and were introduced to new ways of understanding and approaching crowds. The overriding emphasis was on new methods and tactics (such as area cordoning, push-and-shove techniques, formations) and the use of new and more appropriate equipment and weapons (such as shields and the tonfa).[10] Negotiation skills did not, however, feature in this course, notwithstanding the priority given to them in the new policy and legislation. While initiation training was initially done at one central national training centre, it soon evolved into decentralised in-service training with the intention of adapting the course to more localised needs. Somewhat later than the other two courses, a Platoon Commanders' Course was developed to train Platoon Commanders in the planning of interventions, skills in briefing and debriefing, basic negotiation skills, the use of conventional signs, and basic methods and techniques of crowd management.

Both content and philosophy put the new training for public order police in line with international practice which emphasises forward planning, community liaison to pre-empt spontaneous disorder, and improved technology, equipment and tactics that permit more flexible and less forceful responses (see Brearley and King, 1996a).

The new courses, at every level, were a dramatic change from previous training in public order policing. As we have already noted, prior to 1986, police involved in public order operations received virtually no training beyond some rudimentary instruction in riot control: for the most part, officers were simply expected to learn on the job. Senior Superintendent Meiring, one of the longest standing members of the unit nationally, describes his own experience of this:

> When I joined the unit in 1983 we did not really receive training. I did go on a riot control course, but what generally happened was that if you didn't know how to do something, you asked. At that time we didn't have crowd management, we had crowd control. That was aggression. If the crowd didn't listen to what you had to say, there was force. We had no training on the use of batons or formations. The emphasis, you see, was not on crowd management, it was to stop these people from doing what they were busy doing. We told people to disperse and if they didn't, we just used what we had at our disposal – guns, gas and so on.[11]

From 1986 until 1995, training had focused on counter-insurgency methods, with use of dangerous and lethal weapons, premised on a philosophy of crowds as inherently irrational, violent and threatening to social order. Training was paramilitary in both content and style – and certainly there were those who, like this one Durban unit member, claimed to have enjoyed it:

> I joined in 1991. We underwent what was then insurgency training. For me, this was a good experience. We mostly learned about the different firearms and the different ways of retaliating to crowds such as the use of gas or batons. To me, all the firearms training was a great learning experience. Then we were also taught self-defence. They also gave us bush training or a survival course. They would put you in the bush for a week and tell you to find your way out of the camp. They gave you a certain amount of food and water and you had to survive. It was a great experience. It was similar to the kind of training that the military would get.[12]

Others remembered the old training with less fondness. On 30 May 2000, I was driving with a young Inspector to KwaMashu township where one of the platoons was involved in a crime prevention operation. The following discussion was recorded in my research diary:

> We chatted all the way to the township. Inspector De Bruin clearly identified with me as a 'white' person and felt he could tell me how he felt about being a white member of the unit at that time. He said he found it very alienating. I wanted to find out more about his experiences in the unit:
>
> *Monique*: How long have you been in the unit?
> *Inspector De Bruin*: I joined in 1992. I came straight from college . . .
> *Monique*: Did you have any specialised training before you came into the unit?
> *Inspector De Bruin*: Not really. Well, we had some counter-insurgency training as part of the basic training, but nothing much. When I got into the unit I was not allowed to go into the townships unless I had done riot control training.

Monique: What was the training like at that time?

Inspector de Bruin: Well, when I got to Maloeskop [training base] we really did a lot of riot control stuff. We were also taught how to do house penetration, use explosives. We also did bush survival courses. It was very physical. They were really hard on us at the time. They would make us run three kilometres with heavy backpacks. We were given two litres of water between the two of us, and one rat pack. We were told we had to survive on that. You wouldn't believe how much weight I lost during that course, and my eyes were all sunken into my head. I had black rings under my eyes. I tell you, I looked really sick.

Monique: That sounds really taxing. Do you think that the training was useful in any way?

Inspector De Bruin: Not really. It is only useful if you are going to do military operations or if you are wanting to do an armed robbery yourself. But it is useless for what we are doing now. I mean, what am I going to do with bush survival?

The new approaches introduced in 1996 were, in general, embraced positively by unit members of all ranks. For the most part, this was because previous training had left them so patently ill-equipped in the skills they now needed for crowd management that would comply with the new directives. Hardly any officers, prior to 1996, had even had training in the use of shields or tonfas, and it is not surprising that members felt inadequate in the unaccustomed role in which they now found themselves. Yet both rank-and-file members and supervisors readily acknowledged how inappropriate and unprofessional the old methods had been.

The revised training was linked to a broader acknowledgement of the need for comprehensive transformation in the unit in which a very important element would be implementation of new legislation. As Herbert (1998) argues in his study of the Los Angeles Police Department, the law is an important component of the police normative order and plays a key role in shaping police behaviour and the broader police occupational culture. Members of the unit, like their peers internationally, were concerned that their own actions would remain in harmony with the law:

Half-measures?

> The new changes are positive. We now realise that people have rights, and the law allows for people to protest and to demonstrate. So, we can't just forcefully disperse crowds as we did before, which was not right. We are aware that we need new skills and training to be able to change.[13]

Most of the respondents in my 1999 survey, rank-and-file and senior officers alike, felt that the new training did equip them with important new practical skills in crowd management (Figure 6.4) and they valued the theoretical insights it gave them, such as the importance of tolerance in dealing with crowds, though almost all of them also said they still needed in-service training in negotiation and conflict-resolution skills. More senior officers in charge of crowd management operations also felt that the new training put them in a much better position to do good operational planning.[14]

At face value, then, the new training programme seems to have gone some way towards meeting its objectives but at least three problem areas nonetheless remained. In the first place, as with the Policy Document, there was a question mark about the applicability of the new training to the actual daily activities of the unit. At all levels, training was directed toward greater efficiency and professionalism in POP's primary function, crowd management, yet in reality the Durban unit spent most of its time on other, secondary-function operations.

When quizzed about this, the national Head of Training of POP agreed that, yes, it was a problem that officers were being trained for what they did only 20 per cent of their time; his own opinion was that training POP members in the generic skills for crime prevention and regular police work should be the responsibility of those who

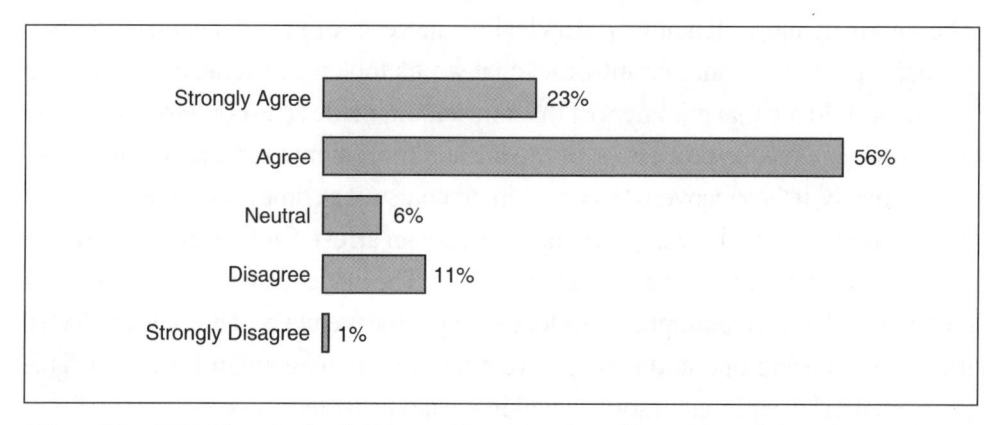

Response	Percentage
Strongly Agree	23%
Agree	56%
Neutral	6%
Disagree	11%
Strongly Disagree	1%

Figure 6.4: 'When I am in the field I am able to use the skills and knowledge I learned in training.'

trained the regular visible police. Rank-and-file members, however, were very concerned about the problem of applicability of training to their daily work. This became evident in informal interactions with them:

> 08/05/2000
> Today I joined one of the sections on a crime prevention operation in KwaMashu township. All of the members in the section were African, and perhaps because of this, they felt at ease discussing some of their problems in the unit openly. As we were 'hanging around' waiting for an instruction from the Platoon Commander, one of the members told me about his frustration with the in-service training programme: 'All we are taught about is crowd management, but as you can see as you are with us now, this is not what we are doing most of the time. We need to learn other skills, like how to use a computer and how to write an affidavit. These are important things for an officer to know. Have you ever heard of a police officer who can only manage crowds and can't do anything else? That is not a policeman. A policeman should know all the skills and be able to do any general policing task. When the community members see us, they don't see a Public Order Police officer. They just see a policeman. We have to know the procedures and be able to help them in any way we can. But, we are not trained for this. Our training is too limited.'

The gaps in training left many officers feeling ineffective in work not related to their primary function. In another informal chat which took place at the unit base, two Sergeants told me that members of the unit seldom made arrests because they had no knowledge of due process or of the basic requirements for making an arrest. Consequently, if they recovered weapons in the course of a crime prevention operation they tended to seize the weapons but not make an arrest, for fear they would run into trouble for not following correct procedure. The inadequate applicability of the new training had serious implications for the way some members of the unit conducted themselves during operations that were not crowd management functions. This problem will be explored in some detail in the next chapter.

A second problem with the new training, again as with the Policy Document, were concerns, expressed particularly by high-ranking officers in the unit, that the principles and procedures covered in the new programmes were not entirely appropriate to the South African context and even less so to the conflict-ridden, volatile environment in KwaZulu-Natal. There was a view that the new techniques were too 'soft'. This was the perception even of the Provincial Head of POP in KwaZulu-Natal:

> The new training works well in Belgium where people are more educated and there is not daily violence and conflict. It is limited in its usefulness in South Africa. It tends to insist on avoidance of confrontation, but there are lots of instances where this model cannot be used. We still need other methods which train members in clear paramilitary skills.[15]

Implicit here may be an unwillingness to let go of familiar tactics in a familiar environment. A similar sentiment was expressed by the Unit Head of POP Durban in an interview in May 1997.

A third reservation emerged when some of the Durban POP trainers expressed doubts about whether Commanders were managing to put their training into practice when it came to planning, directing, and evaluating crowd management operations. Trainers couldn't assess this because there was no provision for on-the-job evaluation in the unit. The point is made by Inspector Bosman, who had had an important role in developing the new training modules:

> One of my real concerns is that our training takes place in a controlled environment. This limits the extent to which individuals see the value of new skills but also means that our evaluation is limited to the classroom . . . Off the top of my head I would guess that Commanders are not entirely following the steps they are taught. So, implementation does seem to be a problem. They leave college with new skills and knowledge, but they don't necessarily change their performance.[16]

On the other hand, some Commanders felt that although they tried to implement crowd management approaches that had been covered in the training, implementation wouldn't get very far if members lacked commitment to the change process. This was reflected in an interchange between a woman Platoon Commander and myself:

10/05/1999

Monique: What role do you think training has played in helping members change their behaviour in the field?

Captain Modise: Training has helped a lot . . . At least members are aware now that a crowd can swear at you, but you cannot harm them. But what is important Monique is that attitude inside. Don't tell members that if they touch a civilian violently they are going to be charged because inside that member there will be no change. They just stop doing certain things because of that fear. We want to change them inside.

Monique: How do you do that?

Captain Modise: Monique, I can't really answer that fully. I just try to motivate my members. I try to command members in such a way that people are respected. I tell them to try to treat other people in the same way you would want them to treat your family.

Training on its own, as Captain Modise implies, cannot change the deep imprint of police culture.

The acid test for training as a transformative mechanism is the extent to which it impacts on the day-to-day exercise of their duties by police officers. However, a straightforward evaluation of the impact of training is difficult because although training may be an indispensable tool for change it is but one influence on police behaviour (Southgate, 1988). Fielding argues that there are a number of other determinants that mediate what is learned in formal training. Foremost is the sense that individual officers make of their own working worlds; this is heavily influenced by their motivations for joining the police in the first place and their understanding of the police role, all of which inform the deep-rooted assumptions and values they adhere to. Ultimately, Fielding argues, 'reform initiatives may stand or fall on their acceptability to those who carry out basic police work' (1988b: 58).

Reference groups within police organisations are also important determinants of whether or not training is effectively implemented (Fielding, 1988a). Younger and less confident officers in particular will seek out more experienced officers that they can identify with and on whom they will model their behaviour as they develop confidence and competence in the field. The reference group becomes even more influential in paramilitary units such as POP where so much emphasis is given to teamwork and solidarity (Jefferson, 1990). Public order work by its very nature involves long hours spent together – on standby, during a demonstration, on patrol. Often this work is risky, putting all the more premium on unit solidarity and mutual trust.

Training can do no more than support change, it cannot direct or drive it. To have real impact it must also be provided at the right time, be tailored to the job, and carry real consequences. Added to this, the work environment must support the changes that training hopes to bring about (Wilms, 1996). Police supervisors and managers must ensure that the conditions of work permit implementation of what is learned in training. Most importantly, supervisors and management must have very thorough working knowledge of what actually happens in training and they must actively draw on this in planning and directing interventions and in evaluating performance. All this requires a management style which is decisive and strategic but also encouraging, supportive and participatory – which, as we shall see in subsequent chapters, was seldom the case in Durban POP.

Recruitment – changing the 'raw material'
While police management had identified policy development and training as starting points for transformation of POP, questions still remained about the personnel composition of the unit. Early in the transformation process it was recognised that existing personnel couldn't simply be replaced, however much 'new blood' might be needed in POP. A number of recommendations were therefore made to address this in the Technical Team Report on Public Order Policing (1995).

- Appointment to POP units should be voluntary, not as in the past where officers were simply assigned to the unit.
- Failure of POP members to act in 'in an impartial and professional manner, regardless of the race, sex, ethnicity, political affiliation or sexual orientation of participants and/or non-participants' (1995: 24) would lead to removal from the unit.
- There should be psychological evaluation and support for all officers coming into the unit and for those already in the unit.
- There should be ongoing evaluation to ensure that officers complied with the unit's mission and code of conduct.
- There should be a maximum period of duty in the unit of five years, putting it in line with international practice where officers serve in any particular specialised unit for no more than three to five years.

The Technical Team was well aware that there would be a limit to how far transformation could go without an inflow of new personnel and the departure of long-standing members not likely to embrace the changes. Revised recruitment strategies will always be important for qualitative change in police agencies; 'improving the quality of people who make up the police department is an unquestionably valid objective of police reform' (Bent, 1974: 11) – and this is difficult to achieve without improving and revisiting recruitment and training.

Whether or not a police organisation can meet transformational goals depends very much on the profile of its personnel. It is obviously important to recruit members who will have the right skills and abilities. But recruitment strategies also have a significant bearing on relationships between the police and the communities they serve (Holdaway, 1991; Brewer, 1991; Goldstein, 1990). Improving police-community relations often means taking steps to make police organisations representative of the society in which they work.

Public order policing reform in Europe has generally put a lot of emphasis on trying to reshape the personnel component. In Spain, for example, in the transition to democracy in the 1980s, a lot of attention was paid to this when the public order units were reviewed. A decade or so later, hardly any members remained, at any level, who had been in the units before the demise of the Franco dictatorship (Jaime-Jimenez and Reinares, 1998). In Germany, on the other hand, corresponding reforms concentrated on replacing high-ranking officers; the rationale here was that top-level officials were best placed to drive philosophical and operational reform (Winter, 1998).

In South Africa personnel change was slower to get off the mark; by 2001, very little had happened, and in Durban POP there was actually a moratorium on members leaving when it became clear how little interest there was in joining the unit either from new recruits or from SAPS officers who might want to transfer from other sections of the service. This had a noticeably detrimental effect on the unit's on-going operations, let alone its receptiveness to reforms. As a result, in February 2000, the Head of Personnel and a senior Operational Commander in Durban POP jointly compiled a document requesting that newly trained police recruits be sent to POP for a 22-week field training programme. Thereafter, the document proposed, the new recruits would be permanently inducted into POP, releasing older and experienced unit members for transfer to the stations. According to this document, in 1999 alone there were 78 applications for transfers by members wanting to leave the unit. There were various reasons for their reluctance to stay: boredom, poor career prospects, work-related stress and depression, or simply that adapting to new ways seemed more than they felt equal to.

For the Durban POP Head of Personnel, the fact that disenchanted members could not be released, however much they wanted to leave, was a major source of frustration. He spoke to me about this informally:

> 20/05/2000
> While waiting to go out with one of the platoons on a crime prevention operation, Captain Naidoo invited me into his office to chat. He looked very perturbed and offered me a seat and he shared with me the cause of his worry.
>
> *Captain Naidoo*: Monique, do you know about our new recruitment document that we put together?
> *Monique*: Yes, I remember looking at it earlier this year. I thought you had some good ideas in there.
> *Captain Naidoo*: You see, we really need new blood in the unit. That is the only way things are going to change around here. We need to get rid of those members who don't want to be here. Last week I sent out a memo asking members if there is anyone who is willing to be transferred out of the unit, and if so, where they would like to go. You see, the problem is that we cannot bring in a new person, or get rid of an old one if we cannot do a swap. So, if a member from the station wants to join POP, we first have to find a POP member who is willing to go to that particular station. This is a bit difficult because all the members who want to leave want to go to another specialised unit, and nobody wants to leave those units to come here . . . So far we have only managed to make four swaps. Our hands are tied. We cannot simply get rid of people or bring new ones in, much as I would like this to happen.

Captain Naidoo had good reason to be concerned as the moratorium was clearly leading to serious discontent. This became very obvious to me during an encounter with a white Sergeant a week after my chat with Captain Naidoo:

28/05/2000

I was busy writing field notes in the reception area while waiting to meet with the Unit Commander. He wanted to have a chat about his ideas of restructuring the unit. A white Sergeant I had interviewed previously came and sat next to me. He told me that he wanted to meet Captain Naidoo (the Head of Personnel) about some health problems he was having and inform him that he wanted to take sick leave. He was in his early thirties and looked depressed and somewhat agitated. We started to talk:

Monique: You look a bit down today.
Sergeant Niekerk: Well, I must tell you, I am not very happy in this unit anymore. I joined 13 years ago. Things were different then. My buddies were in the unit and it was an exciting place to be. We were always on the go and we were active in the communities. Now things have changed a lot.
Monique: In what way have things changed?
Sergeant Niekerk: In those days we knew what was right and what was wrong. We dealt forcefully with people who were causing chaos. We did not tolerate nonsense from people. Nowadays, people can do what they like. We are expected to just watch them and to tolerate things that are not acceptable.
Monique: What are these things that are unacceptable?
Sergeant Niekerk: Well, for example, you can just march in the streets at any time, even without permission, and members of the public can throw things at us and insult us and we are supposed to just tolerate this. I think this is unacceptable. When I joined the unit we were trained differently. The public knew that the police were in charge and that we had authority. Now the police have become a joke. The public know that we can't use force anymore and they are taking advantage of us ... I have tried to get used to these changes, but to tell the truth, I am from the old school ... The other problem is that white members like me will never be promoted. This affirmative action thing has made being in units like this a dead end. This unit is making me sick and I don't have the motivation to come to work anymore. I think it is time to leave.

There are important issues we can unpack here. Sergeant Niekerk is powerfully aware of the influence of his own formative experiences as a policeman – both his training and his field experience. They have shaped him so thoroughly that he simply cannot imagine adapting to the new dispensation, and we could well conclude that new training, and new policy directives, are in the end more likely to confirm his misgivings than dispel them. It is also fairly clear that this white policeman is not likely to rediscover enthusiasm for his job while he contemplates his career path vanishing ahead of him.

Sergeant Niekerk was one of the many who wanted to leave the unit. Responses to the 1999 survey (see Figure 7.2, next chapter) show that almost half the unit members, of all ranks, were thinking of leaving. More than four out of five white members had considered leaving, as compared with just over half the Indian members, more than a third of the African members and two out of three Coloured members.[17] In informal conversations with senior officers, I learned over time that about a third of them had applied for transfer out of the unit (often linked to promotion prospects) and a number had even applied for posts in other policing organisations (including private security firms). For example, two middle-manager officers, both with long service records in the unit, applied for posts in the Durban City Police in 1998.

The disaffection permeated the whole unit, and this can often be the case for police organisations undergoing radical reform. Rippy (1990) writes that frontline police employees usually perceive themselves as bearing the brunt of changes (such as stricter policies, rules and regulations), often producing knee-jerk resistance. Director Wiggins was well aware of the decline in morale:

> To be honest, we are sitting with bad human material. There is helplessness, stress, frustration and poor self-management in the unit. Members think that just being at work is enough.[18]

Members who had joined the unit during the transition period or after the 1994 elections also noticed how difficult the change process was for veteran members of the unit. I had the following conversation with a Sergeant in the unit while sitting with one of the platoons in a courtroom they were policing during a potentially volatile hearing of the Truth and Reconciliation Commission:

08/07/2000
Sergeant Mbambo: You can't force someone to change if they don't want to change. There are people in this unit who don't want to change. I feel sorry for them. Eventually they will become victims of change. You have to go with the processes that are underway, otherwise things change and you are left behind. If you are left behind for too long, you become a danger to yourself and do things that you will be in trouble for. You can't resist the wave of change forever.
Monique: You seem to be someone who is very proud of being in the unit and you feel positive that things are going in the right direction.
Sergeant Mbambo: Well that is true. But, also, I only joined the unit in 1991. By then, changes were already in the wind. So I wasn't really in the unit in the bad old days. Also, I joined when I was already quite old – 32 years. So maybe I came to the unit with a more mature approach. I also had a fresh view of things. Some of these guys have been here forever. It is very difficult for them to change.

Sergeant Mbambo had joined the unit five years before the new training and policy came in. There were, however, a handful of members who joined the unit as 'fresh recruits' having undergone a completely revised SAPS basic training programme. They found it hard to adapt to the way the unit still went about its business and they soon discovered that as new recruits with a fresh perspective there was little they could do to change things. So they learnt not to stick their necks out:

31/05/2000
While I was riding in the Nyala with eight members of the unit, I noticed a member that I had never seen before. He was much younger than the other members and seemed rather quiet. I noticed that he was a Constable while all the other members were Sergeants and Inspectors. I decided to find out more about him.

Monique: Hi there, I haven't seen you around the unit much in the past. Are you new by any chance?
Constable Asmal: Yes, I have only been here for about two months. I am still learning the ropes.

Monique: How have you found working in the unit so far?
Constable Asmal: Well, I only joined the police last year and finished my field training earlier this year in one of the stations. This is really different from the stations and what I have been taught. I am still getting used to it and trying to fit in. It is okay so far, but I must say it is very different from what we learned in the college. We were trained mainly in community policing and human rights. This unit doesn't really do community policing, or they don't see themselves in that way. You just go into an area, do your thing, and then leave again. You don't build relationships with the community. I am very surprised about that. But, I am new, so there is not much I can do about that. I have to realise that members have been here for ten, twelve years. They have a lot of experience that I don't have. These guys are also very militarised, you know. So, I will just have to see how I can try to fit in.

As is nearly always the case in police organisations, instructors in basic training are the 'recruit's first clear role models' (Fielding, 1988a: 69), but their influence may decline rapidly as more experienced officers in the field replace them as the reference group for acceptance as policemen and policewomen. In 1972, John van Maanen studied recruit socialisation in the Union City Police Department in California and concluded:

> It is less a question of the recruit accepting the police system than it is a question of the police system (formal and informal) accepting him . . . the recruit is expected to learn fast or 'get out' for deviations from the work ethic prevalent in the department will normally be met with rather harsh informal – or possibly formal – sanctions (1972: 215).

There are various implications here for police organisations in the process of change. It should not be assumed that an influx of new recruits will necessarily result in new attitudes and practices being role-modelled and accepted. New recruits may be more amenable to change than established officers set in their ways, but this may be of more individual than organisational significance. For recruits to make an impression on the work ethos, they would need to have critical mass: a handful of new recruits in the lower ranks is unlikely to have much effect on the general adoption of fresh attitudes and practices. However, the difficulty of getting satisfactory recruitment strategies in place for the public order units meant that, in Durban POP at any rate, the unit still had veteran members who clearly believed that they were personally unable to adapt. Even for those who welcomed the prospect of transformation, it was difficult to abandon familiar ways of doing things, because this had so much to do with how they judged their own competence in their daily work. Compounding this, the effective stagnation in personnel turnover meant that existing networks and reference groupings continued, along with their influence over members' behaviour.

In short, then, the political and legislative changes that followed in the wake of the 1994 elections left the police with little choice but to embark upon a process of reform. Democracy and a new legislative framework created a huge momentum for societal transformation. But turning around the public service at large and the police in particular was constrained both by the nature of the transition and by the chosen mechanisms for change. South Africa's transition was particularly constrained by the understanding that existing structures would be 'rehabilitated' rather than radically transformed. This meant accepting the fact that seasoned but often tarnished personnel would stay on in the public service. The sunset clauses combined with the unanticipated complications of recruitment for public order policing units produced a demotivated social base, and the old social networks, role-modelling and power relations lingered on. Further complicating this was that veteran members who desperately 'wanted out' discovered that they were stuck in the unit, and had no interest in self- or organisational transformation.

Policy and training were undoubtedly important in the transformation project. Yet in any police organisation there are a host of influences that shape values and assumptions concerning the policing environment and the police role, and hoping that training and policy will induce 'mind change' is perhaps to turn on its head what actually happens in the field. The lessons of training often shift dramatically when real police work begins. The way police see their own role and mission, their organisation and the milieu in which they work, and how they judge the effectiveness of what they do will ultimately be determined by their daily policing experiences.

Did political and legislative transformation, the introduction of new mechanisms for change and limited changes to the social base of Durban POP succeed in bringing about desired changes in Durban POP? This question can best be answered by exploring actual responses, decisions and conduct within the unit, both individual and collective, and is the concern of the next three chapters.

7

New Methods, New Motives?
Durban POP and its Public

A police officer
If you can practice tolerance when all around you are objects of intolerance.
If you can deal in human filth without letting part of it rub off on you.
If you can wash a victim's blood from your uniform and treat it as the dust of your profession.
If you can take the broken body of the child from a screaming mother and hold back emotion.
If you can helplessly watch the courts dismiss a known criminal and still believe in justice.
If you can see your children belittled by their friends because you are 'a cop', and still treat them as friends.
If you can guarantee rights to all, while they are denied to you, and still believe in the 'Bill of Rights'.
If you can accept oral praise rather than a pay-raise because it is politically popular and not complain.
If you can attend church with the same people that curse you on Saturday nights and still see good in all people.
If you can accept a salary less than most welfare cases and still support your family.
If you can accept all these things my friend . . . and not become bitter . . . you are a POLICE OFFICER.

(author unknown)

(http://home.earthlink.net/~piglt/writings.html)

A good many policemen and policewomen, perhaps most, would buy into the self-image of the nameless cop-poet who supposedly penned the lines at the head of this chapter: doing 'shit work in shit conditions for shit pay and no thanks'. Occupying the moral high ground does often help to keep you going, and it matters to police officers, generally, that they should see themselves as working for the public good – never mind that this may turn out to no more than the good of the ruling minority. Add in the memories of triumphs and achievements that reinforce a sense of purpose and principle in policing, and there can be no illusions about the complexities that beset reform in police organisations.

No matter how 'unique' police may consider themselves to be, in a time of democratic transition, police are just one more segment of the broad public service that needs to be restructured and reoriented. And like the rest of the public service – perhaps even more so – it was in the transformation of their service delivery that the South African police (and especially the public order units) were on probation to show their commitment to the political transition. No longer could there be any place for partisan, repressive interventions in a new political climate requiring impartiality and principled commitment to human rights.

The new SAPS had to undergo transformation at three levels. Structurally, it had to be representative of the population it serves, and able to respond to both local and national needs. At the behavioural level, the services it provided had to be community oriented, proactive rather than reactive and subject to processes of accountability. Attitudinally, community-oriented policing had to become its governing philosophy (rather than simply a style of policing) and this meant perceiving the public as 'clients' and even as 'partners' who should be treated with care and respect and who deserve the best possible service.

This chapter is concerned primarily with how police behave. It examines the responses of members of the Durban POP toward the public that they served while carrying out their police functions. A persistent question for this chapter is: Why do police revert to outlawed or discredited and reprehensible ways regardless of reforms in the agencies they belong to? Why is police behaviour seemingly so resistant to fundamental change?

We have to recognise that deep level assumptions, attitudes and values are inevitably difficult to shift. There is nothing unique in the way police officers hold on to established values, perceptions of how things should be done, and views of their environment and the people they serve. They set store by memories of what they recall as the 'golden days' of their careers and these memories continue to shape their sense of what it is legitimate for the police to do. Holding on to established values and assumptions and clinging to nostalgic memories are especially likely when what Chan calls the *field* – 'the historical, structural relations between positions of power' (1996: 116) – has not significantly changed. And the field is difficult to change when rules and policies within the police service are not clear and specific enough, when power relations within the society remain relatively unchanged, and when police supervisors are not directive or supportive enough during change processes.

The burden of the past
The literature of police history in South Africa is replete with narratives of its brutal, unprofessional interventions, like the account an ex-lieutenant of the South African Riot Police gave to lawyer Fink Haysom of his former colleagues:

> [They were] just hitting people. They didn't care if they were innocent bystanders or not. They were running after them even when they were fleeing, hitting them. It seemed to me that they were enjoying themselves, feasting on the people. The Squad stormed the kids like wild dogs. You could see the killer instinct in their eyes (cited in Haysom, 1989: 139).

Or there is the account Waddington gives of the policing of a funeral in Uitenhage in the early 1990s:

> As the crowd participating in the funeral appeared, the Casspirs [armoured vehicles] blocked the road and the lieutenant stood on top of one of the vehicles and ordered the crowd to disperse. When the crowd refused, the lieutenant fired a warning shot which provoked a woman to throw a single stone. The lieutenant replied with the order to 'Fire'. Twenty people were killed by the fusillade that followed (cited in Della Porta and Reiter, 1998: 138).

Members of Durban POP corroborated these accounts many times over when they recalled to me how the policing of crowds took place in the past. These were stories of a unit engaged in crowd control with every assumption of impunity and no respect at all for the ordinary people – particularly the black people – who bore the brunt of these encounters. According to Captain Modise,

> There was no tolerance in the members and the commanders. We did not see any dignity in the people. As a black person, it is your custom to know who to obey, particularly elders. But, at that time, you find the police grabbing an old man, kicking and pushing him. All those kinds of things made me very unhappy. We even used to take young boys and kick them in the face. We never told people their rights or told their relatives what had happened.[1]

The equipment available to the unit confirmed the legitimacy of forceful intervention, as outlined by Senior Superintendent Meiring on page 126, Chapter 6.

Meiring also spoke about the absence of consultation with any interested parties prior to or during a crowd event. All events were policed the same way; the goal was to disperse the crowd and any means would be used to achieve this:

> We did things just the way we were told to do it. Let me give you a simple example. There was a protest meeting at a stadium in Pietermaritzburg. Directly after the meeting we gave the people a certain limited time to disperse. But people had to get buses to be able to leave the meeting. There were thousands of people and there was no way you could get them to disperse in that time. They were still waiting for the buses to come. But then the unit just started to shoot these people. This was wrong because these people were waiting for transport . . . We had this hard rigid approach. You just did what you were instructed to do and what the paper said. We said we negotiated, but really we did not.[3]

And Captain Naidoo, Head of Personnel Services at POP Durban, confirmed that there was no policy of consultation with role players before the mid-1990s. Nor did any kind of briefing or debriefing take place within the unit itself. Briefing police officers prior to intervention is crucial if they are to have knowledge and understanding of the situations they are about to enter. Debriefing is an indispensable means of getting members to reflect on past action and for changing future behaviour where this is necessary. The neglect of briefing and debriefing meant that members simply responded to orders with no real knowledge of the event they were policing. This went along with a general neglect of planning. Events were not individually distinguished; all were simply responded to indiscriminately as problematic situations that had to be contained and terminated and standing procedures envisaged no other approach. According to an Inspector from POP Headquarters, all protests and demonstrations were dealt with the same way:

> The aim of the police was always to disperse crowds, regardless of their purpose. The police were not interested in what the protest was trying to achieve or if there were legitimate goals. We would be deployed with absolutely no information as to the particular event and would be instructed to disperse, usually with rubber bullets or tear gas, but sometimes even with live ammunition. We responded like Robocops.[4]

The Internal Stability Unit, at both provincial and national level, only began to keep proper records of its activities in 1992, with a computer database to record the events or incidents they policed. Each record noted the nature of the event, the police response to the event and whether there were deaths, injuries or damage to property. These records are scant but they do provide insight as to what the activities of the unit were at the time. The Durban records confirm that poor planning, excessive use of force and lack of negotiation were general characteristics of public order policing in the early 1990s, notwithstanding the national political negotiations going on at the time. What is evident in these records is not only the excessive use of force by the police, but also the volatile nature of the crowds they interacted with. There are consistent records in the incident reports of skirmishes between police and crowds. The police were also called upon to intervene in violent confrontations between competing groups, usually in the black townships. The conflict was usually between ANC and IFP supporters and it is widely accepted that police themselves played a role in fuelling this conflict. Rather than make any attempt to resolve the conflict, police were, often as not, prepared simply to resort to the use of deadly force, usually against ANC supporters.

The following four extracts from the Durban records are typical of the records in the early 1990s:[5]

> [August 1992] Warrant Officer N and his members were escorting 1 000 IFP supporters from a rally that was held at Princess Magogo Stadium in KwaMashu. When they passed 'F' section KwaMashu which is occupied by ANC supporters with AK47 rifles, five male IFP supporters were shot and injured. Constable P fired eight rounds with his P38 and Sergeant H fired one round with his R1.

The report does not say how many people were injured or killed. What *is* clear is that a lot of bullets were fired. Other incident reports are more detailed. The language alone of these reports hints at the undercurrent of hostility toward those being policed (mainly black people) and the general intolerance towards crowds. This hostility and intolerance would (in the police officer's mind) legitimise the aggression displayed by the police.

> On 93-12-03 at 08:15, Captain N was called out to the R102 road at Ntshawini where a group of blacks were allegedly stopping buses, taxis and assaulting the commuters. On arrival he was confronted with the group of blacks ranging from youths to adults. This militant group were armed with sticks, spears and stones. The crowd was very aggressive. They refused to disperse. The police tried to stop them from stopping the forms of public transport. In order to avoid violence, injury and the possibility of death, 20 tear gas canisters were fired at the crowd.

Firing off 20 canisters of tear gas hardly seems an avoidance of violence. Tear gas and rubber bullets are often regarded as non-lethal but it is now well recognised that both can cause fatalities if fired directly at their targets and at close range, and children, certainly, are known to have died from respiratory problems after inhaling tear gas. Twenty canisters is a huge quantity of tear gas and firing that much at a crowd could have very grave consequences.

> On 93-01-01 at about 05:00, at Durban beach where Sergeant M together with four members were walking beach patrol. Next to the Cattleman parking they came across a black male raping a black female. The police apprehended the suspect and the crowd around them became aggravated and advanced in a threatening manner. An unknown black man drew a knife and tried to stab Constable M. Constable M fired 1 x 9 mm round to warn the crowd . . . The crowd became aggravated and moved toward Constable M. Constable N fired a 1 x 9 mm round. A Black male of 20 years was shot in the back and taken to King Edward Hospital.

Another record details the ammunition used and the injuries that followed:

> On 93-05-15 at 06:30 at Bambayi area the police witnessed the red band and green band members involved in a faction fight with each other.[6] On arrival of the ISD members, shots were fired at the ISD. The following ISD members returned fire. Sgt P fired 15 x 9 mm rounds; Lieutenant Sergeant G fired 15 x 9 mm rounds; Lieutenant D fired 32 x 9 mm rounds and 6 x No.5 rounds; Sergeant B fired 22 x 9 mm rounds; Constable M fired 6 x 9 mm rounds; Sergeant V fired 30 x 9 mm rounds; Sergeant H fired 2 x gas grenades. The following members from the green band were injured. Black male Mlumna – 18 years – shot on left arm. Black male Vilikazi – 30 years – shot on right middle finger. Black male Mtethwa – 45 years – shot on left leg. Black male Ngcobo – 45 years – shot on left buttock. Black male Kala – 45 years – shot in left palm. Black male Mkolondo – 30 years – shot on left chest and right upper arm. Black male Ndlovu – 23 years – shot in left buttock. Black male Mzinkisi – 39 years – shot on left leg above the knee. Black male unknown – 50 years – shot in head. Black male Ngama – 45 years – shot in head. Black male Sigotu – 22 years – birdshot wound to chest and left eye. Black female Precious – 27 years – birdshot wound to right cheek. Black male Ngcobo – 27 years – shot in right calf and left chest. 12 shacks belonging to the green band were burned . . . Sergeant S sustained minor injuries to his right hand from a rock thrown at him from the crowd.

At least two members of the crowd died in this incident and many more were injured, some almost certainly because of the weapons used by the police. In contrast, one police member was slightly injured. The police freely expended live ammunition, and though the facts of the case are not entirely clear from the report, the crowd almost certainly did not have access to equal or comparable force.

It is clear from the Durban incident reports that during this period it was mainly in the African townships that deaths and injuries occurred as a result of police interventions in crowd events. Most crowd events (protests and demonstrations) in the central business district and in white suburbs were policed relatively peacefully during the early 1990s. Peaceful crowd management in the CBD and suburbs, set against more violent control measures in the African townships, was a pattern that persisted as late as 2001 and various explanations are possible for the difference in response. 'Blacks', and in particular crowds of black people, were automatically identified by the police as 'aggressive' and 'militant' and as 'trouble-makers': in the police world-view, therefore, the use of force in maintaining or creating order was justified. Possibly as a consequence of violent police responses, high levels of antagonism existed between the police and the communities in the African townships; whole areas then came to be defined by the police as dangerous and problematic. Protests and demonstrations in the townships often took their lead from the liberation movement strategy of creating ungovernability, and collective violence was resorted to when peaceful protest failed to achieve it objectives. Over time, localised historical memories accumulated, which created a vicious circle of response and counter-response.

In all these circumstances it could be argued that the kinds of situations that police officers had been exposed to brutalised them and had a deep impact on the way they perceived the communities they policed. General Marais recalled that people in the unit (the ISU and afterwards POP) were exposed to 'bodies blown apart', and that, he said, left a deep impression, particularly on young officers: experience like this confirmed their sense that they were 'going after the enemy'. Police officers themselves were also seriously injured and many died in the confrontations of the 1980s and early 1990s. All too readily, this engendered the belief among those police who worked in the townships that they were indeed fighting a war and that the use of deadly force was accordingly justified.

The following conversation with a Platoon Commander further illustrates this point. We were talking about the use of force in the past and I asked whether the readiness to use force might have been due to the relatively small number of members deployed.[7]

> 10/05/2000
> *Monique*: If you went in with so few members, you must have felt compelled to use forceful methods to achieve your goals.
> *Captain Meetha*: Yes, we used force in those days to achieve our goals. It's not like today when you have to be very careful about what you do. In those days we just used the force we wanted to and we did not even think twice about it.
> *Monique*: How did you feel about this at the time?

> *Captain Meetha*: To be honest it used to worry me because I could see what we were doing. But that is how you had to respond and you just got used to it. But I must tell you that we have seen terrible things in the past. For example, I remember going in to one of the townships and seeing a child whose head and limbs had been cut off. We began to think that black people were just like animals.
> *Monique*: Are there other similar experiences that come to mind?
> *Captain Meetha*: Yes, I remember one day sitting in a vehicle having lunch. Someone threw a grenade at us. I don't know how it happened, but we didn't get hit. But, ten people from the community were standing nearby and ten people were killed. When we got out we found them with shrapnel in their faces and completely dismembered.

A Sergeant who had been working in Inanda township in the 1980s recalled an even more horrific memory:

> ... I will never forget this one scene. There was a little girl, maybe six years old. She had been eating rice. Next minute, someone came and hacked her at the back of her head. Her brains fell into the rice. Can you imagine dealing with such people?[8]

Officers with long service in the unit also recollected horrific scenes following what they termed 'faction fights' (inter- or intracommunal battles ensuing, often, from deep historical disputes) or *muti* murders (murders for traditional medicinal purposes). Bodies would be found with genitals gouged out, or the charred remains of children murdered in revenge, provoking horror and revulsion toward the communities ostensibly responsible for these deeds. Images like these, localised historical memories, brutalising experiences, stereotypes of communities and of crowds, linger on perhaps indelibly and they continued to shape the behaviour of Durban POP members six years after the transformation process in the unit had begun.

Signs of a new direction

My own observations of the unit, reflections communicated to me by members of the unit, and the incident reports provided me with a basis for assessing what degree of change had taken place in Durban POP since the onset of the transformation process.

As we saw in previous chapters, new policy documents and training introduced from 1996 onwards sought to change the behaviour specifically of officers and units involved in the policing of crowds. More broadly, the South African Police Service Act of 1995 and the 1996 Constitution committed the entire police service to the philosophy and practice of community policing. The community-oriented approach called for an entirely new set of assumptions on the part of the police (and the public) and turned the traditional frames of reference of the South African police upside-down. The focus had now to be on individual rights and liberties, with the assumption that crowds have rational objectives and will inherently be orderly and peaceful, and that crowd participants are to be treated as citizens, not criminals. The key responsibility for the police would henceforth be to forestall disorder, not provoke it (Heuns et al., 1998).

The 'new' Public Order Police unit was expected to apply a whole new set of principles and procedures when responding to the public. From now on, its operations were to be guided by international practice that emphasised 'soft', selective, legal, consensual policing, with tolerance of the behaviour and grievances of citizens as the point of departure for averting confrontation between police and public, and recourse to forceful methods considered fundamentally counter-productive (Jaime-Jimenez and Reinares, 1998).

Following the 1996 Policy Document and the new legislation, a particularly significant new dimension to the working routine of the POP units was now to be operational planning, for which a crucial starting point would be good intelligence – accurate, appropriately processed information. Information was not only to be used for planning by Commanding Officers, it should also be passed to front-line Supervisors and those under their command. All unit members should be briefed about the operational plan, and after each event there should be debriefing so that all members jointly review actions taken.

There were now also clear stipulations and guidelines with regard to the use of force. The decision to use force was to be taken only when participants act in ways that threaten life and property. In terms of the Regulations of Gatherings Act, the police have to notify the convener and participants that reasonable grounds exist to use force. Before force is employed, the command structure must be in place, and the weapons to be used must be non-lethal (water canons, tonfas, smoke grenades, chemical agents). Live ammunition is ruled out for the dispersal of crowds in crowd management operations, and the principle of police restraint requires that all officers be provided with suitable protection and equipment before they are deployed. If not, the Operational Commander can withdraw them from the scene.

The new guidelines charged the unit with a significant set of new expectations and these did lead to members of Durban POP seeing their role as having changed significantly. The changes in self-perception are evident in the survey results from my research, but they should also be seen in the context of the decline of violent protest in South Africa since 1994. According to Lodge, since 1994, black South Africans have tended to favour non-violent civic protests, demonstrations, rallies and petitions – which, he argues, 'implies a recognition of authorities' legitimacy' (2001: 12).

The 1999 survey indicated that POP members did think the unit was changing its ways in line with the policy and training reforms (Figure 7.1; Figure 7.2; Figure 7.3). But there were also racialised dimensions to their responses. More than two out of three African members judged that Durban POP had become more community oriented, but less than half the white members agreed with them. Indian members seemed most convinced that the unit had become more community oriented, with almost all of them concurring with the statement. It is not very easy to interpret these findings since it was unclear whether members were referring to their own behaviour, to that of their reference groups (which could be racially based), or to the unit as a whole. But Indian and African officers seemed convinced nonetheless that there was a shift in behaviour, while white officers appeared to be far less certain of this.

The majority of respondents (Figure 7.2) thought that force was used more circumspectly after 1994. Cross-tabulations showed racial differences in responses to this statement too. A high proportion of African, and especially Indian members believed that officers in the unit were now more hesitant to make use of force; somewhat fewer white colleagues agreed with them.

There was fairly uniform agreement that POP now showed more tolerance in crowd control situations (Figure 7.3), suggestive of a particularly significant mind-shift in view of the particular stress given to this in the training and policy document. If taunts and obscenities were hurled at them, and even more substantial missiles, POP members were expected to put up with it. In general they seemed much more ready to do so, and their survey responses indicate that they themselves were conscious of the change.

Between 1997 and 2000, I observed the Durban Pubic Order Police unit in

New Methods, New Motives? 153

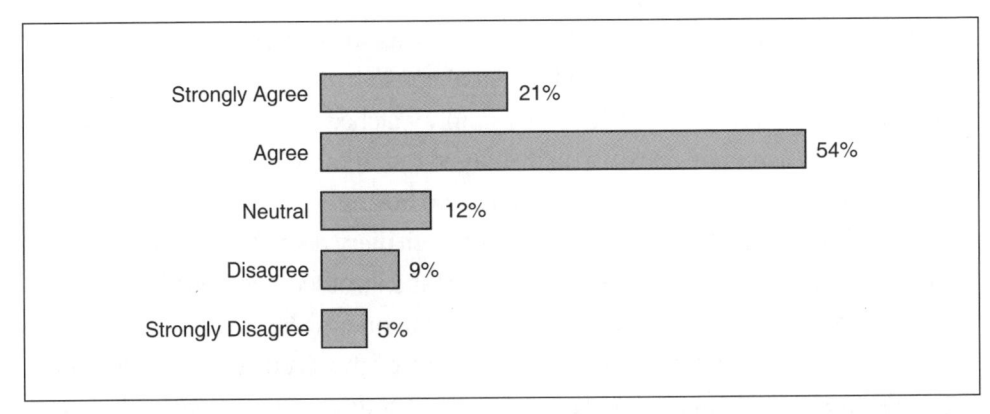

Strongly Agree	21%
Agree	54%
Neutral	12%
Disagree	9%
Strongly Disagree	5%

Figure 7.1: 'Since the 1994 elections, POP has become more community oriented in dealing with crowds.'

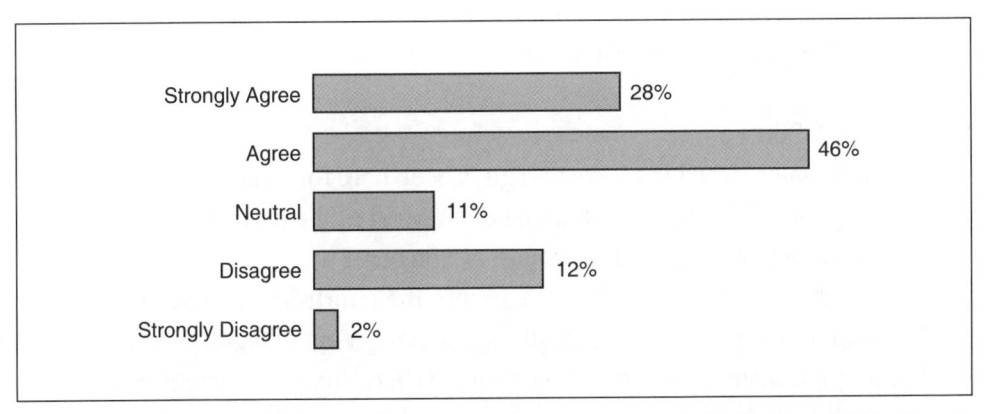

Strongly Agree	28%
Agree	46%
Neutral	11%
Disagree	12%
Strongly Disagree	2%

Figure 7.2: 'POP members are more hesitant to make use of force since the 1994 elections.'

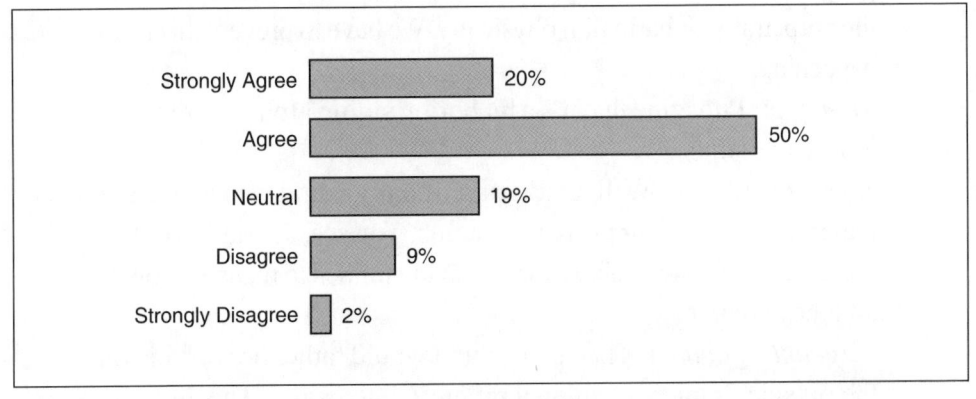

Strongly Agree	20%
Agree	50%
Neutral	19%
Disagree	9%
Strongly Disagree	2%

Figure 7.3: 'POP members are more tolerant in their conduct toward crowds than they were prior to the 1994 elections.'

over twenty crowd management situations. I was impressed by unit members' composure in the face of verbal and physical abuse from the crowds. Even when bottles and stones were thrown at them they simply watched with no sign of antagonism. Unit members (usually African) also displayed remarkable reserves of patience in policing events that turned out to be tedious and boring.

The following incident recorded in my research diary demonstrates new attitudes about what constituted 'good' police behaviour and its outcomes. I had been driving around with a Sergeant who was trying to locate one of the sections. We met up with them at the magistrate's court where some of the Truth and Reconciliation Commission hearings were taking place. Since there was the potential that these hearings would provoke public expressions of anger, disorder was always a possibility and POP were called upon to guard and secure venues where the hearings were taking place. I sat and chatted to some of the members who were in the courtroom waiting for hearings to resume after a break:

> 23/05/2000
> *Monique*: How long have you guys been here for today?
> *Sergeant Ndlovu*: About three hours. Most of the morning.
> *Monique*: What exactly is your function here?
> *Sergeant Ndlovu*: We have to go into the courtroom and see that there is no disruption and that things do not get out of hand. You see, they are dealing with very sensitive things here. Imagine, some people are having to meet the person who injured or even killed one of their family members. It can raise a lot of pain and anger and sometimes people can't contain this pain and anger and they want to shout at the perpetrator or harm him physically. We have to prevent this from happening.
> *Monique*: I imagine that it's a bit boring sitting around here for so long just waiting.
> *Sergeant Ndlovu*: Well, that is part of our job and we have to see that it is done. It is our primary function. You see, the station police are not able to do this job. We are specially trained to manage crowds and they are not.
> *Sergeant Ngubane*: That is true, but I would rather be working on the outside doing something a bit more interesting. This is really frustrating work, sitting around the whole day.

Monique: What would you prefer to be doing?
Sergeant Ngubane: I would prefer to be outside doing proper crowd management stuff. At least there we are active, not just sitting around doing nothing.
Monique: Yes, but sometimes even outside you can sit and do nothing for ages.
Sergeant Ngubane: That is true. But, at least we are monitoring the situation. We are preparing for all eventualities.
Monique: But in most situations, nothing really happens.
Sergeant Ngubane: Well then it is a good day for us. We have not had to resort to any forceful means. That is what we are taught in crowd management training.

The work may be very boring at times, but they see it as their duty to be tolerant and patient when protecting the public. Sergeant Ngubane specifically makes the point that when an event takes place peacefully, this is an indication of good crowd management. New policy and training had clearly influenced cultural knowledge for these two police officers.

The new tolerance is accompanied by notably greater restraint in the use of force. The majority of respondents agreed that officers were now more hesitant to use force than they had been in the past. It is this restraint that was in large part responsible for the low incidence of injury and violence in crowd management situations since 1996, as Table 7.1 shows. Yet while it may well be that unit members were beginning to understand that use of force, in reactive rather than proactive policing, could actually escalate conflict, the more immediate reason for their restraint is likely to have been explicit orders to avoid force and not react to crowd provocation. This would be particularly the case in a paramilitary unit such as POP where there is little space for individual discretion and a strong possibility of disciplinary repercussions for orders not heeded.

Whatever the explanation, Durban POP successfully policed three big international events between 1998 and 2001. Each was attended by many thousands of delegates from all over the world. The large numbers participating and the protests and demonstrations that surrounded these events could have presented a very sizeable public order predicament. In August 1998, the Non-Aligned Movement Summit was held in Durban. Four thousand delegates attended. In July 2000, there was the

Table 7.1: Crowd management incidents 1 January 1992 to 15 June 2000 (Durban).

	Crowd management peaceful	Crowd management unrest	Instances when rubber bullets were used	Instances when tear gas was used	Instances when live ammunition was used	Civilians injured as a result of POP action	Civilian deaths as a result of POP action
Jan–Dec 1993	68 (58%)	54 (44%)	1	22	4	20	4
Jan–Dec 1994	155 (61%)	98 (39%)	15	43	4	5	2
Jan–Dec 1995	169 (75%)	57 (25%)	13	7	1	3	0
Jan–Dec 1996	237 (85%)	42 (15%)	8	17	1	3	0
Jan–Dec 1997	323 (84%)	60 (16%)	4	5	1*	1	0
Jan–Dec 1998	545 (91%)	53 (9%)	4	4	3**	2	0
Jan–Dec 1999	478 (92%)	37 (8%)	4	4	0	5	0
Jan – 15 June 2000	131 (88%)	17 (12%)	1	1	1 (UDW campus)	0	1 (UDW student)

Table drawn from IRIS statistics provided by Operational Centre, POP Durban.
* Live ammunition was fired when police were fired at during a funeral in Chesterville.
**In one of the incidents where live ammunition was used, an armed crowd in Amawoti, KwaMashu, attacked police. In the other two incidents, police fired at warring taxi drivers who had fired as each other and at the police.

13th International Aids World Conference. Twelve thousand delegates participated and there were numerous Aids-related fringe demonstrations and protests close to the conference venue. In August 2001, more than 14 000 delegates attended the World Conference Against Racism (WCAR) at the same venue. In the eight days of the conference, there were dozens of demonstrations, protests and pickets in the surrounding area. Many of these crowd events were potentially volatile and there were large contingents of people displaying open antagonism toward other groups participating in the conference. Prior to the conference there were concerns that public disorder might occur as happened during similar forums in Seattle in 2000 and in Genoa in 2001.

Each of these major events was policed without incident by the security team co-ordinated and led by the Durban POP. At a march by Aids activists during the World Aids Conference, I noticed Durban POP members chatting to participants and reassuring them that they would be protected. The policing of the WCAR was widely praised, the *Sunday Times* reporting that 'intensive planning, strategic deployment of manpower and consultations with groups organising protests had ensured that the police were ready to deal with the high numbers of protesters' (*Sunday Times*, 2 September 2001). Officers stood by unruffled as a large youth gathering sang anti-apartheid songs, shouted taunts at them and rebuffed calls to disperse. Earlier in the week, the police made sure that 30 000 anti-privatisation protesters from the Cosatu and the SACP could demonstrate without incident (*Sunday Times*, 2 September 2001). The policing of the WCAR conference was considered so outstanding that United Nations chiefs of staff proposed that the operation mounted by Durban POP 'be used as a model for international planning and security' (*Sunday Tribune*, 9 September 2001).[9]

The three events were major public proceedings and the presence of the press and the 'eyes' of the international community may in part account for this exemplary demeanour. Della Porta comments in this regard that 'media attention to social protest seems to have the effect of generating a shift toward more tolerant policing . . . The mere presence of journalists, in fact, appears to have a de-escalating effect on the police . . .' (1998: 18). The international spotlight would appear to have a similar effect. The public nature of the venue, the space, in which these events took place, is another important factor. While police may sometimes be more cautious to act in private spaces (such as in cases of domestic violence), when they do act in these spaces their actions are far less subject to regulation and scrutiny than in public spaces (Herbert, 1997).

The publicity will certainly have made a difference but there can be little doubt either that Durban POP members at both supervisory and rank-and-file levels must have taken to heart much of the new guidelines to have been capable of lifting their public order policing to this conspicuous height of success. We could indeed say, following Chan (1996), that changes in organisational field – such as, in this case, policy and training – had a profound impact on two of the levels of cultural knowledge that Chan outlines: directory knowledge and recipe knowledge.

Most POP members were, by 2000, evidently well aware of the new philosophical and strategic principles and capable of putting them into practice with an effectiveness borne out by a dramatic decrease in incidents of violence during crowd management situations. Prior to 1995, a majority of the protests and gatherings that were policed resulted in injury and even death of participants and sometimes the death and injury of police. Significantly, as the Provincial Commander of Public Order Policing in KwaZulu-Natal pointed out to me, there were minimal injuries in crowd management situations in the years 1996–2001.

Table 7.1 analyses the types of crowd management events policed by the Durban unit from January 1993 to June 2000. It records that four years passed without fatalities until the incident, which we shall consider later, at the University of Durban-Westville (UDW) in 2000, where the unit was responsible for the death of a crowd participant. Over a period of seven years, an increasing proportion of events were defined as 'crowd management peaceful', the term used by the POP incident report information system (IRIS) for crowd management events where there are no reports of damage to property, injury or death.

Incidents marred by violence did still occur. For the most part, however, the violence emanated not from the police intervention but from the nature of the crowd itself. For example, if police arrive at M.L. Sultan Technikon and students are breaking classroom windows, the incident will be recorded as 'crowd management unrest', the IRIS category for incidents marred by violence of any sort. Table 7.1 shows that by 1999 only 8 per cent of crowd management events were being recorded as 'crowd management unrest', significantly fewer than in 1993, the year preceding the elections, when almost half the crowd management events would have been so categorised.[10]

The figures also indicate growing reluctance to use force, lethal or non-lethal. From the individual incident recordings of the three instances where live ammunition was used in 1998, it appears that in each case it was used defensively: according to police who were present at these events, members of the unit were fired at by warring taxi owners in two instances and by an armed crowd in Amawoti, KwaMashu, in the other. The UDW incident in 2000 remains an isolated one, to which we shall return.

Other than police conduct, there are two possible explanations for the decrease in 'crowd management unrest' incidents. On the one hand, the new democratic government had made clear its willingness to listen to protestors' demands and grievances and more forceful collective action was consequently not deemed necessary by protestors. And on the other hand, participants in collective action were themselves aware of the Gatherings Act (1993) and willing to adhere to its provisions. But clearly, too, credit must be given to the Durban POP members for the decline in the use of force and the lower casualty figures. The lesson had evidently been learnt, after 1996, that there really are alternatives to the use of force in public order policing.

The decline in crowd management incidents defined as 'unrest' is very important. It indicates a real behaviour change in the unit's primary function of managing crowds. There hasn't been any significant research into community perceptions of the unit but there can nonetheless be little doubt that the fresh approach and the more peaceable outcomes had a positive impact on relationships between the unit and the population at large. I witnessed occasions where people from the community showed their appreciation of the unit's courtesy and even-handedness. I was particularly touched by one such gesture:

> 08/05/2000
> While waiting to go to Umlazi township with one of the sections, I sat chatting to Captain Dada in the Public Relation office. While we were talking, an elderly African woman came into the office and stated that she wanted to talk to Captain Dada. She had made her way to the POP base so that she could speak in person with him. She looked tired, but she had a mission to accomplish. The woman explained that she had been part of a march that Durban POP had just policed. She was, in fact, one of the organisers of the march made up of victims of human rights abuses. The march was intended to end at the Mayor's office where a memorandum was to be handed over calling for reparations from the Truth and Reconciliation Commission. She recalled that the officials in the Mayor's office had been extremely rude to her; they had kicked her out when she tried to hand over the memorandum. The only people, she said, who had treated her with respect and tried to help her were Durban POP members. They had tried to find someone who would accept the memorandum and when this did not happen, they said that they would assist her with writing a letter to the Truth and Reconciliation Commission and would fax it for her if she came to the unit. The woman hugged Captain Dada and held his hands. She then looked

at me and told me how wonderful these police had been. She made the point that this response from the police was completely unexpected. Her encounters with the police in the past had been extremely hostile. She had even been shot by the police during a protest march some years ago . . . I was very touched by the humane treatment the unit had shown toward this woman who could barely speak English and who was illiterate.

Another way of measuring the new acceptability of the unit to local communities is to count the occasions on which POP personnel came under attack, along with the number of officers who were killed or injured. Figure 7.4 shows a sharp decline in the number of attacks on Durban POP members and a correspondingly downward trend in the number of officers killed and injured between 1993 and 2000.

There are deviations from the trend (in 1998 for example) that call for knowledge of the individual incidents but in general the statistics do suggest a lessening of hostility toward the unit. Certainly credit must go to the unit itself for the transformed relations but it may well be that the trend also reflects a more general change in community attitudes toward the SAPS since the transition to democracy.

It is clear enough, then, that important changes had indeed taken place in Durban POP: at the level of structure; at the level of cultural knowledge; and at the level of operational conduct – the behavioural level. But to conclude that transformation was complete would, unfortunately, be premature.

Old habits dying hard

In May 2000, one company of the Durban POP unit was deployed to the campus of the University of Durban-Westville (UDW) to monitor student demonstrations which had been sparked by the university's decision to deregister 540 students who had failed to pay their registration fees. During that intervention, on 16 May, a second year BA student, Michael Makhabane, was shot dead (*Mercury,* 19 May 2000). Internal investigations and two post-mortems concluded that live ammunition had been used by the police (*Independent on Saturday*, 20 May 2000), the fatal bullet having being fired by a member of the Reaction unit, a specialised tactical support group within Durban POP.[11]

Was this simply a case of undisciplined individual action? Possibly, but a number of other reasons could be identified – and were, in subsequent internal enquiries

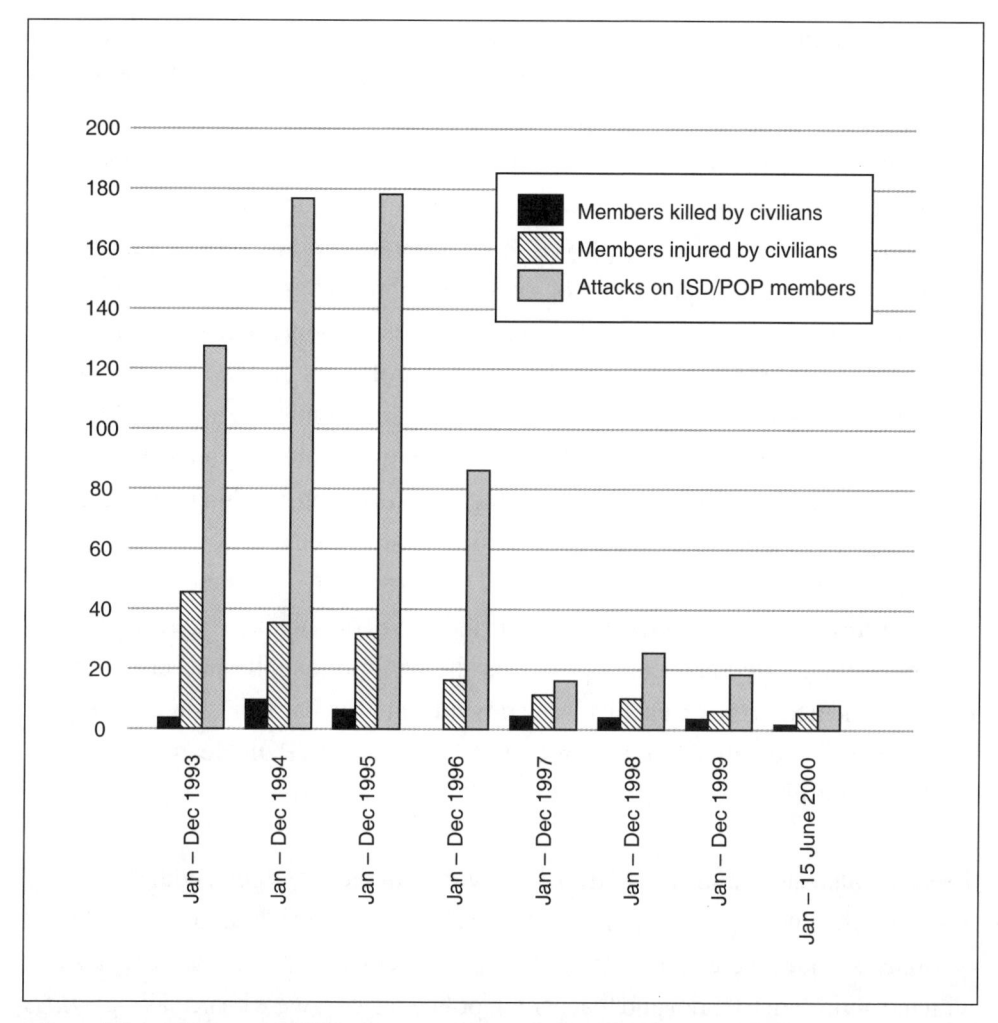

Figure 7.4: Attacks on POP Durban members – January 1993 – June 2000.

conducted at the highest level by POP Headquarters in Pretoria. A POP Headquarters debriefing document issued in June 2000 found that the proper procedures had been ignored – there was no written plan, no threat analysis was done, no joint operation centre was established – and it drew the explicit conclusion that the new philosophy had yet to fully take root in the Durban unit:

> It is of great concern that the POP unit did not implement the tactics and techniques that are taught during training. Durban POP unit is fortunate to

have five of the best trainers in the field of crowd management in South Africa in their personnel. All the officers on the scene of 16 May were apparently trained at the Platoon Commanders' course. It is unthinkable that members did not even apply the most basic principles of good command structure, techniques or use of equipment despite the fact that they were all trained . . . no members deployed in the operation up to very late in the operation were equipped with riot shields or helmets for personal protection against stone attacks. This could have been a reason why members resorted in self-defence to the use of firearms against protesters . . . The Regulation of Gatherings Act, the policy document for crowd management and the training curriculum for operational commanders are emphasising the importance of good information gathering and processing, reaching consensus through negotiation, consultation, in-depth assessment, detailed joint planning, and gradual police response in respect of using protective equipment in order to minimise the use of weapons. Shortcomings on the day regarding the above mentioned aspects implies that the new philosophy had not been implemented to the extent that it can be said that POP Durban is functioning in accordance with the policy of crowd management (POP Headquarters, June 2000).[12]

There are also other indications from this event that old ways persisted. According to one Durban newspaper report, 'UDW staff members said that police had fired on students as they were running away. Several academics said students were pleading with the police not to shoot and that certain police officers were heard saying: "*dit is lekker*" [this is nice/fun], while chasing the students' (*Mercury*, 19 May 2000).

I was not especially surprised to read this in the newspaper. I had been present with the unit on the campus for six days prior to the fatal shooting and had heard a number of individual unit members making comments that indicated they were 'ready for action'. On the fourth day of deployment on the campus, one unit member said to me '*Miskien sal ons aksie hê vandag. Ek hoop so*' [Perhaps we will have action today. I hope so]. On the second day, I overheard members saying that they should just shoot rubber bullets or tear gas at the students during a pushback action on the campus. This, they thought, would 'sort the students out'. Either it would put a stop to the protest or a confrontation would develop and the police would 'have something to do with themselves'.

Statements like this, and the readiness of members to take aggressively offensive action, indicated that there were indeed POP members whose attitudes and assumptions had changed little in the five years since the start of the transformation process. There had been a very long-standing attitude of mind in the South African police that saw university students as trouble-makers and rebels without cause, and by 2000, this old antagonism had, tragically, yet to dissipate. The distorted precedent was given a particularly sharp twist at UDW, a politically charged campus whose student base had historically been disadvantaged black students.

While the UDW incident is one of very few examples of 'retrogressive' police behaviour in the new climate of public order policing, I observed many instances of similar behaviour when members of the unit were out on crime prevention operations – their secondary function. Crime prevention work generally takes place in the townships, which are far more hidden from the public eye than protests and demonstrations (which by their very nature seek to gain public attention). It is in these less exposed spaces that the behaviour of members of the unit was more consistently problematic.

The night of the shooting on UDW campus, I joined another platoon on a night patrol (6 pm to 6 am) in KwaMashu township (already described in Chapter 5). I was in a vehicle with three white and two black policemen and as the night wore on, I grew more and more aghast at their indifference to any rights of the township residents. The following vignette [more extracts from the field notes included in Chapter 5] captures the atmosphere of abuse:

> 16/05/2000
> We drove through a dark alleyway and found a group of young men hanging around on the pavement. The vehicle drew to a sudden halt and four policemen jumped out of the vehicle and pointed their guns at the youngsters. They did a search, shouted at them, and then got back into the vehicle. One of the inspectors got back into the vehicle and said 'Those fuckers have been smoking dagga [marijuana]!'
>
> I decided to find out what exactly was going on in the minds of these policemen.
>
> *Monique*: What made you stop? Surely you are not concerned with dagga?

Inspector Botha: Yes, it is a petty thing. But they told us who the dealer is and where to find him. We won't go there now. We will wait a week and then when he is feeling safe, we will bust the fucker. It is an easy arrest. We keep him in reserve for when our arrest records are low. We are not stupid. We know how to do things in here.

We drove on . . . Both police in the front of the vehicle had their pistols pointed outside open windows ready to fire. Sergeant Marais tried to explain. He said: 'These people [in the township] in this area are not normal. They have no respect for human life. You will see. Life means nothing to them. This is another world' . . .

[Report on the radio of a kangaroo court in an informal settlement, which we head for.]

There were a couple of hundred of community people standing round an elderly man who they had beaten very badly and hit with wooden batons and whips until he was bleeding on his legs, torso, and head. The crowd was furious and clearly wanted to kill this man. They informed the cops that he had been raping young girls in the area for months. While they had reported this to the local police station, no action had been taken. He had raped a three-year-old child that day and the community were furious. The police went to the man and shouted in Zulu 'You fucking Satan. You piece of rubbish!' They then spat on him. The people gathered around laughed. The mother of the child concerned was holding her child close to her and looked very frightened. They searched the man and found numerous pictures of young girls in his possession. They kicked him and shouted, 'you sick fucker'. The man did not respond. He was humiliated and speechless. He had no dignity – his pants had been pulled down and his private parts were present for all to see. The police decided that they would arrest him and take him to the police station. None of the police officers wanted to put him in their vehicle. They decided that they would get him to walk to the nearest tarred road where they would call the station police to come and pick him up and put him in the back of a police van. They told the man to get up. When he didn't move, they hit him over the head with a torch and swore at him. He was escorted down the road by the members of the community and the police ... The sergeant in our vehicle shouted 'gooi die ding in die van!' [throw the thing in the van!].

[We go to the house where there might be Mandrax.]

There was also a small room on the property that they entered – of course, no warrants used. The house was completely bare. On the floor in one room there was one cup, a plate and some cutlery. A man was sleeping in another room on the floor with one blanket. He had not a single other possession. The police woke him and shouted, 'Where the fuck are your drugs, you bastard?' The man said that he did not have any. They slapped him and told him the guys outside said that he had sold drugs to them, and they would come and fuck him up. He cowered into the corner of the room, clearly very frightened. At the same time some of the other members were creating havoc in the small room on the property. They pulled the man and his girlfriend out of the bed and began to shout at them. Sergeant Marais shouted, 'Give us your Mandrax and we will leave you alone. If you don't, we will fuck you up so badly until you speak and we will turn this room upside down!' ... The sergeant walked back into the house and hit the man. He asked him again where the pills were. The man said he really did not know. The sergeant fetched a big rubber rubbish bin and put it on top of the man's head, upside down. He then moved the bin up and down hitting the man's head numerous times. The man cried out in pain. He then started to kick the bin on the top and on the sides, sending the man flying from one side of the room to the next. The man was wailing by this time and begged the policeman to stop. He did not. He carried on for a few minutes and then walked out, having achieved nothing ...

[We drive to the house where the informer has told us there are guns.]

One policeman screamed, 'Open the door, it is the police!' No answer. No lights were on. They continued shouting and banging the door. Eventually a middle-aged man in his underwear opened the door. They swore at him and asked where his gun was. He said he didn't have one. They began to search his house. They found nothing except a holster. They asked again. No response. They then hit him hard on the face a few times. He yelped. They continued. Eventually they got him on the floor and started to kick the side of his body and his head. Still they could not get an answer out of him. He repeated that he had no gun. One of the police then stood on his leg and jumped on it numerous times. The man cried out for him to stop and another policeman hit him on his face and kicked his head and told him to shut up. I was horrified. I didn't want to look but forced myself to. I didn't say a word though I wanted to run up to them and tell them to stop beating this man. Perhaps he really did not have a gun. Perhaps the informer had misinformed them. I said nothing. This continued for about ten minutes. I was petrified that other people nearby would hear the commotion and start shooting at us. Nothing happened. The silence of the night penetrated everything. The only noise was the cries of the man receiving more and more slaps and beatings. Eventually they kicked him one last time and told him they would be back . . . we came to another house. Again, police surrounded the house and shouted for the people inside to open the door. The light went on but the woman inside refused to open the door. 'Open the door you fucking stupid bitch,' yelled one of the Sergeants. No response. They banged the door and threatened to break it down. Eventually, I heard the door open and they went inside. I could see nothing as I crouched on the path outside the house. A few more shouts and banging around inside and the police came out once again: 'The bitch says she doesn't know anything and her husband is not there. She says he is out at work.' I could see they were angry at not finding any weapons. This was not turning out to be a good night for them. We crept back along the path and back into the vehicles. We found out that one of the police from the other vehicle had been shot in his hand and had been taken to a nearby hospital. The police in my vehicle were amused.

Inspector Olivier: Now he can join the team. We have all been shot now.
Sergeant Ndinda: Yes, but he was only shot in his hand and that doesn't count. It is minor. He just won't be able to pick his nose now.

They all burst out laughing . . .

As the night wore on, never was there a hint of concern for due process or the rights of the township residents, let alone anything resembling the principles of community policing. If you were fighting crime you could do what you liked – and this way you would also get good marks for what really counted as performance indicators: arrests and weapon recovery. Here in the townships, my companions assured me, and against such a level of crime, it was simply war – this was a 'chaotic' place to work where you just had to assume people would behave 'atrociously', and where force was the only language anyone understood. You hit hard and everybody respects you, the public and your fellow policemen. Nor did they seem much concerned that their activities would be exposed or that they would be taken to task for them; they were quite sure no one (myself including) would report them. At one point I asked if they were worried that one of the people that they assaulted would lay a complaint: not at all, they said, the harder you '*klap*' (hit) someone, the less likely they are to report you because they'll be scared they'll get hurt even worse next time.

I witnessed the same sort of conduct when I joined another platoon stationed at a Durban hostel, Glebelands, which had been the site of fierce inter-group clashes. Between November 1997 and September 1998, there were 50 murders in the hostel itself (KwaZulu Natal Briefing, September 1998).[13] Durban POP members were deployed at the hostel to 'stabilise' the area and forestall further violence. Hostel rooms were regularly raided for weapon searches and I accompanied seven members of the unit on one early morning weapon raid. I understood well enough that the volatile environment in which these officers were operating demanded extreme vigilance and a show of authority, but I was stunned by their mistreatment of hostel residents:

> 09/071998
> ... The passages were quiet. It seemed like hostel residents were still asleep. I noticed that the floors were dirty and that there was a smell of urine. Empty bottles had been left outside the doors of some of the rooms ... Without knocking, one of the sergeants kicked a door open and the other six members of the unit pushed their way into the tiny room with their rifles pointed in front of them. There was a small table near the door with dishes and cups on it which one of the members knocked over, breaking one of the cups. A man was lying on the floor. The sergeant who had kicked the door open pressed the nose of the rifle into the man's chest and shouted at him in Zulu. When he failed to respond, one of the other policemen present kicked his head and also shouted at him ... Eventually, after searching the room, the police left the room without any recovered weapons. They slammed the door behind them as they walked out into the passage.

The strong-arm tactics and the indifference to individual rights are all too familiar, and in the old dispensation would have been regarded as normal and commonplace. In 2000, the political and legislative environment may have changed dramatically but brutal and arbitrary interventions seemed to have lost little of their legitimacy in the eyes of these particular officers. And there were utterances by political leaders at the highest levels from which they could take encouragement. In 1999, the then Minister of Safety and Security, Steve Tshwete, repeatedly made statements that fed into some very troubling conceptions of what good policing should be. Tshwete made it clear that criminals could be no more than 'scum' in the eyes of the police, and that that was how the police were to handle them. His phrase on one occasion was that criminals should be dealt with 'in the same way that a bulldog deals with a bull' (cited in Laurence, 1999).

Pronouncements like this do little to encourage legitimate tactics in the war against crime, but they stem in part from the pressure on the government to respond decisively to the problem of crime. In the years following the 1994 elections it was (and still is) noticeable that politicians speak rather less of community-oriented, democratic policing and rather more about taking tough action.

> Tshwete ... emphasised the crime fighting role of the police, and ... encouraged a more strong-arm approach to criminals, with far less emphasis on the internal problems of police reform. This discourse has found favour with the South African public which was increasingly concerned about crime, and with a police service which had felt disempowered by the period of police transformation following the first election (Rauch, 2000: 7).

It is not unusual for high crime levels to trigger repressive policing, particularly in countries going through political transition. The police, hard pressed anyway with having to reinvent themselves, get branded as weak and ineffectual, provoking even more calls for tougher action. Needing legitimacy and public support (particularly as autocratic power structures dissolve) they do what people seem to be asking for. And so, just as they try to gear themselves for democracy, they slide back into the old ways – and all too easily when they have behind them a history of militarised and repressive policing (Neild, 2000). In the face of rising crime or the fear of it, public opinion and the media (both of them forces one might expect to press for more democratic policing), may end up provoking the opposite.

My 1999 survey indicated that a large percentage of Durban POP members held onto old ways of thinking about their work, about the environment in which they operated, and about crowds in particular.

How police do perceive crowds and their behaviour most certainly has a bearing on the way they will set about policing them. And the perception is likely to have a decidedly conservative shade: Brearley and King (1996) argue that police philosophy regarding public order is often based on the theories of Le Bon and Smelser that represent crowd behaviour as inherently irrational, emotional and unreasonable. In this view, the individual in the crowd is deindividuated: protesters descend along several different rungs in the ladder of civilisation, with an intrinsic 'link between collective behaviour and irrationality' (Keith, 1993: 79). Critcher and Waddington (1996) argue that police adhere to a Durkheimian view of crowds and disorder: in this picture, dissatisfied crowds speak of an erosion of the social fabric and a breakdown of social control. Rollo similarly contends that policemen trained in riot control in particular are liable to 'view events such as demonstrations and pickets as provocative, likely to cause disorder and [that] therefore [people who participate in these events] are to be restricted and prevented from doing so' (1980: 198). For police who regard crowds as irrational and destructive, strong-arm dispersal tactics are quite legitimate: bad crowd behaviour – throwing projectiles or hurling insults – may be tolerated for a while (since people who participate in crowd events are in any case childish and stupid) but the stage will come when they need to be 'neutralised' and 'disciplined' (Della Porta, 1998).

The revised Durban POP training programme emphasised very strongly that it is the right of all citizens to demonstrate and protest and that crowds are generally rational and peaceful. Yet the 1999 questionnaire uncovered very conservative perceptions of crowd behaviour and crowd participants (Figure 7.5; Figure 7.6; Figure 7.7). In the majority view, crowd violence, for example, sprang from the inherent dynamics of the crowd itself and had nothing to do with the possible conduct of the police. There was much lingering evidence of the theoretical legacy from the pre-1995 'riot' control training, such as the Le Bon/Smelser kind of thinking that circulated in police training colleges textbooks like Van Heerden's *Introduction to Police Science*:

> The barbarism and irrationality of the group is so strong an influence on the individual that, no matter how civilised and rational he may normally be, he descends to the level of an animal and does things he would never do in normal circumstances (1982: 232).

So there was some way to go still in trying to banish the presumption that the job of the police is to curb collective action, not help it along. Nor is the propensity for tough measures too surprising set against survey respondents' generally bleak view of the society they lived in (Figure 7.8).

The police in South Africa are not, of course, alone in holding this view of the world. Reiner (1992a) argues that one of the core components of police culture is a sense of mission. Police view the world with a high degree of suspicion and pessimism and believe that their role is protecting good from evil.

All this tells us that while important aspects of *field* may change in police organisations, and there may even be significant changes observed in *habitus*, the *axiomatic cultural knowledge*, as defined by Chan, can remain unaltered. The basic rationale for policing is the hardest thing to change, yet also the most crucial for the transformation of police culture.

New Methods, New Motives? 171

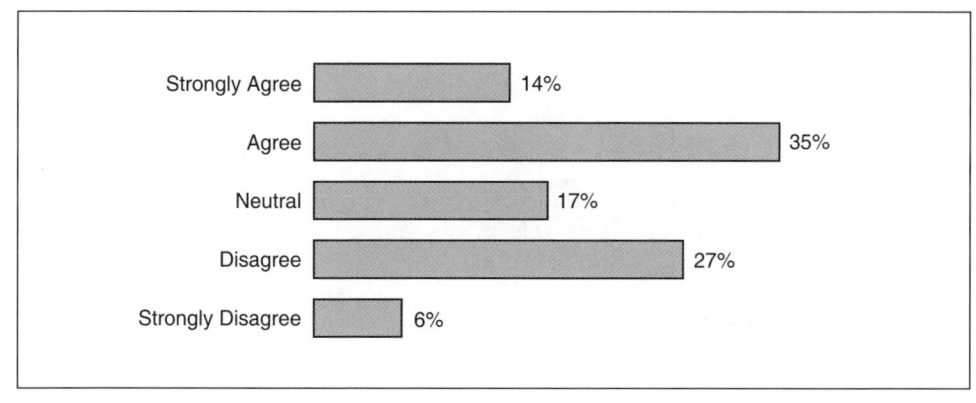

Response	Percentage
Strongly Agree	14%
Agree	35%
Neutral	17%
Disagree	27%
Strongly Disagree	6%

Figure 7.5: 'People who take part in public protests are generally trouble-makers.'

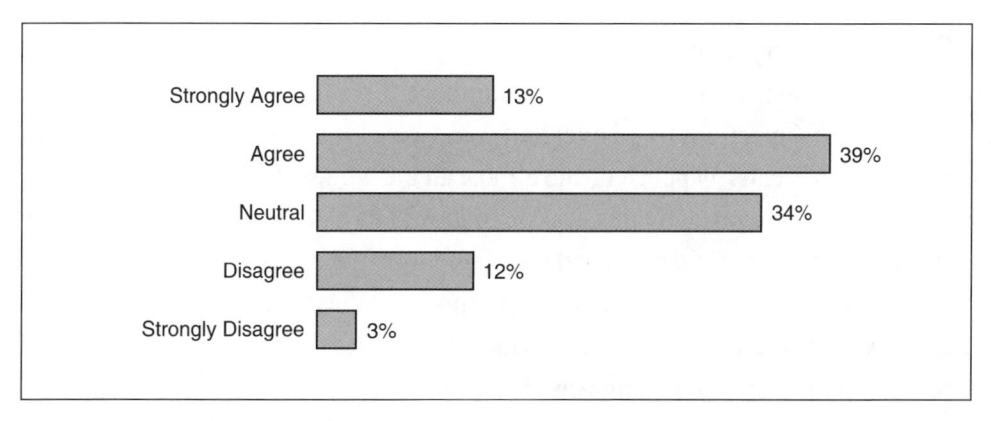

Response	Percentage
Strongly Agree	13%
Agree	39%
Neutral	34%
Disagree	12%
Strongly Disagree	3%

Figure 7.6: 'Crowds tend to be irrational.'

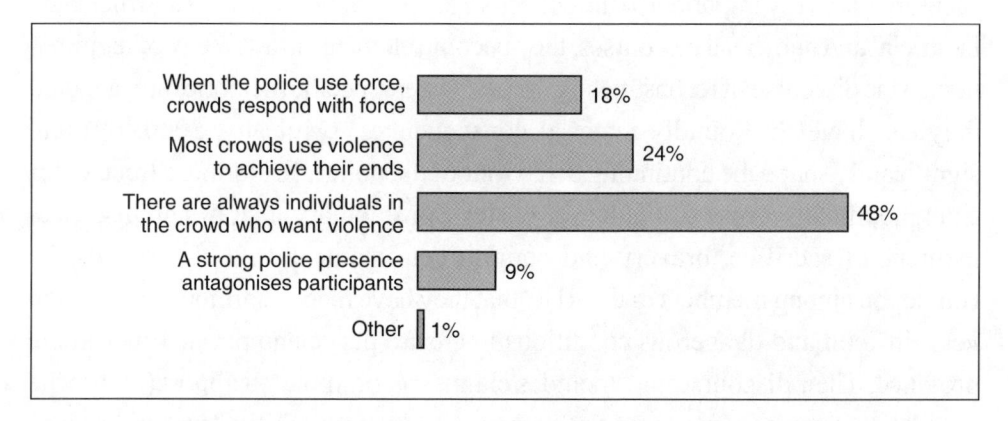

Response	Percentage
When the police use force, crowds respond with force	18%
Most crowds use violence to achieve their ends	24%
There are always individuals in the crowd who want violence	48%
A strong police presence antagonises participants	9%
Other	1%

Figure 7.7: 'Why do you think public events like protests and demonstrations become violent?'

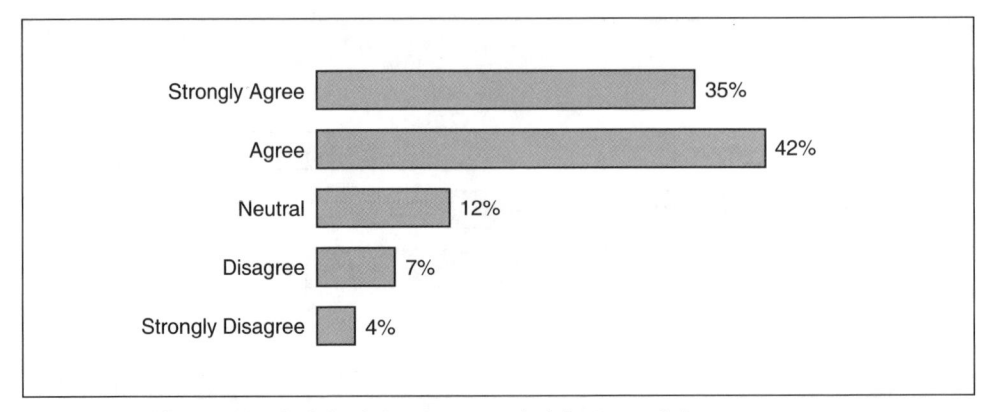

Strongly Agree	35%
Agree	42%
Neutral	12%
Disagree	7%
Strongly Disagree	4%

Figure 7.8: 'Our society is full of dangerous and violent people.'

The most worrying finding of the survey, however, was the respondents' evident nostalgia for past. In response to the statement 'I preferred working in the unit before the 1994 elections) well over half said 'yes': for Indian respondents just 48 per cent, for Africans 59 per cent, and almost all the whites at 94 per cent. There are probably many reasons why this was so. In the old days, officers had considerably greater powers at their disposal and they liked that; the old command system was better; conditions of service were deteriorating – all these were suggested to me in interviews with members of the unit. Whatever their reasons, there was a good deal of unease about the way the unit was changing.

'The old ways sometimes leak out of us'
Memories are very important to the collective identity of police services. Articulated in official and unofficial discourses, they become elements in a strategy of legitimation. In the discourse of reconstructing the past, where specific memories are favoured they can have 'profoundly material consequences' (Mulcahy, 2000: 69) and significantly shape the continuing behaviour of the police. In Northern Ireland, for example, the discourse of the Royal Ulster Constabulary includes an historical memory of sacrifice, bravery and commitment. Mulcahy (2000) records the conviction among members of the RUC that they have made enormous sacrifices in very difficult and dangerous conditions to ensure peace and public order in the province. Their discourse also includes claims of community support (across the population, despite evidence to the contrary) and accountability (via police complaints mechanisms and structures). This memory has in recent years been used to

reject large-scale and far-reaching reform that is crucial to the peace process in that country.

Nostalgia for the past and the importance of remembering it was plain to see in the way Durban POP members spoke about themselves both in formal interviews and more informally while working in the field. Some of the stories were relayed to me the day after the shooting incident at UDW. I had joined one of the platoons (who had not been present on the campus the day before) when they were deployed to the student residences. Students had been asked by the university administration to vacate the residences until the university (which had been closed following the death of the student) was reopened. It was clear to me that the officers I was accompanying still hankered for the days when they could clamp down on student activities however they chose and with no questions asked:

> 17/05/2000
> ... Members were informed by radio that students had broken into the residence the previous night and were being evicted again by private security companies. The students had thrown a petrol bomb at one of the private security officers and they had requested that POP be present. We drove down to the residence in our Nyala [armoured vehicle]. When we arrived at the residence, students clapped and shouted. They were clearly infuriated with the police after the events of the previous day. Members were annoyed and aggravated. One of them commented, 'We should just shoot these students like we used to in the old days' ... We sat and waited. Members knew that they should not act unless this was really necessary. After a while, one of the Inspectors started to talk to me about the 'good old days'.
>
> *Inspector Moonsamy*: Monique, can you see how we are not policemen anymore? We don't even act. We sit around doing nothing. In the past we would have got out of the vehicle and gassed the students by now.
> *Sergeant Pillay*: We have just become glorified security guards now. It is pathetic.
> *Monique*: What would you like to be doing?
> *Sergeant Pillay*: Well, we shouldn't be saying this but we have been

trained over the years to act, not just to sit around. We are used to the old way of being. This is very frustrating for us.

Inspector Moonsamy: Our commanders are useless now. They don't have any backbone. In the past our commanders would have given us clear instructions. We would come to an area, do our job and leave. We had a proper job then. Now, you sit around, do nothing and students swear at you; they think we are a big joke. I miss those times when we could really have action and be productive.

Monique: What is it that you miss?

Inspector Moonsamy: Our best days were during the times of the red and green bands – the war between Inkatha and the ANC. We would go into areas that were on fire that time. We would beat the living daylights out of these youngsters. They were just like barbarians. For example, you would be in the townships and you would see a sea of Inkatha members heavily armed coming up the hill. We would move in and finish them off. Things were hectic then, even in the early nineties. We have seen some terrible things. Children with limbs cut off . . . Shacks had been set alight. We would rush in there and take one child under each arm and get them out of the area. We really worked in those days and we had excellent commanders.

Monique: It seems like you really preferred to work in the unit in the old days. Is that correct?

Sergeant Pillay: That is true. We felt productive in those days. Maybe what we were doing was not right, but we were doing something. We really prevented complete chaos in the township. Okay, there were problems in those days. We Indian members were discriminated against. White members were always superior. If we went out with a vehicle which had white members in it, we would guard the vehicle while they carried out the operation. This was not nice. But, in general I preferred working in the unit in those days.

Inspector Moonsamy: I remember one time, there was a problem in the township. There was a fight between ANC and IFP groupings. We came in and shot so much tear gas that nobody could see or even breathe. We fought a small war in that place.

Monique: It sounds like the past was very turbulent. I want to ask

you a question. I did a survey recently and found that more than half the members of this unit preferred working in the unit prior to the transformation process. What do you guys think of this result?
Inspector Moonsamy: I think most of us feel this way. We are wasting our time in the unit now. We are not able to use our skills and experience. Most of the time we sit around doing nothing . . .
Monique: There is something else I have been thinking about recently. It seems to me that while people have changed their behaviour in many ways, the way they think is still the same. Does this make sense to you?

The members all laughed and nodded.

Sergeant Pillay: To tell the truth, I am not sure that members think differently. We obey instructions in this place. That is the real story. We understand the changes but we don't feel like policemen anymore.

The stories told here by Sergeant Pillay and Inspector Moonsamy reflect a deeply embedded modality of knowledge in relation to the roles of the police, to what constituted appropriate and effective responses, and to the underlying character of particular communities that they served. In this light, the past behaviour of the unit seemed to them perfectly legitimate given the social dynamics in the townships and the political environment, local and national. In the minds of these two officers, the townships would, back then, simply have been zones of chaos and barbarism were it not for the interventions of the unit: this, whatever its connection with historical reality, was the memory that had shaped their identities as policemen and which it was very unlikely they would any time soon purge from their minds. In their view, being a 'productive' policeman meant being active and decisive (and often forceful) in responding to actual or perceived public disorder. That was how they had been trained in the past, and the impact of that training was very long-lasting, equipping them with 'skills' and 'expertise' that they were very unwilling to relinquish. They were quite emphatic that they had preferred working in the unit before 1994, despite their own experiences, as Indian officers, of racial discrimination within the unit.

Memories are partial and discriminatory accounts of the past, and they are also highly selective as the next conversation reveals:

09/08/98

Monique: When you joined the unit in the 1980s it had a very bad name. Did this bother you in any way?

Sergeant Mamela: For me it was a new experience. Whatever was said about the unit, I found was not entirely true. Unless you go into a unit you cannot know for yourself. I think the unit was doing what it had to do. We did our work thoroughly. For example, if there was a situation where there was a big crowd, you control the crowd to the best of your ability. You have then done your work. But you find that you come out and the media had a lot to say and communities always had a lot to say.

Monique: Why do you think the media and communities had these bad things to say?

Sergeant Mamela: You see, what they were trying to achieve they couldn't achieve because of us. We would stop them from doing the things they wanted to do. We were a prevention team.[14]

Sergeant Mamela remembered the 'good work' that the unit did. The unit was unpopular, as he saw it, not because what they did was inherently wrong but because what they did obstructed the goals of others. Like Sergeant Pillay and Inspector Moonsamy, he seems to imply that in the past the police worked hard with a (reassuringly?) simple objective: disperse and control the crowd.

Shearing (1995) argues that training and policy alone will never be enough to engineer real change in police organisations because they lack the capacity to transform the legendary stories. One way these stories can be changed is to expose police to new stories and therefore new tropes and new metaphors, but this will not be easy so long as the membership of the organisation remains essentially unchanged. New recruits who came into the Durban POP unit with fresh perceptions from training, designed to equip them as community policing officers, found it almost impossible to impress their new stories and perspectives on the older and more experienced members of the unit. A young constable who joined the police in 1999 shared his frustration with me:

I was very excited to join the police. I really wanted to help people and to be part of the new police service. At the police college we were taught about community policing. That was in fact what we focused on. Of course we learned other things like how to shoot and we did do physical training, but community policing was what we were mostly taught. After doing my field training, I decided to join POP, mostly because the unit was near to my home. I was shocked at the way the unit behaves. There is no respect for communities. These guys are not interested in community policing. I thought in the beginning that I could talk to them about community policing and the way I was trained. But I have come to realise that they are the ones that are experienced. They know what is going on and how to do things. I don't really agree with a lot of what they do but they have been through a lot and I have no experience compared to them . . . I still think that community policing is right. Once I have enough experience I will probably leave this unit and go to the stations. I don't think this unit will ever follow community policing.[15]

If the identities of officers in the unit were indeed still shaped by memories of the past and if the majority of unit members still preferred that past, why did their behaviour nonetheless change in significant ways? This is a difficult question to answer. There were, of course, those members (mostly African) who could see that apartheid politics were untenable and that apartheid policing was extremely problematic. They were aware of the abusive, unprofessional nature of the old policing style and felt uncomfortable with it, knowing how it provoked antagonism between police and public. But the majority of members, it would seem, went along with the changes simply because they felt they had no choice. Those were their orders and, in the military ethos of the SAP, orders were not to be challenged. As Sergeant Beatrice Ngobo told me:

No one actually told us how we were supposed to change. But you get to know this from the instructions given. The police force is the military. You must be able to take instructions and have discipline. If you can't do that, you are not a policeman. Members must obey commands that are given to them . . .[16]

A more senior member of the unit, Captain Padayachee, concurred:

> No matter how much you talk about change and transformation, you as a person have to take that information and act on it. The one thing about the police, though, is that you have to follow instructions and commands, so sometimes you have no choice . . . Whether members like it or not, in some ways they have no choice about changing. Eventually members will see that they have to change. Some members who were negative a few years ago are now a lot more positive . . . I would say about 30 to 40 per cent are willing to change.[17]

Sitting in the training office one morning, I listened to a conversation between Sergeant Gumede, probably the most experienced trainer in the unit, and an Inspector who had, reluctantly, presented himself for retraining. They were discussing whether or not change had taken place in the unit in the light of the fatal shooting incident at UDW:

> *Sergeant Gumede*: How would you say change has happened in the police?
> *Trainee Inspector*: It was forced down our throats. We had to follow instructions to behave in new ways. We had no choice. Otherwise we would have to leave the police, but where would we go? There is nowhere for us to go, except maybe private security.
> *Sergeant Gumede*: Do you think that we have really changed?
> *Trainee Inspector*: Probably not.
> *Sergeant Gumede*: You see, Monique, police have changed because of instructions. But, when I am alone, my feelings dictate my responses. POP is always in the public eye. Therefore, we have to act properly. When we are out of the public eye we go back to our old behaviour. When faced with change, there is no real mind change. So, old ways sometimes leak out of us.

The conclusion would seem to be that officers in the unit could so far detect very little fundamental change in values and beliefs in the minds of many of their colleagues – and if behaviour was indeed changing, well then that was because people were simply complying with instructions. So we could also conclude that the bureaucratic and hierarchical make-up of the unit did in fact make change possible, since members felt they had no option but to follow instructions. However, as Sergeant Gumede so eloquently warns, the problem with directed change, when policemen look on the past as the 'golden age' of their calling, is that the 'old ways leak out'.

Changes in attitudes, values and assumptions in Durban POP certainly seemed to lag behind more instrumental behavioural change. To borrow terms used by Ogbonna and Harris (1998), we can perhaps see this as an instance of existing values having been 'reinvented' or 'reinterpreted' (rather than fundamentally reoriented) in the minds of many members of the unit. Durban POP went on telling stories that, reinvented or not, still preserved the old memories and the tropes and the metaphors embedded in these stories continued to justify old habits and old attitudes.

We could also note that reversion to past behaviour seemed particularly likely in Durban POP when members used individual discretion, when supervision and leadership was weak or absent, when planning was poor, and when police actions were not directly open to public scrutiny.

Real change in police organisations requires changed attitudes on the part of both rank-and-file and management. This involves, among other things, a constant process of review – good front-line supervision in particular – so that there can be reinforcement when the changes go well and sanctions for regressive conduct. And it is no good if close supervision is simply imposed on rank-and-file: for police to wholeheartedly embrace new values there has to be an environment where all officers actively participate in the processes of change. Inevitably this means a fundamental shift from traditional top-down management towards more participatory practice (Reiner, 1992a; Bayley, 1994) so that members do not feel that change is 'forced' upon them. Participatory management and supervision were very slow to take root in Durban POP and in the next chapter we shall examine how this slowed transformation.

8

Shifting Gears or Slamming on the Brakes?
Management and Supervision

It is essential that discipline be uplifted before the point of no return is reached ... It is a fallacy that democracy reduces the need for discipline – policing in a democracy is so complex and demanding that higher disciplinary standards are an absolute necessity (Fivaz, 1997).

POLICE SERVICES PLACE high value on disciplinary practices and codes. Regardless of how internally democratic they may wish to be, some degree of discipline is always necessary in police organisations and it is therefore unlikely to disappear from police 'culture' (Shearing, 1992). Disciplinary codes and practices not only keep police in check, they also have the potential to spur on behavioural change, since police officers are expected to follow orders. However, behavioural change by decree is liable to be mechanical and unreflective and with police values and assumptions apparently so resistant to change it is likely that police will revert to old and familiar ways whenever the opportunity is presented. This is particularly so when supervision and leadership is weak, when planning is poor, and when the actions of the police are not directly open to public scrutiny.

SAPS National Commissioner Fivaz is right when he says that disciplinary standards are important in 'complex and demanding' times, but reliance on discipline alone is more likely to harm reform programmes than move them forward. They also require a thorough revamping of the way police work is organised; real commitment to a changed culture is unlikely without transformation of workplace practices and relations (Wilms, 1996).

Police leaders play a crucial role in police transformation because they have the capacity to reinforce and embed police culture through the issues they emphasise and in the way they measure and control performance. Schein underlines the importance of good management and supervision for any attempt to modify police culture. Managers need to be both directive and supportive to rank-and-file members:

> The key to producing change . . . is first to prevent exit and then to escalate the disconfirming forces while providing psychological safety. This is difficult to execute, but precisely what effective turnaround managers do. By using the right incentives, they make sure that the people who they want to retain in the organization find it difficult to leave. By consistently challenging old assumptions . . . they make it difficult for people to sustain the old assumptions. By consistently being supportive and rewarding any evidence of movement in the direction of new assumptions, they provide some psychological safety. If psychological safety is sufficient, members of the group can begin to examine and possibly give up some of their cognitive defences (Schein, quoted in Chan, 1999: 131).

Effective change in police organisations requires a managerial and supervisory style that especially promotes cultural revitalisation. I see three significant ways to achieve this:
- by employing participatory management styles: This promotes understanding of what is expected from police members and why, and it also encourages rank-and-file officers to 'buy into' change processes. Democratic and participatory management practice also provides police with a model for democratic practices in their interaction with the public.
- by providing clear direction and supervision: This, likewise, presents an object lesson for officers to learn what good operational practice is like and what operational conduct should be rewarded or reproved.
- by providing appropriate measures of performance: This sets up incentives for good work and clarifies understanding of how work is evaluated.

Direct, active supervision coupled with participatory management can accelerate transformation of police cultural assumptions but, as we shall see, neither were adequately developed in the Durban POP despite legislative and governmental pressure, and rank-and-file unit members were left feeling excluded from decision-making or ideas for change. Leadership deficiency also created uncertainty and confusion about appropriate ways of responding to the public. Ultimately, the contradictory combination of inflexible yet irresolute leadership led to serious alienation between top management and the lower ranks. Officers did not get the support they needed in the change process and their commitment to the unit was compromised. All this impeded the potential for real deep-level cultural shift and goes some way to explaining the incomplete nature of behavioural change in the unit.

Changing the style and culture of management
After 1994, there was a great deal of emphasis, particularly on the part of central government, on both professional service delivery and democratised labour relations in the public service. Legislation passed shortly after the political transition underlined the need for new public service management and human resource practices. In particular, the Labour Relations Act of 1995 established the principles of 'employment justice' – the protection of employees from unjust and unfair relationships with their employers.[1] The Act stresses that every person is entitled to fair labour practice. This includes the right to form and join trade unions and other representative organisations as well as the right to bargain collectively. Employee participation in decision-making in the workplace is also promoted in the Act. In short, the Labour Relations Act is aimed at more open, flexible and participative management structures. SAPS members are considered to be 'employees' or 'workers', and they are 'now accorded internationally recognised labour rights or freedom to work; to associate; to collective bargaining; to withhold labour; to protection; and to development' (Bouwer, 1997: 395).

The Labour Relations Act (informed also by Chapter 2 of the South African Constitution of 1996 and the Bill of Rights) created an entirely new labour dispensation for the public service. Previously, public service labour relations were enmeshed in a deeply paternalistic and rule-bound system. This began to change somewhat in the mid-1980s when the trade union movement started organising in the public service. Black public servants began to make their grievances heard and by the late 1980s had in fact become a very volatile labour sector with a number of significant new labour unions coming into being. In 1989, the Police and Prisons Civil Rights Union was formed, organising mainly black police officers and prison wardens, followed in 1993 by the South African Police Union (SAPU) which organised mostly white police members (Marks, 2000b; 2000c). Between 1989 and 1993, South Africa witnessed the biggest strike waves in the history of the public service. This unionism within the public service was a very clear signal of the need to transform public service labour relations. Attainment of such a goal, as enshrined in the Labour Relations Act, 'entailed overcoming racial and gender imbalances, a commitment to education and training to develop public servants' skills, eliminating discrimination in salaries and benefits, and changing the public service's authoritarian culture and outmoded work practices' (Adler, 2000: 13).

Aside from the Labour Relations Act, other measures pertaining specifically to the public service called for improved service delivery in tandem with improved labour practices. The White Paper on Human Resource Management in the Public Service (1997) requires human resource management in the public service to become a model of excellence in service delivery that takes account of the needs of both the organisation and the employees. This, the White Paper acknowledges, will mean a fundamental change in the human resource management culture:

> Turning into reality the vision of a diverse, competent and well managed workforce, capable of and committed to delivering high quality services to the people of South Africa, will require something close to a managerial revolution within the Public Service. Central to this revolution will be a shift from administering personnel to managing people (1997: 10).

The intention is that this will create a revitalised public service far less over-centralised, rule-bound and bureaucratic, with, in particular, a new approach to performance management in which managers must henceforth assess individual employees' performance annually against mutually agreed objectives. The White Paper insists that diversity must be valued, affirmative action practices be improved, and representivity be evident in the workforce. All employees should have written contracts that detail the terms and conditions and the period of their employment. Employees must know what is expected of them; managers must evaluate them according to those expectations. Poor performance should be identified and rectified, and good performance should be recognised and rewarded.

The accompanying White Paper on Transforming Public Service Delivery (1997) – known as the *Batho Pele* (People First) Paper – likewise stresses the need for performance management and measurement, stipulating that both individuals and groups in the public service be given appropriate recognition for performing well, particularly in regard to customer service. Service delivery improvement programmes are to be developed and should include proposed service standards and how they will be monitored, along with supervision and appraisal measures to ensure that staff put into practice the overriding *Batho Pele* principle. The main concern of the programme is to improve service delivery to the public. Again, this requires a fresh conception of management style: 'to implement a service delivery programme successfully, public service managers require new management tools' (1997: 11). In particular, managers are expected to delegate managerial responsibility to the lowest level, take individual responsibility for decisions about the use of resources, and reward innovation and creativity. In so doing, the 'energy and commitment of public servants will be freed up to allow for the best possible service delivery to the public' (1997: 13).

Despite the various legislative attempts to transform public service labour relations and service delivery, public service management was less than entirely amenable to change. Adair and Albertyn (2000) comment that by the end of the twentieth century, the public service in South Africa remained highly centralised with hierarchical management structures, a rule-bound rather than goal-oriented culture and a management system that was both unskilled and unproductive. Similarly, Adler concludes:

> Notwithstanding massive efforts to transform the old public service, and the increasing importance of collective bargaining in place of unilateral determinations by the old Public Service Commission, managers still do not 'manage'. They are responsible for ensuring that employees abide by a complex set of rules and regulations, rather than concentrating on output and service (2000: 35).

This slow pace of change in management systems and workplace culture was also true of the SAPS in the same period (Marks, 2000b). This is hardly surprising given that police organisations everywhere are, typically, highly centralised and bureaucratic, and designed on a principle of division of labour and unity of control (Birzer, 1996). Police managers are inclined to be preoccupied with the need for 'discipline', to which they see participatory management as a direct challenge. As Jefferson argues, police forces aim to produce officers who are 'disciplined agents expected to follow orders within an organized bureaucracy with militaristic leanings' (1990: 62). Bureaucratic, militaristic management styles are even more prevalent in paramilitary public order units such as Durban POP.

Democratising management in Durban POP

In October 2001, I asked the Operational Commander of Durban POP if the Platoon and Company Commanders had any idea of how to be participatory managers. He gave me the following answer: 'To be honest, most people who are in management positions in the police in South Africa are there because of their rank. They simply got promoted and are now in management positions. But they know nothing about managing.'

The lack of management skills among the police is not confined to South Africa. Bayley argues:

> For years police organisations have been criticized for failing to develop skilled managers – that is people who can manage complex organisations as opposed to commanding field operations. Senior police have been called 'reluctant managers' who do not anticipate needs and reshape their organisations to accomplish new objectives (1994: 85).

Police managers want to be respected, and to ensure this they create 'an elaborate hierarchy of command, an insistence on compliance, and punitive supervision based on detailed rules covering almost everything that a police officer may do (Bayley, 1994).

Decisions are traditionally made at the top and passed down what is referred to as the chain of command. 'Decision-making is rarely participative or collegial across rank lines' (Bayley, 1994: 61). Officers who are in closest touch with operational problems have little opportunity to shape policy, and there is a premium on compliance rather than on initiative (Van Heerden, 1982). Police managers, Goldstein (1990) argues, are not good at innovation or handling new ways of supervising, tending to be preoccupied with internal procedures and maintaining efficiency.

This management model is especially characteristic of public order units. This is because in times of riot or disorder the police must quickly form themselves into a tight, focused unit of operation, where 'a clearly defined and strict chain of command becomes critical to applying force efficiently and to initiating a quick response to social upheaval' (Birzer, 1996: 9). Such units generally also have a military-style structure and operate as squadrons, further entrenching the preference for a command leadership style (Jefferson, 1990). Captain Mahomed, in charge of training in Durban POP, captured this very well when he told me: 'The rank-and-file must be like Robocops. They must respond quickly to orders. They are not here to learn to negotiate. Their job is to respond without question to the commands they are given'.[2]

There have, however, been some shifts in police thinking on management styles in the past twenty years. According to Reiner (1992a), in recent years (particularly in Britain) there has been a concern to develop high quality police management (what Reiner has called a 'corporate management style') that does incorporate a participatory management element. This coincides with 'the emerging consensus around a service-based, consumerist approach to policing' (Reiner, 1992a: 267) in which police see themselves as service providers to a client base. To secure the best quality service delivery, management itself is expected to show high levels of competence directed by clear measurable objectives.

The introduction of localised, community-oriented policing is one dimension of the new service-based emphasis in policing and creates its own need for more participatory (if not also corporate-style) police management since it requires especially flexible responses to community problems. That means police supervisors must actively promote, not limit, creativity and problem-solving approaches (Birzer, 1996).

While community policing may present its own rationale for more participatory management, there are also intra-organisational arguments for promoting this kind of shift. Goldstein (1990) argues that participatory involvement is crucial for police organisational change, since the changes must make sense to those at the front-line; if they don't, then rank-and-file officers are likely to feel threatened by the process and suspicious that it may not be in their best interest. So reform must be designed from the bottom up, and not from the top down (Dean, 1995). The more comprehension there is of change process the more likely it will be acceptable to police members, and the more likely, too, that individual officers will be motivated to actively participate in the process (Washo, 1984; Sykes, 1986). Better morale promotes pride, efficiency and harmony, and in turn heightens the acceptability of the police in the eyes of the 'client' community and enhances the quality of service (Van Heerden, 1982). Excluding the rank-and-file from information and decision-making may leave them feeling disillusioned, manipulated, frustrated and demotivated.

The importance of participatory management in organisational reform is not peculiar to police services. Wilms (1996) concludes, from ethnographic studies of four American companies undergoing change, that developing new work practices and cultures requires changing the very system of work itself.[3] He argues that if the work structure is not altered then ingrained beliefs will be difficult to change because existing authoritarian power relationships (not conducive to learning processes) remain the same. And training, he says, is not an adequate tool for changing culture. Wilms notes that in companies that had introduced innovative forms of participatory management there was also evidence of deeper change: personnel were personally committed to doing high-quality work; managers not only involved workers in planning and problem solving, but also guided them in how to do their work better and supported them in the change process.

Conversely, there also had to be a leadership force strong enough to propel the reforms, 'powerful enough to cancel out individuals' natural fear of letting go of their core beliefs' (Wilms, 1996: 252). This force will be found in a leadership style that brings the entire workforce together in an atmosphere of trust, encourages them to seek common ground on mutual obligations and allows them the space to disagree and express unpopular points of view. For Wilms 'no serious restructuring can take place if it is mandated from above. It must be embraced fully by employees at every level of the organization' (1996: 284).

Existing beliefs are hard to change because they have been 'reinforced by experience for years, [and] give direction and security to individuals as they navigate through their daily lives' (Wilms, 1996: 152). For police to take on new systems of values and beliefs there has to be an environment where all police members can actively participate in the transformation, particularly difficult in an organisation that takes pride in discipline and following orders. It is even more difficult in specialised units accustomed to the hierarchical command structure of a military formation (Waddington, 1991: 136).

It is hardly surprising, then, that participatory management had not really been developed in Durban POP.[4] But there were indications of a less overtly military style, possibly due to the broad campaign in the SAPS to demilitarise. I often noticed that members spoke freely amongst themselves across ranks. Military-style saluting, compulsory before 1995, had ceased and parades were now infrequent. Even low-ranking officers acknowledged the changes, as the following conversation demonstrates:

> *Monique*: Would you say that the police service has changed since the elections?
>
> *Sergeant Mbele*: Yes. Management is better now. You can say something to the management. Before 1994 there was a closed-door policy. Management did not take care of us. Today you can tell the Unit Commander directly what you feel inside.[5]

Captain Naidoo, one of the Platoon Commanders, supported this sentiment. He told me:

> The military structure of the police has been dismantled. There is now more openness. Previously we were told to act, now we give reasons. There is more of a focus on self-development and upliftment. We now have the opportunity to air out our views and there is more room for choice.[6]

Yet many members still felt that there were serious weaknesses in management and supervision. In fact, when members were asked what the chief problem was in the unit at the time of doing the survey, poor management was identified as the second biggest problem. The biggest problem, not surprisingly, was a resource issue (Figure 8.1).

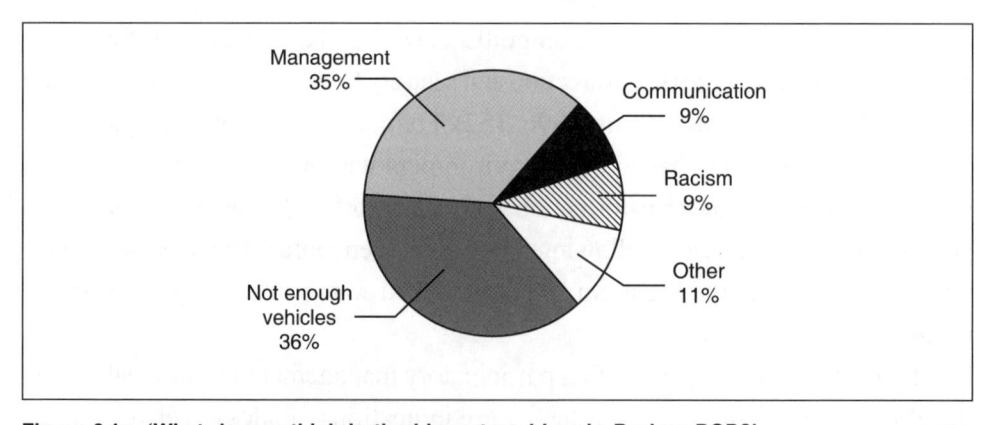

Figure 8.1: 'What do you think is the biggest problem in Durban POP?'

- Management 35%
- Communication 9%
- Racism 9%
- Other 11%
- Not enough vehicles 36%

Even the KwaZulu-Natal Provincial Unit Commander was aware that there was a problem with the calibre of managers in the unit, middle managers in particular.[7] Asked whether he thought that Platoon Commanders and Section Leaders were adequately equipped to lead the unit, his answer was:

> No. There are many captains who have not been on an officer's course. They have not had any training to be different from other guys. They have had no management training. They don't seem to realise that officers have to motivate members and be responsible for state property. They also lack skills in communication, and, as I have said, they are not capable of motivating members.[8]

Indeed, while Platoon Commanders, Company Commanders and Operational Commanders had had training in planning and carrying out crowd management operations, there had been no training to provide them with organisational management expertise. Not a single officer in a management or supervisory role in the unit (including the Unit Commander) had ever had training in any way geared toward participatory management. So it is hardly surprising that the discourse for high-ranking managers continued to be autocratic and disciplinarian. The following conversation with one of the Operational Commanders was noted in my research diary:

> 18/05/2000
> *Senior Superintendent Patel*: The problem in this unit is that the members are not disciplined. They don't want to work with their commanders. You see Monique, they are not even worried about the consequences of their actions. They are not here to work. From now on I am going to do something to the members so they know what they need to do. I am going to write up what is expected from them and make them sign it. If they do something wrong, I will get rid of them.
> *Monique*: Would it not be wise to involve members in deciding what is to be expected from them? That way they might feel that they have some ownership over the criteria used to evaluate them.
> *Senior Superintendent Patel*: There is no way I am going to do that. I know what is expected of them and I am simply going to tell them what to do. That is the end of the story!

Rank-and-file members were well aware of the autocratic inclination of supervisors and managers but this did not mean they were still willing to acquiesce. In early 2000, a group of rank-and-file members formed themselves into what they called the 'Empowerment Committee'. This committee met regularly to discuss problems in the unit and to try to strategise mechanisms for changing the way the unit operated. Even though both middle and top management were sceptical about this committee they allowed it to operate. Members of the committee were vociferous in their belief that there had to be a radical change in management style. I had the following encounter with one of the members of the Empowerment Committee:

> 28/07/2000
> I was sitting in the canteen reading a newspaper when one of the Inspectors from the unit came and sat next to me. I had been on two field operations with his section so we were familiar with one another. He offered me a cigarette and he told me that he was becoming an 'activist' in the unit. I thought this was a strange word for a policeman to use to describe himself – particularly this policeman who had been a long-serving member of the unit.
>
> *Monique*: What exactly does it mean to be an activist in the unit?
> *Inspector Moonsamy*: Well, I am one of those people who is trying to change this place. You know, there are so many problems in this unit. There are many Hitlers in this unit. They are so authoritarian. I thought Hitler died a long time ago, but that is not the case in this place. He is still alive in this unit.
> *Monique*: I am still not clear what you mean.
> *Inspector Moonsamy*: The commanders here don't know how to treat us. They behave toward us like we are children. They just order us around and treat us like we can't think for ourselves. They never ask us what we think, or what we feel about things. It is pathetic. Our Platoon Commander is a real problem. He just tells us that he knows his job and that we must respect him. Respect doesn't come like that. We are going to the labour relations guy to tell him that we want to get rid of our Platoon Commander.

The survival of the old autocratic tendencies reflected a strong element of glorification of the past with its conviction that 'discipline' was the key to 'real' policing, a sentiment that the 1998/1999 acting Unit Commander conveyed to me very plainly:

> We need to get back to the military set-up I spoke about earlier. Although discipline was harsh and rigid, it happened. Discipline is lost from the force now. I will give you a good example. Nobody salutes an officer anymore. In the old days, if an officer walked past in the morning someone would shout attention. It was a sign of respect, and it gives the police pride in themselves. Nobody comes to salute anymore. We are talking about basic things, Monique. They [members] must get away from this sloppy approach and go back to saluting an officer. It is very sad. We just need to ensure that our buckles are shining and that our shirts are tucked in and our shoes are clean. We have to present ourselves in a certain way to the community. The quicker these police start to do it, the better.[9]

Even though most rank-and-file members were unhappy with the autocratic management of the unit, they seemed to go along with the view that police organisations are intrinsically militaristic. One young woman officer had the following to say in this regard:

> The police force is like the army. You must be able to take instructions and have discipline. If you can't do that, you are not a policeman. Members must obey commands that are given to them. The police will always be the same. It will never change. So, when you come into the police force you will know that that is what is expected from you.[10]

Members did think that maintaining discipline in the unit was important but they were also disheartened and frustrated by the fact that they had little opportunity to contribute to decision-making or planning and policy. They expressed deep alienation from middle and top management. As Sergeant Mbele told me:

> What actually happens is that by the time the communication comes down, it is often too late for us to have any say. It would be better if we had a say because we do the dirty work. The person at the top just throws things down. So, I can say that even if we look at the Unit Commanders they have not changed. They are just the same . . . those above your immediate peers, like your Platoon Commanders and those above them, we only see them when there is an instruction. You will try to get on with them but we never

come into contact with the top leadership . . . I actually never see them. I don't even know what kind of people they are. Even the Platoon Commander, I only get to know him when he tells us what the Commander says.[11]

Asked whether Platoon Commanders or Company Commanders had ever discussed the policy document or the change process with them, rank-and-file members were unanimous that this had never taken place:

The Unit Commanders never have proper discussions with us about what is happening in this transformation thing. In my unit, the only time we have a meeting is because members are complaining about transport. Of all the changes, I have never heard such a discussion. Maybe the senior officers talk about it. When we raise things with them, we never get feedback.[12]

Although it had been made clear to middle management that they were expected to develop a new management style (participatory management) they had little idea of what this was supposed to mean. Most thought that participatory management meant simply allowing members to express their grievances. Never having been trained in management skills – let alone participatory management skills – they were at a loss to know how to promote a common vision and a shared approach in the platoons and companies, how to develop a relationship of trust and respect between themselves and their 'subordinates'. This *they* found demoralising, as the following extract from my research diary brings out very clearly:

30/05/2000
. . . It is only a few days after the fatal shooting incident at the University of Durban-Westville, and both middle and top management seemed to be in a state of delayed shock. There was much discussion and debate taking place in the unit. Questions were being raised as to who was ultimately responsible for the disastrous incident. Rank-and-file members blamed commanders for giving unclear direction, and commanders blamed rank-and-file members for not obeying instructions . . . I wandered around the unit talking to members of all ranks about the incident. Everyone wanted to talk to me and share his or her point of view. Captain Govindsamy, whose platoon had

been deployed on the campus on the day of the shooting, came and chatted to me. I noticed that he looked dejected and concerned:

Captain Govindsamy: I don't really know what to do about the members in my platoon anymore. They keep putting me before a firing line and telling me how useless I am. I really feel that my members are against me.
Monique: What are they saying?
Captain Govindsamy: They tell me I am not instructing them properly and that I am very autocratic. They tell me I am a bad manager.
Monique: What do you make of all of this?
Captain Govindsamy: I am really trying to do my best. I try to ask them what the problems are but then they refuse to listen to my instructions. I have informed them that I am going to pursue disciplinary action against them for their conduct at the University of Durban-Westville. I am not prepared to fall on my own when they are the problem. They must account for their behaviour. They think I am very wrong to be doing this. I really need advice as to what to do. I don't know who to turn to. What do you think I should do?
Monique: I can't really comment on this. It is not my place. But I do think that you guys have been put in a really difficult situation. You are trying to bring about changes but you yourselves have not been trained in new styles of managing. I really think that all you managers and supervisors in the unit need to have some training in how to implement participatory management. What do you think?
Captain Govindsamy: I think it is really important. We are instructed to hold participant management meetings but we have never really been told what this means. So I am trying, but I am not sure if I am doing the right thing. Now there is this Empowerment Committee and they are organising against me. I am not against this committee, but really, I have my limits as to the amount of attacks I can take. I have tried to be reasonable about this but the members are really making my life difficult at the moment.

There was clearly conflict between Captain Govindsamy and his platoon members and this was distressing and confusing for him as Platoon Commander. There seem to have been three underlying causes for this discordant relationship. In the first place, Captain Govindsamy had had no training in how to give clear instructions while also involving his platoon members in decision-making and planning. Secondly, he invited the platoon members to tell him their grievances while continuing to insist on his authority to discipline them. Thirdly, implicit in his complaint is lack of support from top management for middle management trying to introduce new management styles. They were expected to be participatory managers (an entirely foreign concept to police management in South Africa), but with no training or advice as to how to do this. This left middle management feeling vulnerable and the rank-and-file frustrated and angry.

While the discordant interactions in Captain Govindsamy's platoon may have been more acute than in other platoons, commanders and rank-and-file members from other platoons indicated to me that similar dynamics operated throughout the unit: no learning environment here where old assumptions could be challenged or new attitudes acquired.

Leadership and supervision
Participatory management is likely to be a decisive ingredient in police reform: drawing in all personnel helps build a common purpose, allowing members to buy into the process and promoting trust between managers/supervisors and rank-and-file. This, in turn, creates the space for learning and co-operation. But it is equally important for managers and supervisors to be capable of giving appropriate leadership when new ways of responding and acting are in the balance.

Supervision is especially crucial when police are on the streets or in the field. Goldstein (1990) argues that front-line supervisors are perhaps the most important leaders in police organisations, since their guidance and direction has such an immediate bearing on the day-to-day working lives of police officers. Supervisors should, ideally, be present and visible when rank-and-file members are 'on the job', actively directing and monitoring the work of rank-and-file.

In public order units organised along military lines, like Durban POP, these issues assume even more significance. Waddington points out that public order interventions depend very much on co-ordination and discipline that require closer control and supervision than regular (more individualised) policing does (1991: 136). Waddington argues that officers in public order policing often become very emotive because they are so 'close to the action'. Public order or civil disorder events are often unpredictable, generating high anxiety levels for the officers policing them and consequently also strong pressure to resort to forceful action. To prevent this, 'it is essential that officers engaged in public order situations are carefully supervised and controlled, for internal controls on behaviour are unlikely to prove reliable' (1991: 137).

And the stakes are still higher where there has been a history of abusive policing and when both culture and practice must change. Here police leaders and managers carry a heavy responsibility for instilling new paradigms of cultural knowledge. Following Chan's paradigms (see Chapter 3), in the case of Durban POP these are the shifts that had to be engineered: *axiomatic knowledge*, the police mandate, had to shift from control of crowds and war-on-crime to management of crowds and crime prevention; *dictionary knowledge*, categories of people and environment, had to replace racial and ethnic stereotyping with open tolerance of all social groups and positive acceptance of diversity: officers to appreciate the social, political and economic circumstances of the people that they serve; *directory knowledge*, appropriate methods, had to shift from forceful intervention to problem solving and negotiation – no longer just looking for the quickest way out, but taking the best procedural route to reach the best long-term outcomes; and finally, *recipe knowledge*, basic values, had to centre on a real respect for the rights of all persons: in particular, respect for the right to freedom of expression, freedom of assembly and freedom of political opinion.

Shifts in cultural knowledge do not develop spontaneously, nor simply as an outcome of changes in training and policy. Transformation of this order has to be forged on the streets where the police meet their public (Waddington, 1999a) – and this is where the leadership must be to steer them in their adoption of new and appropriate practices and in the renegotiation of practices that are familiar and established; this is where, whenever possible, front-line supervisors should be visible and present when rank-and-file officers are 'on the job'. It is the supervisors who need to ensure that operations are directed by proper planning, that there is correct assessment of the equipment and the tactics to be used and careful monitoring of the actions of rank-and-file members prior to and during interventions, with proper briefing and debriefing.

Briefing and debriefing is very important in police work. Proper briefing establishes a common understanding of what is to be done, knowledge about the circumstances in which officers will be operating, and the rationale for particular interventions. With such shared insight and understanding, rank-and-file members are more likely to see themselves as active agents rather than as Captain Mahomed's automaton Robocops. Debriefing allows police to reflect upon actions taken, to commend good work done and to learn from mistakes. However, results from the survey conducted in 1998 indicate that briefing and debriefing was very inconsistent in Durban POP (Figure 8.2). Barely a quarter of unit members considered that adequate briefing and debriefing was taking place.

One reason for the inadequacy of briefing and debriefing was that commanders were too seldom present when active policing was taking place. From my own observation and from interviews with members of all ranks, it became clear that far too often supervisors and commanders were simply not there when the platoons were deployed.

On 29 April 1998, I joined the Durban POP trainers on field visits. Trainers wanted to observe members in the field to ascertain whether skills and procedures learned in training were being implemented. We left the college at 9:30 am and went to join a platoon that had been deployed at Mariannhill Police Station. Mariannhill is an African peri-urban area and a new Indian station commissioner had recently been appointed at the station. Rank-and-file officers at the station were unhappy about the appointment; they felt an African commander should have been appointed. They had threatened the new Station Commissioner with physical abuse and declared that they refused to work under his command.

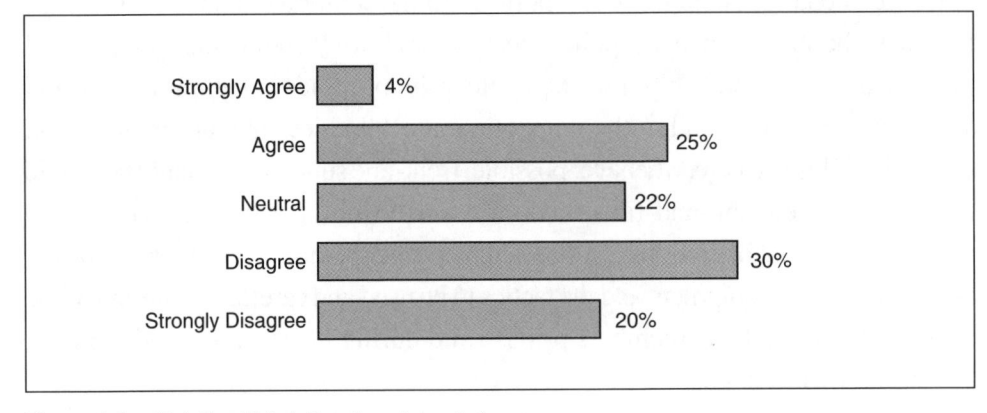

Response	Percentage
Strongly Agree	4%
Agree	25%
Neutral	22%
Disagree	30%
Strongly Disagree	20%

Figure 8.2: 'Briefing/debriefing is adequate.'

The Station Commissioner had called in the Public Order unit because protesting officers were organising strike action which, for the police, is illegal in terms of the Labour Relations Act. When we arrived at the police station, the Indian Station Commissioner and two other Indian officers were on the point of leaving because they feared being injured by African officers at the station. A Durban POP platoon was present, as well as a small contingent of the Defence Force. POP members were talking and simply hanging around. When I asked them what instructions they had been given, they informed me that none had been given and that they were unclear what action should be taken. Furthermore, there was no Platoon Commander present. At no point did any commissioned officer speak to either the POP members or the protesting police officers to find out what was happening or what the role of POP was. There was no briefing, assessment or debriefing at any stage during the event. (We stayed at Mariannhill until the Provincial Commissioner of the SAPS intervened and POP was instructed to withdraw.)

Once POP was withdrawn, we joined another platoon that was deployed at the provincial government administrative offices. Young school students from the African townships were protesting against the quality of education they were getting: lack of teachers; poor facilities; and insufficient textbooks. A large contingent of Durban POP was present, but once again no Platoon Commander. The only instruction that the platoon had been given was to monitor the situation and make sure no incidents occurred. Rank-and-file members complained to me that they had been deployed in the hot sun with nothing to do. They were extremely bored and no provision had been made for anyone to take a lunch break.

In both these instances, Section Leaders had been present with the platoons. But Section Leaders are not responsible for the planning of operations; this is the function of Platoon and Company Commanders. Nor have they had training in the command of operations. They are non-commissioned officers with very limited powers of command and deployment. It was therefore very problematic that no officer with authority was present during these events since proper monitoring could not take place and unit members were left feeling directionless.

These experiences were not uncommon. In fact, interviews with both rank-and-file and more high-ranking officers corroborated these experiences. I asked a Sergeant why this happened so frequently. He responded:

I don't know why this tends to happen. It is a bad thing. When I was in charge of the bike unit temporarily, I was always out there to sort things out. When there was even a small problem, I would be there to sort things out. I had to take over when the Captain in charge took medical board. But even when he was in charge, he was never with us when we went out into the field. It was a big problem. I told the Commander that it is a problem to have someone with the same rank like me in charge of the others. That is why we need a Captain in the first place. But the Captain that was supposed to be in charge would only rock up ten minutes before we were going to leave the operation. While he was not there, we simply had to take action and then say that he must take it up with the Director if he had a problem since he was never there.[13]

Captain Botha, the Head of Personal Development in Durban POP, agreed that this was a major problem:

Commanders know that there are seconds in charge, like an Inspector, who is capable of doing the work. So, 90 per cent of the time they are either not there or they don't want to be there or they have other things to do . . . This is wrong. They shouldn't do this. I mean, I am sure you have heard this from others as well. I don't think they show any interest anymore. They should never have been made officers in the first place. Really, members who are not capable or willing should leave the police force. If a platoon doesn't have a good commander it will go backwards.[14]

Captain Modise, a female Platoon Commander, stated that she was always present with her members when they were deployed and that those Platoon Commanders who did not join their members were contributing to low productivity and low morale in the unit:

What I know is that members tend to be negative because they think we, the commanders, don't care about them. We send them into the hot sun for a whole day. Maybe the commander is not around. He just leaves them in the field alone and goes home to do his own thing. You will find that there are no Platoon Commanders in some operations . . . I can tell you, if you can go through the commanders in this unit, you will see those who don't go to work with the members. Their platoons have low productivity. The Platoon Commanders just come to greet the Company Commanders at the unit, show that they have pitched for work, and then they just disappear. The guys stand around doing nothing. They are bored. They are stressed. They say, 'Hey, I am tired of working in this unit. I am tired of using that fucking broken-down vehicle.' They do nothing. If you work, there is no time to complain. That is why you need to keep them busy. The Unit Commander should be visiting the platoons when they are operational to see if the Platoon Commander is there or not. If the Unit Commander just stays in his office thinking that his members are working outside, nothing can change . . . you need to get the members involved physically and show them how things must be done. You must show them how to love the community. This will create better communication and interaction in the unit.[15]

Captain Modise felt strongly about leading by example, and joining rank-and-file officers in the field to boost morale. It particularly irked her that the Unit Commander was so office-bound because that meant there was poor monitoring of the performance of lower-level commanders and commissioned officers.

For Bayley, it is management at the very top that counts for most police reform. In a monograph published by the United States Department of Justice, *Democratizing the Police Abroad: What To Do And How To Do It*, he makes the point:

> Sustained and committed leadership by top management, especially the most senior executive, is required to produce any important organisational change. This is probably the most frequently repeated lesson of reform management . . . Significant reform cannot be brought about by stealth from below against the indifference or hostility of senior managers (1999: 20).

Managers and supervisors in Durban POP did not seem to be providing 'sustained and committed' leadership. I observed a number of operations where it was evident that supervisors were unable to provide direction to unit members and that planning had been inadequate. In the days leading up to the fatal shooting of the student on UDW campus (see Chapter 7) it became obvious that those in command had no clear plan and were in fact quite confused about what the jurisdiction of the unit was on the campus. The next extract from my research diary illustrates this very clearly:

15/05/2000

Captain Meetha and myself arrived at the University of Durban-Westville at 9 am. Students were protesting. 540 students had been excluded from the university because they had failed to pay fees. University authorities had told the police and the student body that they would not allow students to conduct a protest march on campus. Students were also informed that if they wanted to hold a public meeting, they could only do so in one place on the campus. When we got to the place where Durban POP was congregating, we found two Platoon Commanders trying desperately to determine what action the unit should take. Four Platoon Commanders were standing next to a car having a heated discussion. The platoon members were smoking and talking about ten metres away from where the Platoon Commanders were meeting. A heated discussion was ensuing between two Platoon Commanders as to what action should be taken.

One of the Platoon Commanders was arguing that they should form a police line and push the students off campus and they would then have to protest on the streets. Another Platoon Commander was arguing that the campus was private property and that the police had no authority to prevent the students from protesting on campus. The following conversation ensued:

Captain Paral: The university administration has told the students that they cannot march on campus and that they can only meet in the concourse. Campus security has stated that they want students to move off campus if they want to organise a protest demonstration. I think we should try to push the students onto the street where they can protest as much as they like.
Captain Padayachee: We can't do that. We cannot infringe on the students' right to protest unless they are endangering life or property. If the campus management doesn't want students to march, they must enforce this and not us. We can't act in the interest of management alone. We can only be here on standby in case something happens.
Captain Paral: The decision to do a push-back was made by the commander who was here yesterday. We need continuity.

Captain Padayachee: Yes, but this is not the right thing to do. We are not authorised to do this.

Captain Paral became very upset at having being contradicted by a peer in public. Eventually all commissioned officers present decided to hold a quick meeting to decide what course of action should be taken. They concluded that it was the responsibility of university management to limit the movement of students on campus. One of the Platoon Commanders reported this back to the platoon members. The platoon members had witnessed the interaction that had taken place and one of the Sergeants asked: 'How are we supposed to know what to do if our management doesn't even know what is right and what is wrong?'

This incident highlights a number of problems in the unit. Middle management were unclear about the role and limitations of the unit; rank-and-file members seemed unconvinced that Platoon Commanders were capable of making informed decisions and took a dim view of this. Throughout that day Platoon Commanders held regular meetings with campus administration. They would then simply hang out together in a group making virtually no effort to consult rank-and-file members or give them feedback. Nor had there been prior planning, which meant that those in command were not in a position to brief unit members or provide direction. The lack of planning and the uncertainty about the jurisdiction of the unit indicated that senior officers were not implementing the skills (i.e. planning of crowd management operations) that they had ostensibly learned in training, and that they were not in fact abreast of the legislation and policy pertaining to crowd management.

It was very soon after this diary entry that the fatal campus shooting took place recorded in the previous chapter. In the debriefing document drawn up by POP Headquarters in its aftermath, lack of planning and direction on the part of those in command were identified as the key factors in this operational catastrophe. The document explicitly detailed the procedural lapses (no written plan, no threat analysis, no joint operation centre), drawing the following conclusion:

> The absence of written instructions or planning left the door open for uncoordinated actions and the use of inappropriate equipment and force . . .

> Planning was not used as an opportunity to share information and initiate new and creative tactics to enhance co-operation and reduce the risk of violence . . . The deficiencies in the negotiation, assessment and planning subsequently resulted in weak command and control . . . All the officers on the scene on 16 May were apparently trained in the Platoon Commanders' Course. It is unthinkable that POP members did not apply even the most basic principles of good command structure, techniques, or use of equipment despite the fact that they were all trained. It is clear that the will to implement an acceptable approach to crowd management is lacking even at command level in the unit (Public Order Police, 2000).

Two weeks after the shooting incident at UDW, I accompanied a senior officer on a visit to Mangosuthu Technical College in Umlazi Township. Students and staff were in an uproar following the fatal shooting of a student by private security officers on the campus. That morning, students had gone on a rampage destroying campus property. Durban POP was called to the scene. No commanding officer was present when we arrived and unit members were not sure what they should be doing. The Section Leader was concerned that if a problem arose, and officers responded without clear orders from the Platoon Commander, the unit would be compromised again. According to Captain Paral, the Platoon Commander was on sick leave and no one had been sent to replace him. The Section Leader told us that his section had been at work monitoring one of the township hostels when they were called out to the college campus. Since they had been doing crime prevention work, they had no crowd management equipment with them. No meeting had been held with either students or campus administration to find out exactly what the situation was or to plan appropriate police intervention should a problem emerge. The following conversation between Captain Paral and the Section Leader was recorded in my research diary:

> 08/06/2000
> *Captain Paral*: Where have you guys come from?
> *Sergeant Ngubane*: We were at S.J. Smith Hostel looking for drugs and weapons. We were just told to come here but we have received no briefing yet. Can you imagine? There are only six members down at this meeting of students. If something happens, we are just sitting ducks. These students are very angry.

Captain Paral: What equipment do you guys have?
Sergeant Ngubane: Three of us have side-arms [pistols]. We have no shields and no helmets. And, no one has briefed us as to what we are expected to do. Captain, this is not a good situation. We don't feel safe like this. What are we supposed to do if a riot breaks out? Go out with our bare hands and try to push people back? Honestly, we are not prepared for this situation at all.

The inadequacy of direction and planning was not confined to crowd management events. It was also evident when the unit was involved in crime prevention duties, as the following extract from my research diary illustrates:

18/03/2000
... The Inspector parked the armoured vehicle in a park and everyone took out their lunch. African members shared lunch with one another while Indian members shared lunch among themselves. Those who were not eating lunch lay on their backs and smoked cigarettes. After sitting around for about an hour-and-a-half doing nothing in particular, the Platoon Commander arrived. He called the members together and informed them that they should go and 'do crime prevention work' in the central business district. He did not explain what exactly this 'crime prevention' exercise would involve, or why it was necessary. Members did not ask for clarity. After this short and imprecise briefing, the Platoon Commander said he had to leave and that he had other responsibilities to fulfil. I accompanied him as he walked to his vehicle and asked him what he meant by 'crime prevention'. He responded that it meant doing things like picking up people who were drunk in public. I thought this was a very poor description of crime prevention and was curious to know how platoon members interpreted their very vague instruction. I asked them what they intended to do and they replied that they would just drive around town and in so doing create a police presence in the area. They had no plan as to what they would do or which areas they thought were most in need of crime prevention work. The Section Leader in the vehicle gave no further direction and no discussion

was held as to what could or should be done. Both the members present and myself were aware that this 'mission' was simply about passing time . . . We drove into town, found another recreational area, and parked the vehicle. I asked how sitting in a vehicle in a recreational area constituted crime prevention. I was informed that just by virtue of the fact that they as police were visible would detract people from engaging in criminal activities. I was also informed by one of the Sergeants that members of the platoon had no intention of going out and doing 'hard work' such as arresting criminals. This, he said, would reflect positively on the Platoon Commander and they had no intention of 'creating a good name for him'. I felt perturbed by the racialised informal interactions that were taking place. I was appalled by the lack of initiative and interest on the part of the members. I realised, however, that this whole situation is a result of poor management and supervision.

In the previous chapter we saw that there were certainly occasions when rank-and-file members, in the presence of Section Leaders, conducted themselves unacceptably when commanders were not there to supervise the activities of the platoons. The fact that there were not more deaths and injuries during these operations, whether crowd management events or crime prevention exercises, was perhaps attributable more to the generally peaceable disposition of the crowds – and maybe some fear of reprimand after the event – than to sound judgement on the part of the unit members.

Measuring performance

Proper performance measurement (both of individuals and of the organisation more broadly) is crucial in any organisation, particularly when it is undergoing reform. Performance measures help in assessing the success of particular programmes and in identifying areas where performance is weak or strong. They point the way to better allocation of resources, better-focused training needs, more uniform promotion procedures and more equitable structuring of workloads. They can also be a good starting point for the development of reward systems (crucial for building morale and organisational commitment) and in clarifying roles and expectations.

The 1997 White Paper on Human Resource Management stresses that the success of the Public Service in delivering its operational and developmental goals depends primarily on the efficiency with which employees carry out their duties. Managing performance is therefore a key human resource management tool to ensure that

- employees know what is expected of them;
- managers know whether the employees' performances are delivering the required objectives;
- poor performance is identified and improved; and
- good performance is recognised and rewarded.

The White Paper advises that performance management should be a continuous process in which employer and employee work together to improve the employee's individual performance and his or her contribution to the organisation's objectives. For this, appropriate individual performance indicators have to be developed and applied. At the same time there must also be performance evaluation for the organisation as a whole.

These recommendations were for the whole of the public service, but it was the SAPS that was most under pressure to match up to them (Leggett, 2002). However, research into the effectiveness of performance evaluation in the SAPS has suggested that too many indicators were set and that 'target setting did not relate to any independent set of criteria about optimal performance' (Shaw, cited in Leggett, 2002: 57). In South Africa, and indeed internationally, the public sector has lagged behind the private sector in developing measures of performance. 'The near monopoly that public service bureaucracies have, their multiple purposes and diffuse clientele, and the belief (unshaken until recently) that because their formal goals say they do good, they actually must do good, help account for this' (Marx, 1976: 1). Performance indicators for police organisations are perhaps even less well developed than for other sectors of the public service. Vanagunas and Elliot (1980) point out that there are many problems in measuring police productivity. It is not possible to translate police output to a monetary value. Police output is a service and requires qualitative and quantitative measurement but some aspects of it simply cannot be measured; they are too intermeshed with other expectations such as trying to provide a community with a sense of security. For the wide range of functions that police perform, assigning relative value to individual tasks is almost impossible (Leggett, 2002).

Over the past two decades, however, there has been a concerted effort on the part of government in most liberal democracies to improve public sector performance indicators including those for police. In Britain, for example, a Policing Performance Assessment Framework has been devised by the Home Office to assist with assessing the performance of local police services. Best Value Performance Indicators (BVPIs) have been devised as a way of measuring successful public service delivery in line with corporate assessment frameworks and these BVPIs have been adapted to the various police agencies in Britain (North Yorkshire Police Authority, n.d.).

However, despite moves to define what good police performance is and how to measure it, police services have generally been reluctant to abandon more traditional performance expectations, in particular the belief that arrest rates indicate productivity. But arrest rates are not a good indicator. Why? In the first place, those that are arrested are not necessarily guilty of committing crimes. Secondly, questions remain as to whether arresting suspected offenders will make any difference to the problem at hand. Thirdly, arrest rates may have nothing to do with the policing objectives of the agency: a high arrest rate does not necessarily reflect success in the peaceful policing of protest events or the prevention of youth delinquency. Fourthly, the focus is on the rate of production rather than the process by which it is achieved, yet process is crucial to the effectiveness of community policing. Fifthly, and perhaps most importantly, focusing on arrest rates, clearance rates and response times will not speed the delivery of new strategic plans.

Bayley (1994) suggests that in police organisations there are both direct and indirect performance indicators. Direct indicators are those that indicate what the police have actually accomplished in the community: a decline in particular crime rates; fewer complaints against the police; police willingness to assist the public; and reduced fear of crime. Indirect indicators measure what the police have done but not their impact on the quality of community life. These include arrest rates, response times, the recovery of stolen weapons, the number of patrols, and clearance rates. And it is the indirect performance indicators that police most often attend to – which is unhelpful, since on their own they do not reflect the impact of police actions on the community. Increased arrest rates, for example, do not necessarily make the community feel safer; this is simply a presumption that police make. Police themselves prefer to be rated indirectly and police managers prefer to focus on what the police do most visibly and what can be quantified (Bayley, 1994).

Durban POP is a classic instance of the shortcomings in the traditional criteria: performance measurement was a very low priority, and the performance indicators were invariably the indirect ones. Only about one in three members in Durban POP considered that there was regular individual performance evaluation (Figure 8.3).

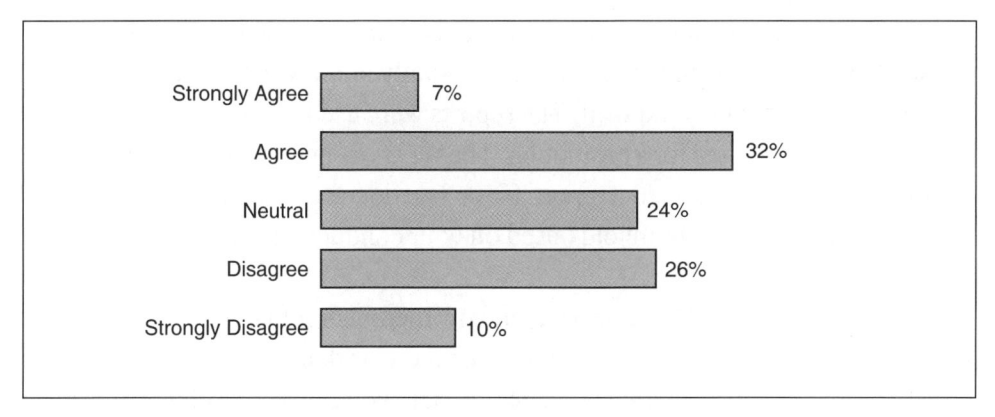

Response	Percentage
Strongly Agree	7%
Agree	32%
Neutral	24%
Disagree	26%
Strongly Disagree	10%

Figure 8.3: 'We continually evaluate our individual performance in Durban POP.'

Perhaps there were some Section Leaders and Platoon Commanders who informally conducted individual performance evaluations. In practice, however, this was not something supervisors were expected to do. A programme for evaluating individual performance was only introduced to the unit in October 2001, and a month later still no evaluations had begun. According to Captain Zungu, a Platoon Commander in the unit,

> We have never really done individual performance evaluations. In fact, until mid-2001, we did not even have proper job descriptions for the various ranks in the unit. These were only drawn up in about July 2001. This is a big problem. How could we be expected to evaluate our members if we did not know what exactly they were supposed to be doing?[16]

Before October 2001, supervisors in Durban POP were expected to keep 'conduct records' of their subordinates. These focused mainly on disciplinary matters such as whether or not officers were absent from duty, drunk on duty, or had been involved in criminal offences. The conduct records tended to operate punitively and cannot be said to have enhanced individual performance or built individual morale. According to a senior training officer at Durban POP:

> We have always had individual conduct reports which immediate supervisors are supposed to fill in four times a year. These reports never really evaluated the jobs people did as such. They never added up to a formal acknowledgement of a person's work. They were used, negatively, if I can say that. What I mean is that they were usually about what somebody did wrong, not what they did well. The reports were used against you. Say for example you applied for a promotion. The supervisor concerned would take out your individual conduct report. If you had done something wrong, your promotion would be withheld based on your conduct report.[17]

The conduct records had little bearing on how members actually performed in the field. In fact, as is the case in many parts of the world, evaluations tended to be based on 'conformity to internal bureaucratic standards, which may have little to do with how well a [police officer] does his job on the street or what he does' (Marx, 1976: 2).

The absence of structured performance monitoring left members feeling that their skills and contributions were neither recognised nor rewarded. Linked to this was an absence at any level of career planning or individual development programmes.[18] One of the Captains who had recently completed his honours degree in psychology expressed his frustration at the lack of recognition for his expertise:

> I have my degree now. I am working here. It is good, I don't have a problem being here. But no incentive is given to me for having this degree. There is no structure in place to say 'okay, these are his skills and this is where he will be most effective'. It doesn't have to mean an increase in salary. It is about looking at the development of individuals. It takes place, but really in such a small way. That is, members are waiting to see if they can do better somewhere else. Frankly, that is what I am waiting for as well, and I have applied for a position in the City Police.[19]

Rank-and-file members also expressed frustration at the lack of performance appraisal and the lack of recognition of 'good work':

> Usually your Section Leader is supposed to reward you. But most of the time this doesn't happen. A person must have something that will stimulate him to do better work. Maybe if you find a stolen firearm or make an arrest

you should get a medal with your name on it. Like those medals they are giving to members who are serving in the police for a long time. Once a month they should see which members had successes and give them medals. Everybody would want to work more . . . at the moment we are not recognised. If you recover a stolen car, the Section Leader will be happy. But the Section Leader gets praise for this, not us. If we were rewarded maybe the police who are hesitant would feel more motivated. But I can say that they don't motivate you in the police.[20]

This Sergeant makes an important point: recognition of your achievements boosts your motivation and commitment. But what she understands as 'good performance' are still the traditional indirect indicators: arrests, recovery of stolen weapons and vehicles.

Indirect performance indicators *were* used to evaluate and reward platoons. Until the middle of 1999, each month the Unit Commander would announce the 'Platoon of the Month'. This would be the platoon that had the highest record of arrests and the highest recovery tally of stolen weapons and vehicles. The 1998 Unit Commander kept a set of statistics that indicated the number of arrests and recoveries for each platoon. When he wanted to indicate which platoon was being productive, he would bring out his statistics and point out which had good arrests and recovery statistics. At no stage did he critically evaluate who was arrested or whether those arrested were ever convicted of any crime. Nor was he interested in how weapons were recovered. In other words, there was no questioning whether members of the platoon used legitimate means to recover these weapons or whether they followed community policing objectives in their crime prevention work.

The fact that arrests were viewed as one of the key performance indicators meant that members would in practice arrest anyone vaguely suspected of a criminal offence, even if there was no substantive evidence of this. This became clear to me when I joined platoons on their various crime prevention operations. One of the platoons arrested a young township resident simply because he looked as if he could be trading marijuana. When I asked what evidence they had of this they responded that they knew what people like that looked like and if they were 'forcefully questioned' they would admit to buying marijuana. Their chief motivation was that if they arrested a large number of suspects they would be regarded by the Unit Commander as a productive platoon. At no time did they attempt to make any sort of connection between these traditional indicators of 'good performance' and the supposed objectives of the unit. Traditional indicators thus reinforced old behaviours (unsubstantiated arrests and discriminatory profiling) and blocked any evolution of new standards.

The Head of Labour Relations spoke to me about the fact that Durban POP Commanders had not reconsidered their performance indicators:

> At this point in the unit we don't really have proper performance indicators. I suppose if you do a march and it goes without incident this is seen as good. But other than that we don't have indicators. There is no real way of evaluating the unit. We have geared our work toward the recovery of vehicles and firearms. But these are not proper indicators, particularly for crowd management. Management are still with the old mindset about criteria. It doesn't look like things are really changing . . . The other big problem is that Platoon Commanders are not really evaluated when they are appointed. There are no performance indicators or job descriptions for them either. Once you are a Platoon Commander, you can stay in that position forever because no one will be evaluating you. There is no mechanism for ensuring that members are doing things properly or that they are effective in their work . . . Also, no one looks at how members behave when they are actually doing operations. They should be evaluated according to what their conduct was in an operation on any given day. How did they actually carry out that operation? The only way of reviewing is through debriefing, but this is not being done in terms of proper evaluation. There is nothing in place to ensure that Section Leaders or Platoon Commanders meet regularly with individuals under their command. A mechanism and criteria for evaluation should be given to the Section Leaders and Platoon Commanders.[21]

The continued use of the old performance indicators in platoon evaluations is problematic for two reasons. They are indirect, and consequently provided no measure of whether the unit had any positive impact in the community it served. And they are associated with crime prevention work while the primary function of the unit was that of crowd management. So no incentives existed for better crowd management performance: no recognition for problem solving, for negotiating with interest groups, for successfully keeping the peace at crowd events.

Support, motivation, commitment

The deficiencies in management, leadership, performance evaluation and career guidance all had their effect on morale. Survey responses (Figure 8.4) indicated that almost half the officers in Durban POP had considered leaving.[22] But there were also significant differences between the various race groups in this regard, with white members the most disaffected. This is hardly surprising since they saw themselves as having the most to lose in the transformation process, particularly with the departure from the unit of white managers and supervisors. Members also claimed that they lacked motivation to work and found the work in the unit unstimulating. As a young white sergeant told me:

> To be honest, I feel really bored. We sit around doing nothing most of the time. I come to work and sleep in the office. I am not being challenged anymore. I am getting fat and more and more stupid. In fact, to tell you the truth I am embarrassed to wear a police uniform in public these days. When I go to the shopping centre I don't even wear my cap anymore. I can't be a policeman with pride anymore. I am really not doing anything that makes me feel like a policeman. I don't feel very motivated.[23]

He had, he said, been far more motivated before the transformation process began. He felt that Unit Commanders had been more supportive in the past and the work more exciting. Yet he also indicated that he would not consider transferring to any of the stations as he enjoyed the flexibility of working hours in the POP.

There were many other members who told me they intended to leave the unit,

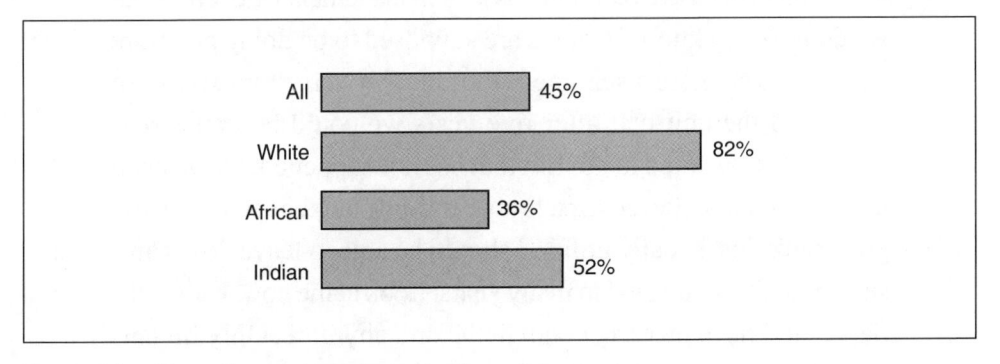

Group	Percentage
All	45%
White	82%
African	36%
Indian	52%

Figure 8.4: 'Recently considered leaving the unit.'

but what they wanted, often, was transfer to other specialised units. The following encounter with another white Sergeant illustrates this:

> I sat in the canteen and worked on my laptop. I was waiting for a meeting with Captain Pillay. While I was sitting there, a female trainer came and sat with me. She brought me a cup of tea and a cigarette and we chatted about babies and other 'girls' stuff'. While sitting with her I noticed a white Sergeant who had waved to me. I decided to go and say hello.
>
> *Monique*: Hi there, how are things going with you?
> *Sergeant Meyer*: Well not too bad. I am just filling in a form at the moment requesting a transfer out of the unit.
> *Monique*: Where are you wanting to go to?
> *Sergeant Meyer*: To be honest, anywhere. To any other specialised unit. I applied to the child protection unit, but they did not accept the transfer. So, now I am applying to the water wing unit. I don't know exactly what they do, but there are no other applications to that unit from here at the moment. I just want to get out of here.
> *Monique*: Why do you want to get out so badly?
> *Sergeant Meyer*: I have been in the unit for sixteen years. That is a really long time. When I got here, we were trained completely differently. I am used to the old style. They expect me to change now, and to be honest I cannot change. I am used to that old way of doing things. You can't teach an old dog new tricks. I am also finding it difficult to get used to the new style of management here. I find that we don't really know what we are supposed to be doing anymore and there is no more discipline in the unit. We were promised when we joined the unit that after five years we could be transferred wherever we wanted to go. But that has not happened. I have been trying to get transferred for a few years now, but they won't let me go. I think this is really unfair. I should be able to leave. You can't stay in a unit like this for so many years. Look at me now, I am still a Sergeant. I have no career path in the unit anymore. Only Indians are being promoted. At the moment, they have put an Indian in charge

of the bike unit. I tell you, he knows nothing about biking at all. This is very frustrating. At this point, if I were given any job outside of the force, I would leave the force altogether.

I tell you, I am going to apply to transfers to any other specialised unit until I get it. Even if this means filling in forms for the next month. When I joined this unit it was great. We were just like a family. I need to be somewhere where there is a strong team spirit.

Sergeant Meyer was plainly unhappy, and while there were a number of reasons why he wanted to leave (including his sense that he was unable to change), much of his frustration centred on the current management in the unit. Poor career prospects were a particular point of resentment for a white officer who felt that Indian members were getting preferential treatment. But there were also many Indian members who wanted to leave, both rank-and-file and commissioned officers. In May 1999, I accompanied one of the sections to a township hostel. Driving back afterwards, two Indian Sergeants spoke to me of their desire to leave the unit. One told me that he was currently seeing a psychologist. He was hoping that the psychologist would diagnose him with post traumatic stress disorder and that he would then be found medically unfit. That would enable him to leave the unit with a severance package which he could use as capital to start a small business. The other Indian sergeant asked me if I had any contacts in the Royal Ulster Constabulary as he hoped to apply for a job in Northern Ireland. They both claimed that there were no career prospects in Durban POP.

A number of Indian Captains in the unit also spoke to me about wanting to leave. In November 2000, the Head of Labour Relations left the unit and joined the SAPS Provincial Labour Relations Department. The Head of Training was transferred to POP Headquarters. The Head of Intelligence applied for a job in the Durban City Police, but wasn't accepted. Another Captain told me that he was saving money so that he would be able to open a fast food franchise. These high levels of discontent and apathy indicated a lack of commitment at all levels and were undoubtedly one more obstacle to transformation.

Successful organisational change depends very much on the level of individual members' commitment to the transformation, since the changes must be geared toward 'restructuring' the people as much as the organisation. For individuals to come on board the organisation has to be experienced as a 'holding environment' –

somewhere safe, accepting and trustworthy (Stapley, 1996) – and it is management and leadership who have to create that holding environment. A good holding environment is one that has structure (predictability) and offers members a sense of security and protection while encouraging individual growth and identity. If the holding environment is not perceived to be 'good enough', organisation members will seek to develop a culture that serves them best under the circumstances. They may resist changes in various ways – rejecting responsibility, eschewing identification with the organisation – if they see no corresponding outreach to them on the part of the organisation. Alternatively, a poor holding environment may produce an overwhelming fear of being wrong which eclipses any appreciation of the need for change and leaves organisation members apathetic and dependent (Stapley, 1996; Hogg and Terry, 2000). This kind of organisational environment leaves people feeling that changes are simply being imposed on them over which they have very little control. In the case of Durban POP, many members clearly felt that the unit environment was unsupportive and took no account of them as individuals. The response was their lack of commitment and inclination simply to get out.

Ultimately, police members have to register the positive impact of new ways of doing things. There has to be positive feedback from managers and supervisors when changed behaviour is attempted, and, if possible, positive reinforcement from the recipients of police services. Police need to be aware that new methods do in fact work. This often requires a fundamental rethinking of systems of reward and indicators of 'good' performance (Bayley, 1994). Otherwise, as with Durban POP, police members (particularly at the lower levels) remain in doubt about what desirable behaviour is. Conversely, they may disregard new objectives since their performance is not monitored, sanctioned or rewarded.

Much of the responsibility in all this rests with front-line supervisors, who need to be both encouraging of good work and familiar with the work that their 'teams' are engaged in. This involves frequent discussions about problems and opportunities, and ways of responding to these. Goldstein argues that good police leaders during times of transition must be

> comfortable in criticising the past, confident in their grasp of the complexity of the police function, and open to new ideas. They must be willing to invest substantial time to studying the behaviour problems their agencies must handle, to search for new responses to them, and to evaluating these responses.

They must be prepared to abandon long-held notions about the nature of some problems when confronted with the hard data that redefine them, and be open to challenges of the value of existing responses. And, they must be willing to assume some of the risks entailed in departing from traditional policing (1990: 155).

Supervision is of course just one important ingredient in changing police culture. It may assist in changing what Chan refers to as the *habitus*, but the *field* also needs to change (see Chapter 3). There must be clarity about policy; civil oversight bodies must be vigilant in monitoring police behaviour; government must demonstrate commitment to equal treatment of all and to eradicating poor practice in public services. Citizens must be given both the opportunity and the resources to challenge bad behaviour on the part of the police, making it plain that they will not tolerate police misconduct, but also showing respect and sympathy for the police where those are due. The police must, in turn, know very clearly and specifically what their legal powers are. Finally, there needs to be both co-operation and unity of purpose internally within the police agency – not easy to achieve when there are internal social cleavages, such as those based on race and race thinking, which will be the focus of the next chapter.

9

Division in the Ranks

WHEN I FIRST encountered Durban POP in 1996, I was struck by the very lopsided composition of the unit. The Unit Commander was a white man and his middle managers were either white or Indian men. Most women members were concentrated in administrative positions, though there were a few, around a dozen, who worked operationally in a unit of over 860 members. The majority of members at lower ranks were African men.

By 2001, Durban POP looked rather different. The Unit Commander and his deputy were both African men. Middle management was far more diverse and even included two high-ranking African women Commanders. The lower ranks remained mainly African and there were very few white members left in the unit. Equal opportunity and affirmative action policies had clearly had an impact on the social base of the unit. However, spending time with the unit and observing them more closely it became clear to me that more fundamental cultural change was extremely slow and that the unit remained deeply fragmented. This deeper level disunity in the ranks presented Durban POP with a major transformation challenge – freeing the organisation of discriminatory practices and codes and creating a public agency representative of the broader South African population.

Given the history of racial discrimination in the South African public service (and in South African society more generally), for many police members transformation signified affirmative action and the representation of black (and to a lesser extent women) police officers at all levels of the SAPS. While it was generally accepted that adapting to community policing practice was the cornerstone of police transformation, there was also a widespread belief in the SAPS that transformation was synonymous with affirmative action (Van Kessel, 2001).

A demographically representative police force is not necessarily a legitimate or effective one (Cashmore, 1991). Nevertheless, there are at least three reasons why it is important to look at questions of representivity and affirmative action in Durban POP. Firstly, both were noted by unit members themselves as salient markers of transformation. Secondly, representivity was a key element of the stated goals of police transformation in South Africa. Thirdly, and perhaps most importantly, discrimination and group stereotyping internal to the police themselves are liable to extend also to their interactions with the community they serve; if there are prejudices the police fail to transcend in their own organisation, it is unlikely that they will provide a fully equitable, non-discriminatory service to the public.

It is hardly surprising that discriminatory codes and practices persisted in Durban POP, and indeed throughout the police service. The cultural knowledge of the police has been infused over many decades with racist and sexist assumptions and stereotypes. As Brogden and Shearing point out, there is a legacy in the police in South Africa of white Afrikaner (male) ascendancy. Since the 1920s and 1930s, they contend, white police have been recruited who have been socialised to believe that their 'special mission is to safeguard white (and especially Afrikaner) civilization against "*die Swart Gevaar*" (the Black Peril) . . . [P]otential recruits to the SAP were heavily indoctrinated into police racism' (1993: 44). This racist culture was (and continues to be) reinforced in the police canteen and in daily police work. Black members, say Brogden and Shearing, willingly adopted this racist police culture in their concern to prove themselves as members of the force. There was further reinforcement from the religious and political discourses of white rule in South Africa – a world-view the police service itself was internally structured to reflect. White police officers had higher status and greater life chances.

Police cultural knowledge likewise embraces gender-prejudicial values and assumptions that give rise to chauvinist practices and ideologies. This is for the most part a reflection of the sexist nature of the broader social environment. The South African cultural context has been, and continues to be, strongly male chauvinistic – 'a man's country' (Morrell 2001: 18).

This sexism, and the masculinities it generated, was reproduced in all institutions in South African society. In the police, women were excluded from operational duty, clustered in the lowest ranks of the force and expected to conform to traditionalist 'feminine' conduct and appearances (Cawthra, 1993). Until the late 1980s, unmarried mothers were not accepted into the police force. Women officers were expected to obtain approval from their senior male officers before they could marry, and police standing orders insisted that they wear skirts which restricted their ability to work operationally.

In general terms, South African society is characterised by deep social cleavages at every level and in all institutions. Bowling et al. (2001) argue that where societies are divided by ethnic, class and racial differences, it is to be expected that the police service too will be affected by these divisions. If police officers share existing stereotypes about ethnicity and gender, this is very likely to influence the ways in which officers from different backgrounds relate to one another. Police prejudice is not simply the expression of individual racist or sexist attitudes, it reflects the racism and prejudice of the society from which police are drawn, together with the localised experiences that police have in working with particular groups in society (Chan, 1997).

Racist and sexist practices have become institutionalised, even formalised, in police organisations, and institutional racism and sexism is very difficult to dislodge. Explicit manifestations of racism and sexism in policy, and less explicit, 'informal' practices persist; racism and sexism, however subtle and indirect, are still pervasive and they are practiced by overtly prejudiced individuals. They are also entrenched in the general mode of operations of police organisations and even when they are, often enough, unintentional or even unwitting they are no less damaging than more formalised racial policies (Lea, 2000). In the South African police, an interplay between existing police culture, institutional practices and codes, and the social and political environment continues to preserve racial and gender cleavages.

Police representivity and equality in context

Since the 1960s there have been attempts in many Western democracies[1] to boost representation of minorities in police services. This coincided with deteriorating relations between the police and minorities, particularly in Britain and the United States (Decker and Smith, 1980; Brown, 1997). Police authorities, policing analysts and policy makers all agree that for the police to build good relationships with minorities in the communities that they serve, it is essential to recruit officers from minority communities. According to Weitzer, since the 1960s in the United States

> an official consensus has emerged on the value of proportional representation of minority officers in the cities they serve: Greater diversity is expected to

result in improvements in police treatment of minorities and also to provide a symbolic sense of 'ownership' of police departments (2000: 313).

Yet despite affirmative action and equal opportunity programmes, women and minorities continue to be under-represented in Western police services. In England and Wales in March 2000, ethnic minorities made up only 2 per cent of police personnel despite the fact that they represent around 7 per cent of the economically active population (Bowling et al., 2001). In the United States, where affirmative action and equal opportunity policies for women have existed since the 1960s, it was estimated that in 1990, women represented only about 10 per cent of police personnel. The proportion of women in supervisory roles was also very small – approximately 3.3 per cent at municipal level and 0.7 per cent at the state level (Prenzler, 1995).

The continued under-representation of ethnic minorities and women in police services can be attributed to patriarchal and Western norms permeating all aspects of police work. Neither supervisory officers nor their seniors appear to be concerned with challenging and changing these aspects of police culture (Bowling et al., 2001). The lack of interest of police managers and supervisors in dealing decisively with the discriminatory aspects of police culture is a serious impediment to transforming police organisations.

Police leaders play a major role in embedding and reinforcing organisational culture and there are a number of mechanisms through which they do this. What leaders pay attention to and measure; their reactions to critical incidents and organisational crises; role-modelling and teaching; criteria for allocation of rewards; criteria for selection and promotion: all these influence police assumptions, values and schemas (Schein, 1997). Ultimately, police leaders are responsible for integrating the different sub-cultures 'by encouraging the evolution of common goals, common language and common procedures for solving problems' (Schein, 1997: 275). Police managers must themselves be committed to reform and capable of generating involvement and participation of force members if they are to play much part in tilting things in the direction of genuine equity and tolerance of diversity.

Representation and discrimination in the South Africa police

The South African police have also had to confront issues of representivity. Relating to the recruitment of women, these issues are played out along similar lines to those in typical Western democracies. Racial representivity, however, has been a different matter. There have always been a significant number of black policemen in the South African state police. Black police were recruited even in the time of the British colonial administrations. By the late 1980s, there were almost equal numbers of white and black police. By 1995, the SAPS was 35 per cent white, 54 per cent African, 8 per cent Coloured and 3 per cent 'Asian' (Cawthra, 1997).

Although black police have always been a component in the police forces in South Africa, the way they have been treated presents a long history of discrimination. No training was provided to black police until the late 1930s, nor were black police members expected to be literate, which institutionalised career inferiority. They were not allowed to arrest white people, and they could enforce the law only in certain designated geographic areas: until the late 1970s they wore different uniforms. And they earned roughly two-thirds of the pay of their white colleagues (Brewer et al., 1988).

Black police were excluded from certain career rungs. Not until 1978 did the SAP appoint its first black Major; its first black Lieutenant Colonel was appointed in 1980 (Brewer et al., 1988). In 1980, the first black police officer was given authority over white police and the first black station commander was appointed in the same year (Brogden and Shearing, 1993). In 1993, white officers occupied 93 per cent of the highest-ranking positions in the SAP (Scharf and Cochrane, 1993). The low representation of black police in management structures has been the most enduring legacy of institutional racism in the South African police.

Accompanying the 1994 political transition were concerns about the representation of historically disadvantaged groups. The new government was particularly concerned that there should be adequate representivity and equity in the public service (including the police), and a number of formal interventions were introduced to eradicate racism and sexism. Chapter 10 of the White Paper on the Transformation of the Public Service singles out 'representativeness [as] one of the main foundations of a non-racist, non-sexist and democratic society, and as such . . . one of the key principles of the new Government' (1995: 52).

Targeted groups (black people, women and people with disabilities) were, through affirmative action programmes, to be identified and appointed at all levels of the public service. The White Paper also outlines a timeframe for affirmative action: 'within four years, all departmental establishments must endeavour to be at least 50 per cent black at management level'. During this same period, at least 30 per cent of new recruits to middle management and senior management echelons should be women.

Following the Constitution and the various White Papers pertaining to the public service, legislation applying to the SAPS states that there should be representivity at all levels of the service, including the highest, to reflect the diversity of South African society. Affirmative action programmes were the means to confront the legacy of inequality, but linked directly, too, to the need for better performance on the part of the police. In the words of the 1998 White Paper on Safety and Security, 'improving service delivery is directly related to the creation of a representative, democratic and accountable Department of Safety and Security' (1988: 2).

In 1997, the SAPS decided to formulate its own equity policy in line with the general directives for the public service. The SAPS Credo for Affirmative Action (1997) states that by 2000, the service shall attain a minimum of 50 per cent black personnel at management level. Women should comprise 30 per cent at middle and senior management levels. Paradoxically, it was predominantly white police managers who were responsible for ensuring this took place, which also meant that white managers were responsible for phasing themselves out – a difficult task to imagine. To speed this up, processes were subsequently set in place for fast track promotions, accelerated management training and shadow postings.

When the transformation of the South African police began in the mid-1990s after the elections, the issues confronting the service were less about numerical representation of black police members and more about the proportion of black officers at the top levels and about rooting out discriminatory practices against black police. Gender numerical representation was also made a priority for the new police service.

By 1998, there had been only limited achievement. The total SAPS force was roughly 130 000. Nearly 70 per cent were black (African, Indian and Coloured). But in high-ranking and leadership roles black members were still significantly under-represented. Of a total of 12 182 commissioned officers, only a third (4 064) were black (Marks, 1998). This meant that those in the steering positions were still for the most part white. This problem was even more acute at the level of middle management. At Superintendent level, for example, of 2 530 officers, three-quarters (1 928) were white.

The poor representation of black officers in management positions led to accusations of racism in the SAPS and in 1998, an Independent Commission of

Inquiry into Racism in the SAPS was appointed. The Commission found that institutional racism was indeed widespread in the service and evident in the rank breakdown according to race. The Commission concluded that 'the occupational pyramid of the SAPS displays a white apex with an overwhelming black base... from the rank of Sergeant down to that of the Constable, white officers are under-represented by a margin of 10 and 20 percentage points respectively below what their normal representation in these ranks should be' (Report of the Independent Commission of Inquiry into Racism in the SAPS, 1999: 22).

The 'white apex' in the SAPS fed into experiences and perceptions of racism amongst black members in the SAPS:

> The promotion of Indian and white officers over Africans is a long-standing grievance. Since its inception in 1994, the provincial government's Safety and Security Portfolio Committee, which has representatives from all seven of the provinces' political parties, has repeatedly voiced its concern about racially-biased police promotions and appointments. They have criticised the lack of affirmative action policies in the force, of training programmes and of transparency – especially the failure to provide accurate statistics on the racial breakdown of police management. Chris Serfontein, KwaZulu-Natal Provincial Commissioner, finally released statistics to the committee on February 2 1999 showing that out of 182 police stations in the province only 29 had African station commanders... Jacob Zuma, the ANC provincial leader went further... he accused the police of deliberately attempting to sow racial divisions between Africans and Indians. The promotion of Indian police officers into senior positions had been designed to raise tensions between them and their African colleagues, he said (Helen Suzman Foundation, n.d).

The discriminatory practices in the SAPS were an ongoing point of mobilisation for the police unions, the Police and Prisons Civil Rights Union (POPCRU) in particular.[2] Despite the serious repercussions it was likely to have for its members, POPCRU eventually decided to resort to industrial action in protest at the continued appointment of what they called white racist officers to management positions. Over a period of nine months in 1998, POPCRU in KwaZulu-Natal embarked on a number of actions against local and provincial police management. This included an illegal sit-in at police headquarters.

The purpose of the sit-in was to demand the resignation of the provincial commissioner on the grounds of what POPCRU alleged was his unwillingness to transform the service (*Mercury*, 11 May 1998). On another occasion POPCRU members engaged in a work-to-rule action at the main Durban police station: about 100 members left their workstations and congregated in front of the main gate, disrupting services and blocking access. This time the grievance was the promotion of white officers and the poor representation of black police in management positions (*Daily News*, 5 May 1998). Subsequently, 29 members who had taken part in the collective action were dismissed from the police. But this time police management did commence a series of discussions with the unions about fast tracking the affirmative action process. In October 1998, POPCRU launched a national programme of action. One of its main campaigns was described by spokesman Siyavuya Jafta as taking a 'decided sweep at the old guard of the police force notorious for its racism' (*Mercury*, 31 October 1998).

High-ranking officers also created their own representative organisations to fight against racism. In June 1998, the Black Officers' Forum (BOF) was launched. The BOF was likewise concerned at the lack of affirmative action. But unlike POPCRU, they were more troubled that black police in management positions were 'not challenging the existing culture and power relations within the organisation' (Marks, 1998). The BOF opposed what founding member Mpho Mutle called 'token affirmative action' whereby black members of the police were placed in management positions, not having had appropriate training to carry out their functions.

On the issue of gender representivity, the SAPS official website noted in November 2001 that women made up 12 per cent of the total organisation, which compares well with the pattern in Western police services (www.saps.org.za/profile/icomp.htm). But they were notably under-represented in the specialised units and were in short supply at high-ranking levels. A Provincial Status Report on Transformation in the South African Police Service in KwaZulu-Natal for the period June 1998 to May 1999 noted that women were barely represented in the senior management echelons despite affirmative action. Women constituted a total of 5 per cent of senior management in the province of KwaZulu-Natal.

Annie get your gun – Women in Durban POP
Very few women chose to join Durban POP. By May 2000, there were only nineteen women officers in the unit, which had a total strength at that stage of 816 members. Of those nineteen, only seven were operational. This is not surprising: Jefferson

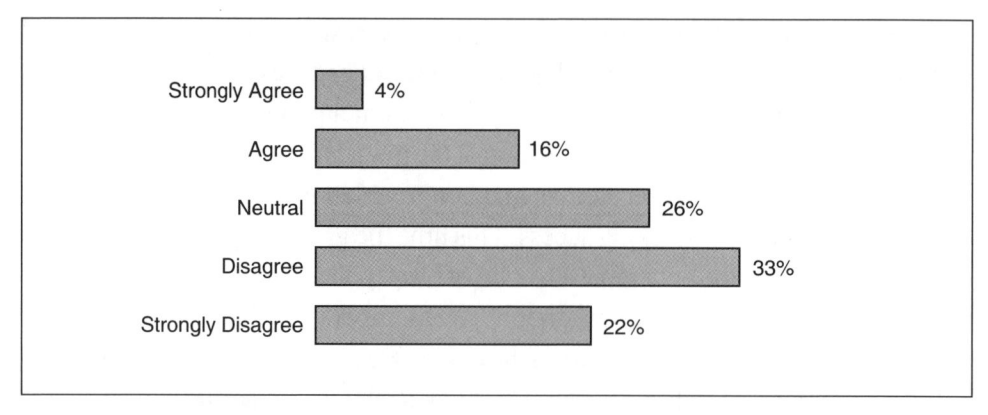

Strongly Agree	4%
Agree	16%
Neutral	26%
Disagree	33%
Strongly Disagree	22%

Figure 9.1: 'Easy for women to gain acceptance in POP.'

remarks that paramilitary police units are 'the province of men' (1990: 115) and that the entry of women into these units will inevitably be resisted. Members of Durban POP who were surveyed (almost all men) acknowledged that women coming into the unit would face difficulties (Figure 9.1). Male officers, for the most part, seemed to think that if there was any role for women in the unit it was merely to create a tranquil environment. In general, rank-and-file members simply considered them a nuisance. Asked why so few women joined the unit, a male Inspector told me:

> We do not have a need for women in the unit. If you work in the township, what is a woman supposed to do there? A female cannot go into the township and do what a male can do. Men see it as disrespectful to take an order from a woman. Although we sometimes do have a need for women in the unit. This is particularly important when we do searches on women in the community. Females can also look after the criminals when they are arrested. When we penetrate a house and there are kids and women inside, female members can calm them down . . . Female members get associated with a mother figure which can be important. There are those advantages to having women in the unit. But, I would say that there are more disadvantages to having them in the unit than there are advantages.[3]

Yet even against these odds, a few women did elect to join the unit. Women were first allowed to be part of the specialised public order unit in the early 1990s, but were restricted to administrative duties. It was only in 1995 that policewomen were permitted to participate in the operational duties of Durban POP and they encountered notable antipathy from men in the unit. Inspector Marike Vosloo, one of the first white women who opted to work operationally, shared her experience with me:

> I was one of the first three women to work outside in the unit. That was in 1995. Prior to that we were only allowed to work in the operational room and in administration. And, it was only in 1994 that we were allowed to work in the ops room. It was a big fight to get to this point. We had to fight with management. The Provincial Director of the Public Order Police unit was opposed to this initially. I think it was because he had a daughter of his own and he was worried about the dangers of working outside. He is very protective, you see. Initially it was only white women who wanted to work outside. Personally, I wanted to work outside because I didn't join the police to work in an office. Why did we get trained in SWAT and other things if we couldn't get to utilise our skills? But, I can tell you, it wasn't easy to become part of the platoons . . . You get tired of being a woman in a male's world. If a man can run 100 metres, you have to run 150 metres. You need to show all the time that you have the ability to do things like a man, even better. The first mistake you make, men come down hard on you. You see, a lot of men in the unit don't want to work with females. They feel that they need to protect you all the time and this makes their work more difficult. When you divide into groups, men will not choose you to go into their groups.[4]

African women who became operational in the unit later that same year corroborated Inspector Vosloo's experiences:

> *Monique*: How did it feel to join POP as a woman?
> *Sergeant Mary Nene*: Hey, we were very much afraid. I remember when we first arrived from the college, they told us that they really don't like to have women in the unit and that there was a certain officer that did not take shit from anyone. We were very frightened then . . . I just knew that I had to do what I was told. Before that, I was working in the leave office in the unit writing leave forms for people when they were sick. We were not allowed to do operational work at that time. They used to make us make tea and whenever there was an operation they would say: 'No you ladies can't go out.' So, we said 'No man, we were trained to be police not tea ladies.'

> But in those days, they wouldn't let us go out. We just had to sit there and do admin, make tea and such things. This was very painful for us. So, one day, my friend said: 'No Mary, this is enough. I am going straight to the Commander and ask him whether I was trained as a tea women or a police officer.' Then after that they stopped telling us that we can't go outside. But they still argued that keeping us in admin was for our own safety. So, we said, 'No, we want to go outside. When we joined the police we wanted to serve the community. How can we serve the community making tea for the officers?' Eventually in October 1995, we were allowed to join the platoons . . . Most men think that they are better than the females, but we are proving them wrong.[5]

Getting into Durban POP and working there was tough for women members. The discrimination which confronted them subsequently led to distinct schisms in the unit as male members closed ranks in their own status groups. This was certainly one factor in the continuing low levels of representation of women in the unit and the general lack of gender diversity in the platoons.

Intra-organisational factors were not the only ones that determined gender representivity. Whether or not women would or could enter the unit and work operationally was also, to an extent, dependent on their individual family circumstances. The demands of the job called for partners who were supportive both emotionally and physically (especially in terms of sharing household responsibilities). Inspector Marike Vosloo, despite her passion for operational work, decided to return to administrative work in January 2001 because, as a single parent, she felt the demands of the job were impacting negatively on her daughter's well-being:

> Earlier this year, I had to go back to administrative duties in the unit. You see, I am a single mother and my daughter started to be very anxious about my work. You see, I had a boyfriend in the unit. He got shot and my daughter was very upset by this. Every time I put on my uniform, she would cry and tell me not to get shot. She doesn't have a father and so I think she worries a lot about me getting hurt or dying. So, for her sake, I stay in an admin job now. I see myself primarily as a mother, and then as a policewoman. If I was married with a supportive husband maybe that would be different. But, to be

honest, I am bored in admin. I really want to be operational but what can I do?[6]

Captain Modise, on the other hand, had an accommodating husband and this freed her up to work in an unpredictable environment with long periods of absence from home:

> I think what scares a lot of women about the unit is the night shift and the times that you have to go away. But there is nothing wrong with the night shift. It is the same as the day shift. But you have to have somebody like your husband on your side. If your husband is angry at you doing night shifts, you won't be able to do anything. You will just have to work in administration. On my side, it is another story because my husband supports me in the work that I do. He is a good man with a big heart. Sometimes he stays with the kids for a month, or for two weeks, and he doesn't complain. But you have to compromise. You have to see that the house is in order before you leave. The cooking and washing must be done and then you can convince your husbands, motivate them.[7]

Although rank-and-file policemen seemed sceptical about incorporating women into operational work, management were supportive. Captain Modise was in fact one of the first woman Platoon Commanders to be appointed in the country. In 2000 she was promoted to Company Commander, and in 2001 another African woman was appointed as a Company Commander. The Unit Commander told me that it was very important to encourage women in the unit and to try to recruit more:

> We really need more women like Captain Modise in the unit. We noticed early on that she had excellent potential. So, we promoted her to Platoon Commander. Men in the unit were not very happy at first, but look now, she is one of our best Platoon Commanders. Most of the members in her platoon are happy and they are doing very well. I wish we could find more women like her to incorporate in the unit. But, it is not easy to find women who want to join this unit.[8]

Captain Modise greatly appreciated the support she had received from the unit management. She believed that she had demonstrated her competence as a

Commander and that men in the unit would, as a result, shed their gendered assumptions. She also thought that women bring 'special qualities' and skills to the unit:

> At the time I became Platoon Commander, the platoon was full of members who used to drink on duty and misbehave. That platoon was restructured and I was put in charge. I did not feel afraid that I had been given such difficult men to deal with because everything depends on motivation and I am able to motivate my men at all times. And things have happened. I have turned the platoon around. Now there is discipline and productivity in the platoon. The platoon was useless before. So now I have seen that I joined the unit, became a Platoon Commander and I have worked with these members and things have changed. In the beginning they were unwilling to co-operate with me . . . They came to see that no, this woman is good and is even better than a man. She understands, she listens, she can cope with our difficulties . . . I can do anything they can do. Look how fat I am but I am fit and I am excellent in weapon training . . . I actually feel that at least half the Platoon Commanders in this unit should be women. We would then achieve a lot. There will be no booking off sick and no taking long leave. You know what happens now? If I am not at work, my members phone me at home and ask, 'Mammie, why are you not at work? We are missing you a lot. Please tell us that tomorrow you are coming' . . . So, I can say that if we put more women in the field, society will gain a lot. If I go to the university to solve a certain problem, students don't go crazy because of the wonderful thing they see before their eyes. Instead of seeing a man with a gun, they see a woman smiling, waving hands and talking to them nicely. In all instances, people co-operate with me.[9]

Analysts who focus on police gender issues would recognise Captain Modise's sentiments. Jennifer Brown, for example, argues that while men in police organisations tend to concentrate on 'external issues and prefer to exchange hard information, women talk to establish or reinforce a personal connection or exchange experience' (1997: 23). She is therefore a strong advocate of equal opportunity policies as holding out a real possibility for creating better working environments.

Antagonism persisted in Durban POP despite – or for some members because of – the example of Captain Modise. According to Inspector Marike Vosloo:

Division in the Ranks 229

Many males feel negative toward Captain Modise. They are threatened by her and perhaps there is also jealousy toward her. They feel she has been fast tracked unjustifiably just because she is a black woman. They don't understand how oppressed we women have been in the police for such a long time and that we deserve a break. Men in the unit think very negatively about women in the unit. They think we are promiscuous and that we get where we are by sleeping with men. Do you know what they call women in the unit? State mattresses! Can you believe that? They really treat us with no respect. But, I have to say that when you work consistently with them in the field, they do eventually change their attitudes toward you.[10]

Even though management did seek to improve gender representivity and tackle gender stereotyping, women continued to be under-represented in the unit and men continued to question their presence. Affirmative action, unsurprisingly, triggered resentments; Crosby and Clayton (1990) are not the only commentators to note how it can often have negative consequences, provoking or reinforcing prejudice and drawing attention to someone's minority status, while those not targeted by affirmative action feel frustrated and unfairly victimised (see also Taylor, 1995).

The gender divisions in Durban POP were still very apparent five years after the transformation process was first set in motion. It is unlikely that Durban POP or any other public order police unit in South Africa will ever attain the target of 30 per cent representation of women as set in the Credo for Affirmative Action. However, appointing women to supervisory positions and including them in operational work will quite probably produce a shift in the organisational culture of the SAPS, particularly in the gendered dictionary knowledge of both men and women officers.

Racial division in the organisational field

Chan (1996) argues that racist cultures are likely to persist in police organisations so long as the 'field' in which police work remains racially prejudiced and stratified. The organisational field of Durban POP was racially determined in two ways: the working platoons were racially constituted and supervisors in the unit generally were not trained in the management of race relations.

Table 4.2 indicates the racial profile by rank of Durban POP in May 2000: Africans 53 per cent overall, Indians 37 per cent, whites 9 per cent, and Coloured members just 1 per cent of the unit. While the Unit Commander was African, Indian members occupied the majority of top and middle management positions. This meant that most of the Platoon and Company Commanders were Indian. This, as we shall see, created antagonism and resentment between the various race/ethnic groups.

A further structural problem was that, as of March 2001, the platoons and companies were still racially skewed (Figure 9.2). Of the 37 white members who were operational in the unit, 32 were in the specialised platoons. The Charlie and Delta companies were almost entirely constituted by African members. Although Indian members were present in all companies they were poorly represented in the Delta Company and barely represented in the Field and Reaction Platoons. The

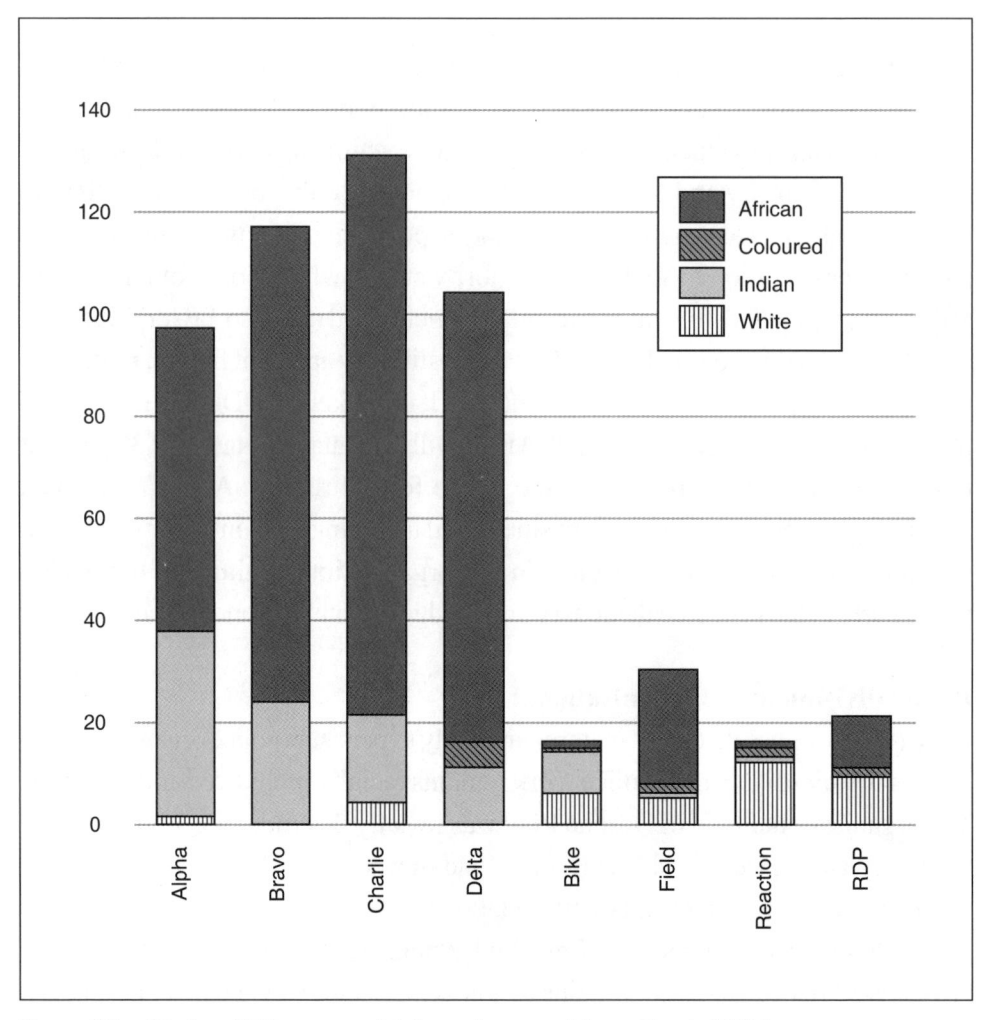

Figure 9.2: 'Durban POP company/platoon demographics – March 2001.'

over-representation of white members in the specialised platoons led to much controversy in the unit. African and Indian members complained that white members were getting preferential treatment since these specialised platoons had better resources than the others. Officers in these platoons also got more overtime payment. The following conversation took place when I joined a largely African staffed platoon on a crime prevention operation in KwaMashu township:

> 14/09/2000
> *Sergeant Ngema*: You see, white members are all in this RDP platoon. They come into the area for a short time and then they leave again. If there are any problems with the way in which they conduct themselves, we who are permanently in the area have to deal with it once they leave. We [African members] are the ones who have to work in dirty conditions and at the end of a shift we have grease all over our uniforms and have to go home and wash them before we can wear them again the next day. The RDP unit are always clean. They don't get to do the dirty work. They are also paid overtime for the same work that we do all the time but don't get paid extra for. So, we can only say that blacks and whites are treated differently in the unit.
>
> *Monique*: What about Indian members? Are they treated differently to African members?
> *Sergeant Ngema*: Well, look at the unit. What do you see? Indian members are all doing office jobs. I think that is not right.

The precedent that had been set in Durban POP was that officers worked most often with others of the same racial group. Despite the animosity that this created within the unit, officers also spoke of feeling dislocated when members of the same racial reference group as themselves were not present. As a white Sergeant informed me,

> This unit has changed a lot in the last few years. One big change is that there are no white members anymore. I don't mean to be racist, but now I feel like an outsider in the unit. Before there were a lot of whites. I enjoyed being

with them. We spoke the same language. At the moment, I feel like a German in Zambia. Most of the white members have left, and in the unit where I work, I am the only white member at the moment.[11]

Around the middle of 2000, the Unit Commander began to inform rank-and-file platoon members that he intended to restructure the platoons to make sure that racial integration did take place, hoping that this would put an end to the perceptions of preferential treatment. However, officers in the specialised platoons made it clear to me that they would do everything in their power to prevent this. The following conversation was recorded in my research diary:

15/05/2000
Inspector Botha: Monique, do you know that the new Unit Commander is thinking of disbanding the RDP unit as part of his restructuring plan?

Monique: I have heard that.
Inspector Botha: That is very stupid of him. We are the hardest working and most productive members in the unit. Let me show you our performance records. (Takes out a book with recordings of their 'successes'). Last month we arrested 43 suspects, recovered 25 vehicles and recovered 18 guns. Now, that is what you call productive. The other guys in the unit don't have half of our recoveries and arrests. In fact, probably the whole unit together doesn't get the same results as us.
Monique: You may be right.
Inspector Botha: Well, the Unit Commander will never succeed in shutting us down. We will cause chaos in the unit if he tries to do this. We will get the support of the Area Commissioner and the KwaMashu community and we will organise a petition.
Monique: That sounds pretty serious. Why do you think the Unit Commander wants to disband you in the first place?
Inspector Botha: Because these fucking lazy Indians have got it in for us. They claim that we get preferential treatment in the unit. What they don't report is how productive we are and that we are really

committed to being policemen. These Indians have no stamina. They have no backbone. They won't do anything that is a little bit dangerous. They don't take risks. It is their nature to be like this. Those Indian Captains are just pathetic. They don't know what they are doing but it is only Indians that are promoted in this unit. But when there is a real problem, they call us okes [guys] to come and sort it out.

Sergeant Marais: I can tell you one thing, if they close down our platoon, I will take permanent sick leave. There is no way that I will go and work with those guys in the other platoons.

Members of the specialised platoons had a vested interest in ensuring that they were not disbanded. They were comfortable with their platoon colleagues and they felt they had developed a good modus operandi. But what they had really created was closed status group within the unit, and their language was loaded with negative stereotypes about other groups (racial and functional) in the unit.

The racial clustering into particular companies and platoons meant that integration was limited in the daily working lives of members of the unit, which undermined the effort to create racial diversity and equality. This in turn compromised the overall organisational change programme since diversity itself can be such a potent generator of solutions and opportunities (Kiel, 1994; Schein, 1997).

A second structural problem in the unit was that middle and top management had received no diversity training and felt ill-equipped to deal with racial tensions. They were as much products of their environment (social, political and organisational) as were their subordinates, with no extra skill in resolving or mediating racial tensions in the platoons – or at being role models for racial reconciliation. In fact, a number of Platoon Commanders told how much they felt at a loss to resolve the racial cleavages in their platoons or handle accusations of racism.

There were various occasions when I noticed that both unit leaders and rank-and-file members socialised only with colleagues of the same racial groups. Even where platoons contained members of all racial groups, during rest periods members invariably chose to associate only with those of their own reference group which was usually racially determined. I recorded the following observation in my research diary:

11/05/2000

Things settled down a bit on the campus and the unit retreated to the sports field. The Platoon Commanders had instructed members to withdraw and to relax until they were called upon to intervene. It was by now about 13:00 and some members decided it was time to have something to eat. They took out their lunch and started to share with one another. I noticed that Indian members sat with one another and shared with one another, across the rank boundaries. I asked the Indian Platoon Commander present if his platoon was made up only of Indian members. He pointed to a vehicle where about ten African members were sitting. I asked why they were sitting separately from him and his peers. I was told that African and Indian members seldom mix socially and that this would take at least fifteen years to come right . . . The African members were sitting in the Nyalas [armoured vehicles] talking; some were lying with their eyes closed. African members were in one vehicle and Indian members were standing around together talking and eating food, which they were sharing with one another. I asked one of the Captains why this was happening and he informed me that this was just how things were and that it was because members come from such different 'cultures'. It became clear to me that even while members from different race groups may work together, there is little attempt or interest on the part of members to develop social relationships across racial divides.

Far from being pace-setters for racial integration, Platoon Commanders, too, tended to retreat into their own reference group comfort zones. Social cleavages remained unchallenged and the dictionary knowledge of members of the unit continued to be infused with stereotypical schemas of 'the other'.

There was rampant racial and ethnic stereotyping in Durban POP. Stereotypes 'explained' divisions and allegiances at all levels. A white Inspector explained to me that white and African police share certain characteristics that are not common among Indian police. That, he argued, was why white and African police are able to work collaboratively:

> White and black members work much better together. It is not a political thing. It is not a racial thing. It is just that they link up much better together. The Indians in this unit are totally useless. When there is a shooting, they are

not willing to give assistance. They are not even prepared to open the door of an armoured vehicle to pull in an injured man into it. They worry about themselves whereas if you look at the Zulu man, he is a warrior. He is not scared of anything. Similarly, a white policeman will not be indoctrinated. He will do what he thinks is right. If somebody shoots at him, he will take the necessary action without hesitation. So, the African and the white have similar thinking and they work very well together. Even if you interviewed an African member, he would tell you that he prefers to work with whites than with Indians . . . There is a lot of talk that Indian members are only concerned about themselves. And Indian members easily become involved in drugs and things like that. Indians will not do things on their own. They are cowards. In my platoon I don't have a single Indian member and I like it like that. A policeman is a breed on his own, I think. You have to have balls. Whites and Africans have balls, but not these Indians.[12]

High-ranking officers were just as much given to stereotyping. The 1998 acting Unit Commander, for example, insisted to me that it wasn't a good idea to deploy a racially diverse group on a long-term project because they had such different social practices:

Say you send the guys out on an operation for a few days, or longer. Say that there are 60 Africans, 39 Indians and one white. Now who does this white guy speak to? Who does he relate to and so on? We would have to keep this white guy back. This is not because it is a racial issue, but because there is not familiarity. Let me give you an example. We whites bath in a bath and we shower in a shower. Africans don't do this. They wash their bodies and their faces in a washbasin. So, there is friction. The guys don't understand these differences. It is just that different people have different cultures. We have to accept these things, Monique.[13]

Instead of challenging stereotypes and building diversity, unit leaders reinforced race thinking by continually invoking those stereotypes. So racial and ethnic self-identities persisted, often rationalised by linking race and ethnicity with 'cultural' practices. As an African trainer in the unit informed me,

> There really is no racial interaction in the unit. I think it is because we come from different cultures. Even the food that we eat is different. Africans like to have meat that is cooked with a fire. Indians like to bring their sandwiches with curry inside. And whites like their own food. Africans like soccer. Indians like volleyball. We are different, and there is nothing that can change this. And then there is also the language barrier. African members feel resentful that they are always expected to speak English and there is no effort by other members to speak Zulu.[14]

What preoccupied these officers, grappling with all the convolutions of change, was, invariably, not diversity but difference – and for them differences were inherent, not socially determined.

Challenging division and discrimination

Despite the fact that Durban POP members from all race groups at all levels subscribed to racial stereotyping, African (and some Indian members) were nevertheless concerned about racial discrimination and inequality in the unit. African members in particular were convinced that affirmative action was taking place too slowly.

Affirmative action and fast track promotion did in fact take place in Durban POP and we have already noted the appointment in January 2000 of an African Unit Commander, made possible by the resignation of the (white) Unit Commander the previous year. The new African Unit Commander was an outsider; he came from another public order unit where he had been a Superintendent and was fast tracked to level of Director, which allowed him to take up the appointment as Unit Commander. Some white and Indian members in the unit regarded this appointment as problematic. A white female inspector told me:

> Members generally are very negative about the black management at the moment. They feel that they haven't been through the proper ranking processes. They feel that the new managers are not here because of ability but because of affirmative action.[15]

An Indian Superintendent predicted that the new Unit Commander would face a lot of difficulties because of his ethnic status:

> I don't think that the new Unit Commander is going to have an easy time. You see, he is a Sotho and most members in this unit are Zulus. Sothos are the softest people around and they don't know how to deal with Zulus. A Zulu will never be happy to take orders from a Sotho.[16]

Despite these views and 'predictions', the new Unit Commander did not in fact face much antagonism or insubordination. African members welcomed his appointment arguing that an African commander would understand their own circumstances better than the previous white Unit Commanders, and also the African communities that were the primary clients of the unit.

In addition, the military structure of the unit once again turned out to have its advantages. Many members, across the racial spectrum, told me that they would respect the authority of the new Unit Commander as they would any other Commander, so long as he performed 'competently'. Those who did feel animosity toward him did not display this openly nor did they challenge his authority. The new Unit Commander was optimistic about his reception by the unit, also announcing his intention to make significant changes:

> I have not had many problems coming into this unit. Most members have welcomed me into this unit. They know that now I am in charge and they have to get used to this. But there are many problems in this unit and there are things that I am going to change, which is going to make some members unhappy. Things must change and eventually members will accept this. We cannot continue to have platoons that are made up of certain racial groupings. We cannot have Indian members in all the management positions. Once I am more familiar with the unit, I am going to shake things up a bit.[17]

In March 2001, he presented a restructuring plan to the unit in which he proposed reshuffling the platoons to improve their racial balance and also disbanding some of the specialised platoons. His restructuring plan was set in motion over the next few months. While officers at all levels indicated to me that they felt unsettled by this restructuring, they did not directly oppose it. What did happen was that most members of the RDP and Reaction Platoons applied for transfers out of the unit into an even more paramilitary and centralised unit, the Provincial Intervention Unit.[18] The number of white members in Durban POP was thus further depleted.

Following the appointment of the new Unit Commander, two senior African officers then joined the unit. In January 2001, Senior Superintendent Zungu was appointed as the new Operational Commander – a key function in a public order police unit. In November 2001, a female Superintendent, Anna Letsholo, was appointed as a Company Commander. Both Senior Superintendent Zungu and Superintendent Letsholo came from Pretoria and were new to Durban POP. Approval for these two appointments had to come from national and regional SAPS management, but Zungu and Letsholo both told me that it was the new Unit Commander who had encouraged them to take up their appointments, which they were more comfortable doing because there was an African Unit Commander. These appointments dramatically altered the profile of the top management echelon of the unit and had a notable effect on the way unit members regarded affirmative action. African members began to feel that affirmative action was now being speeded up and saw it as a real sign that transformation was finally starting to happen:

> I feel now that changes are really happening in the unit. African people are now in positions of power and I hope this means that things will get better for the rest of us in the unit. But we will just have to see how things work out. It is still too early to say, but I would say that African members are feeling more positive now.[19]

White and Indian members, on the other hand, were less enthusiastic, and doubts were expressed about the abilities of the new management.

There were also concerns that giving advantage to members of particular race groups was discrimination in reverse and a signal that the career prospects of members from non-targeted groups would be jeopardised:

> We Indians may as well just leave the unit now. We will never be promoted again. It seems that if you are not African, you have no career prospects in the unit. I am busy looking for other options in the police at the moment. I don't want to stay in this same position forever. I can't grow old doing the same thing and never being promoted. Don't you agree?[20]

Taylor (1995), Holdaway (1991) and Crosby and Clayton (1990) have all noted that affirmative action can produce a backlash from non-beneficiaries who feel frustrated and unfairly treated, and generate fresh animosity that slows transformation.

Structural adjustments and affirmative action tend to be top-down mechanisms of change. But change in Durban POP as it affected representation and equity was not solely top down; there were also initiatives 'from below', such as the Empowerment Committee (see Chapter 8). Its stated aims were to promote equity in the unit and devise ways of improving productivity. Initially the Committee was concerned with the lack of representation of African commissioned officers in middle and top management positions. The minutes of its first meeting, which were circulated to the unit Commanders, declared that 'racism is still rife in the unit and African members are still being discriminated against. We feel that in order for the unit to be truly representative, 70 per cent of the commissioned officers and management should be African'. Nineteen members of the unit attended this first meeting, most of them of Sergeant and Inspector rank. There were three Indian members present.

I was invited to attend the second meeting of the Empowerment Committee. This time 20 members were present. The majority were African and male but there were also two African women, both of them administrative staff, and five Indian members. The main topic was the need for unit managers to undergo management training, since, in the view of the committee, they lacked personnel management and communication skills. According to members present, Platoon Commanders were ignorant about the Public Order Police Policy Document and were consequently failing to give 'appropriate commands and instructions to platoon members'. The second item on the agenda was to plan a meeting with the new Unit Commander at which they would raise their grievances and present their suggestions for change. He would then be aware of their problems and so they would begin a process of consultation. They were confident that the new Unit Commander would take their issues seriously and that he was well placed to speed up transformation and equity in the unit.

The formation of the Empowerment Committee signalled a real need on the part of members in the unit to come together to discuss their concerns and dilemmas. A forum had been needed to represent the collective voice of (black) members in the unit and to allow members the opportunity to contribute to and shape the change process in the unit. The committee was, perhaps, a localised version of the Black Officers' Forum discussed earlier in this chapter. It is difficult to say how effective and influential the Empowerment Committee was but it certainly served as a pressure group and opened up space for discussion. Social change is unlikely to get very far from top-down initiatives alone. Rank-and-file members of police organisations are also agents of change. By their mere existence, groups like the Empowerment Committee present a useful challenge to traditional police hierarchies. They can also keep a watchful eye on management commitment to progressive transformation.

Despite all these initiatives Durban POP was still, as I knew it in 2001, beset by racial and gender splits. These were reinforced by the structural make-up of the unit and by the inability of middle management to come up with more creative ways to organise the unit and manage interactions between its members. Racial, ethnic and gender stereotypes still persisted and continue to legitimise divisions. The deep-rooted assumptions, schemas and values that informed these stereotypes supported a dictionary knowledge very resistant to change.

Racism and sexism, and poor representivity, are perennial hindrances to police transformation. So long as the schemas, perceptions and values of police culture remain unreconstructed, interactions both within the police and between the police and their client communities will be compromised.

10

Conclusion

Contradictions of Police Organisational Change

WHETHER OR NOT the police like the changes that are happening in the arena of their work, change is nonetheless inevitable. For the police in South Africa there is still a long road to travel and various paths that they could follow. If they see that innovations actually work they are more likely to be convinced by reform agendas. The better the feedback (from their managers, from government, from the public) for new approaches, the greater the likelihood of committed transformation. But even then there will be backwards glances to the safety of known ways. Police organisations have an intrinsic cultural capital that does not readily accommodate change, particularly when times are tough. Police transformation is always beset with contradictions and is slower than reformers would prefer.

So, has there been real police transformation in South Africa? Looking back on the story of the Durban POP, we must remember that the SAPS as a whole is a diverse organisation with many different units, each with its own history, each with its own measuring scale for reform. And police change also has to be assessed against the broader socio-political context. In South Africa, the advent of democratic governance and the attendant reforms in the public service both frame and reflect the changes that are taking place within the state police.

In 2004, South Africa celebrated the tenth anniversary of its freedom. There were many reasons to rejoice, not least a new and widely praised constitution; the democratic government has overwhelming electoral support; where once it was universally condemned, the country is now fully integrated into the international arena and its leaders are frequently called upon to guide the peace initiatives of others; and 'more people identify with the nation than ever before' (Klandermans et al., 2001).

Even so, at the coalface of institutional change, particularly of public service organisations, we can begin to discern the limits of state transformation (Klinck, 2001). It is this level of change that will determine whether South Africa continues to be the 'miracle' nation for the world at large.

Jonathan Jansen reminds us that we need to be critical of the idea that government policy is inherently rational and coheres with institutional practice. A host of influences shape institutional practice: the leadership of organisations, public demand, membership buy-in and commitment, resource availability, government dedication to building democratic institutions and fostering community empowerment (Jansen, 2003). Permutations of all these have meant that institutional change in South Africa has been both slower and more uncertain than many had hoped for.

These limitations in state transformation have not gone unnoticed by government itself: a ten-year review of institutional change published by the Policy Co-ordination and Advisory Services (PCAS) in 2003 concludes positively but acknowledges a variety of continuing impediments to institutional transformation:

> most evidence suggests that government has made remarkable progress in transforming the State machinery to make it more responsive to the needs of citizens and to make it more accountable . . . Challenges, however, remain around performance, corporate governance and commitment of some of these institutions to the overall development objectives of government (PCAS, 2003: 12).

The report makes the crucial point that 'transformation is a protracted process' and that 'success has, in the detail, given rise to new challenges' (PCAS, 2003: 74): the reach of institutional change is determined by informal social modes of interaction that precede change processes; both officials and recipients of services may behave in ways that constrain the implementation of new policy (with, on this point, officials in the criminal justice system getting particular mention).

The tone of the report is admirably open and self-reflective; nevertheless, it leaves aside the contradictions of change at the micro level, in particular or local institutions. And it is at this level that important questions remain, which cannot be answered through broad reviews of government sectors: What stories are told and how do they shape behaviour? How do organisational members from different status groups relate to one another? What are the institutionalised labour-management practices and do they favour change objectives? Do organisations have clear targets for change and how is their attainment measured? In short, what are the 'details' that continue to generate fresh challenges?

This book has attempted to answer the big questions about institutional change in South Africa by focusing on the small ones. It is an exploration of a single unit of the SAPS going through a time of fundamental organisational change. It is a tale that (I hope) captures some of the stories, trials and tribulations of the men and women who worked together in the unit and offers some insight into the dilemmas of institutional change in South Africa during the past ten years. I shared in the daily life of Durban POP, looking to understand its structural make-up and comprehend the behaviour and values of its individual members. Readers of this book will, I hope, have some basis for drawing their own conclusions about what may have been achieved of the transformations aimed at in policy and legislation. Maurice Punch says that it is through ethnographic studies that we understand what is happening at the '"sharp end" of policing in diverse settings' (2003: 4), and perhaps, in time, further ethnographies of the South African police will give us a kind of patchwork quilt of 'insider' pictures of police organisational change.

Meantime, I offer here some conclusions about the dilemmas of police transformation in the Durban Public Order Police unit and some suggestions about possibilities for internally generated change in police organisations.

Did Durban POP really change?
There can be little question that there was real transformation in Durban POP, as even the most cursory review of the unit would confirm. The unit of 2001 was barely recognisable from what it had been in its former embodiments, the Riot Unit and the Internal Stability Division. In the first place, the unit was far more representative (in terms of race) of the communities that it served. The majority of its rank-and-file members were African and there was a proportional representation of Indian and white members; even in the top management echelons, high-ranking African officers predominated. Secondly, there was no longer any question of indiscriminate brute force against protesters and demonstrators. Nearly all public order incidents appear in Durban POP incident reports as 'crowd management peaceful' – very seldom were there incidents where injury to person or property resulted from police intervention. Disorderly crowds were quite likely to be regarded now with a positive and patient tolerance previously unimaginable. Thirdly, there were more than just

tokens of 'demilitarisation': camouflage uniforms were a thing of the past and rank divisions less rigidly enforced; unit members were no longer expected to salute their superiors; relations between rank-and-file and management were far more relaxed.

These significant shifts resulted in large part from changes in what Janet Chan refers to as the field, or the structural conditions of policing. The transition to democracy gave a clear signal that new principles of governance were to be incorporated at all levels of South African society. State institutions, in particular, had to show real commitment to equitable, participatory and professional service delivery. The expectation of democratic reform was laid upon all public institutions, both internally (sound and participatory labour relations and representivity) and externally (non-partisan, participatory and accountable service delivery). In the case of the public police, new legislation, training and oversight bodies provided strong external pressure to impel organisational change.

However, training, new policy, even dramatic changes in the mode of national governance, do not automatically translate into real transformational outcomes. Structural changes may come about as a result of these external influences, but the informal values and norms of practice which are embodied in police culture are much more difficult to change, created as they have been through historical daily experiences on the streets and reinforced in the stories the police tell and the memories they hold dear. Police officers are also agents in their own right: they interpret their environment each in their own way, and while welcoming some changes, may well resist or challenge others.

Change in Durban POP (as with any organisation in similar circumstances) was certainly uneven. Sub-groups within the unit (reflecting cleavages of race and gender) had developed their own sets of police 'sub-culture' and each responded differently to the challenge of transformation. Some, especially white members, resisted change by rebuffing management attempts to restructure the platoons. Others felt that transformation (particularly as it related to affirmative action) was happening too slowly, and formed their own representative body, the POP Empowerment Committee, to campaign for speedier action. In consequence, the transformation outcomes were disparate and even contradictory, as became clear to me when I tried to analyse the evolutions of Durban POP cultural knowledge – the unit's assumptions, values, and beliefs.

It was clear there had been a shift in axiomatic knowledge. Unit members seemed to have accepted that the basic rationale for their work had changed. Managing crowds rather than controlling them was plainly the way forward for a more community-oriented style of policing. They knew that political changes meant they now had to do things differently, and their awareness was sharpened by the new legislation and policy directives they had to take on board – legal particulars, as always, being a priority for police officers (Herbert, 1997).

While the changes that took place in the axiomatic knowledge of the unit clearly impacted on other levels of cultural knowledge (dictionary knowledge, directory knowledge, recipe knowledge), change at these other levels was more uncertain. The new emphasis on crowd management and community-oriented policing presupposes shifts in dictionary knowledge (the categories according to which police classify their environment). POP members clung to many of their old assumptions about crowds and about status groups in South African society. Most continued to regard crowd participants as irrational and provocative. Consequently they always went into crowd event operations heavily armed, prepared for the worst possible outcome. For white members particularly, African townships remained barbarous territory where heavy-handed crime prevention was self-evidently justified. From my own ventures with the unit on operations in the African townships I saw for myself that township residents were regularly assaulted and verbally abused. Regression to this kind of policing tended to happen when operations took place away from public scrutiny and in the absence of supervisory oversight. Within the unit, too, members held onto the old stereotypes of race and gender, in turn reinforcing internal cleavages and lingering prejudicial practices at all levels.

Transformation of directory knowledge (informing strategies and tactics) likewise remained shallow. Members had received substantial retraining in new public order policing procedures and tactics, and for the most part, they applied them in their public order operations: the principle of minimum force was generally adhered to; negotiation with relevant stakeholders did take place; and public order policing methods generally conformed to approved international norms. Yet still there were times, as in the case of the student killed at the University of Durban-Westville, when excessive and undue force was used. There were also times, particularly in crime prevention operations, when members of the unit fell back on old practices: dealing out beatings on mere suspicion of criminal intent, wrecking property in forcefully entered homes.

So too, plainly, was the recipe knowledge (conceptions of normative behaviour and basic values) still very imperfectly altered, amongst rank-and-file at any rate.

Officers may have understood and even accepted the political imperatives for developing a human rights culture within the police, but it cannot be said that, by 2001, these values were unconditionally installed. Members of the unit clung to fond recollections of past practices and norms, a majority (see Chapter 7) claiming that that they preferred working in the unit during the apartheid era.

Intractability of norms and cultural knowledge

Why, then, this intractability of norms and cultural knowledge? Before tackling the question, two general points need to be made. In the first place, the state police are, inevitably maybe, part of the repressive apparatus of the state. They are trained and mandated to use force and will do so when they deem this necessary and justifiable. But aside from this, there is also always a multiplicity of factors that shape police behaviour at any point in time: the political opportunity structure; the historic relationship between the police and geographical communities; levels of crime and public disorder; the legal framework; and others besides. So Durban POP was not unique in its regressive attachment to the use of force or its disregard of individual liberties. All the more reason, then, to pinpoint, so far as we can, just what it is, specifically, that keeps members of a unit – of this unit, Durban POP – tied to the old ways and values.

In the case of Durban POP, five principle aspects of the organisational field certainly seemed to contribute to the problem. This was reform initiated by top-down fiat within the unit, without adequate performance indicators, in the context of a still largely unreformed managerial ethos, with much of the old racial and gender stereotyping still persisting both within the service and in the society at large, and with the police still effectively shielded from public criticism and repercussions by the continuing social and economic disempowerment of vulnerable and marginalised communities.

Supervisors and managers in Durban POP *instructed* members of the unit to change their behaviour in line with new legislation and training. These directives were important and behavioural change did result. But it did not go very deep. Lasting change in police behaviour, it would seem, requires close and directive supervision, and, by all accounts, unit supervisors failed to provide ongoing direction to rank-and-file members. Platoon Commanders and Company Commanders were often absent when members were deployed to carry out crowd management and crime prevention operations. While unit members generally (including non-commissioned front-line supervisors) were aware of the general framework that was meant to guide their interventions, they felt unconfident and insecure about responding to old problems in new and unfamiliar ways. Police tend to learn 'on the streets' (Waddington, 1999a) as they carry out their daily work. Changing behaviour that has historically proven to be 'effective' requires direct experience of the positive results of new responses and strategies, with ongoing encouragement and approval from supervisors. There could be very little of this kind of feedback when the supervisors themselves so often failed to turn up for operations in the field. Nor did regular briefings and debriefings take place in Durban POP, so important for learning from mistakes and reinforcing positive results.

Durban POP supervisors and managers failed to develop proper performance indicators. The behaviour of individual members and of the unit as a whole could not therefore be systematically measured and appraised. 'Good behaviour' was accordingly not positively reinforced and deplorable behaviour was at best erratically reproved. Nor did the unit attempt to assess how operational interventions were experienced by its 'clients' – the general public to whom service was rendered. Both direct and indirect performance indicators were lacking.

Leadership style continued to be shaped both by the traditional policing managerial ethos and by the long-established authoritarian management conventions of the South African public service more generally. New directives notwithstanding, Durban POP managers, particularly the middle managers, still held the view that in a paramilitary unit such as POP 'discipline' had to be paramount and that this required strict lines of authority and unquestioning compliance with orders. The few middle managers more willing to experiment with participatory styles of management lacked the knowledge and skills to do so because they had been given no appropriate training or guidance. Nor is this peculiar to the police in South Africa: Cowper notes that police organisations internationally have struggled to break with management style based on 'authoritarian, centralised control of mindless subordinates' (2004: 113). This is because, he argues, they have had little if any leadership or management training yet are routinely confronted with crisis situations. They tend then to 'fall back on top-down decision making and total submission to ensure their authority and status within the hierarchy and retain operational control' (2004: 119). For Durban POP this meant that rank-and-file members were left excluded from decision-making and problem solving. They were not party to discussions as to why and how change would take place in the unit and they certainly did not feel like partners in the change process. Mutual respect, trust and support remained in short supply. This, compounded with the uncertainty generated by change itself, led to low levels of commitment; almost half of the members indicated that they wanted to leave the unit.

We have seen in Chapter 9 how there was a three-way reinforcement and legitimisation of racial and gender stereotyping and division: (a) The racial diversity of the unit was not reflected in many of the platoons. Some were made up of mainly African personnel while in others Indians were the majority. White members dominated the highly specialised platoons, leading to accusations of preferential treatment. (b) Managers and supervisors developed informal or social relationships only with members (rank-and-file included) of their own racial groups. They were unable (and perhaps unwilling) to provide leadership in valuing diversity. (c) Gender representation, particularly with regard to operational functions, was extremely skewed: by February 2002, there were only nine policewomen in operational roles. This low representation of women reinforced assumptions that men are best suited for paramilitary police work. Very little attempt was made to recruit more policewomen even though there were two (African) women Company Commanders – some gender affirmative action at the top, but little that permeated through to the broader social base of the unit.

Finally, although the country saw tremendous political and legislative change in the course of the decade, social and economic conditions remain much as they have been for the majority of citizens, and in some instances have even worsened as levels of unemployment increase. South Africans may have unequalled constitutional assurance of their political and human rights but their access to these has been far more uneven. Poor and marginalised (generally black) people lack the confidence, the knowledge or the resources that would admit them to the networks of power where such rights are effectively still adjudicated, and the police, aware of this limited access, continued to act in ways that flouted an ethos of rights when they policed marginalised groups and communities, secure in the knowledge that the still disempowered would be less likely to challenge abuse and mistreatment. Added to this, individual police officers themselves in so many respects bore the same scars of apartheid as their fellow citizens and were trapped in the same web of unequal access and influence.

While the study of Durban POP cannot be generalised to the entire SAPS, it does highlight some of the impediments to police organisational change. Moreover, the contradictory and uneven experience of change in this unit is very likely to be shared by other public institutions in South Africa. Deeper cultural change at the level of dispositions, assumptions and values will never come easily while management systems seem impervious to new workplace philosophies and when institutional members cling to stories and memories that venerate the past. And change within powerful public institutions will also go slowly so long as the citizens they serve still cannot readily challenge or refashion them.

Added to this, as institutional environments change, so too do the change agendas. As crime, rather than public order, takes centre stage as a policing priority, Durban POP, as noted in the introductory chapter, is being 'made over' once again. Now reincarnated as the Area Crime Combating Unit (ACCU), crowd management has ceased to be its chief function, and this has, I am sure, raised questions all over again in the minds of officers in the unit about the years of transformation from 1994–2001. Present unit members will without doubt once more have to reorient themselves to new policy and undergo new training programmes. The outcome of this new phase of change will again depend on the strategy and style of management for these changes, availability of supervisors to guide rank-and-file members on the streets, new assessment indicators, and the readiness of unit members to 'buy into' another change process and to reorient their self-identities. Without doubt the prospect will be daunting. So I was not at all surprised when the ACCU Training Manager asked outright in a recent interview: 'How many times can a unit reinvent itself?' That would be a good question for another ethnographic study.

What can the police themselves do to facilitate change?

There are three dimensions to police transformation – structural, behavioural and attitudinal. Each has to be addressed for the changes to really take root. Police are pragmatists 'concerned to get from here to tomorrow (or the next hour) with the least amount of fuss and paperwork' (Reiner, 1992a: 128). They like to focus on observable and tangible outcomes. Police managers and supervisors tend to concentrate on structures and conduct and they give much less attention to transforming values and assumptions. While structural and behavioural change does produce shifts in belief systems, deeper transformation of values and assumptions requires a radical reconceptualisation of the role and self-image of the police organisation and of individual police officers. I would accordingly like to outline five possible areas of intervention for ongoing police organisational transformation:[1]

- flattened, more participatory work structures;
- directive leadership;
- representative employee forums;
- installing new stories in the institutional memory; and
- lateral entry recruitment programmes.

Flattened work structures
Police supervisors and managers have an indispensable role to play in police reform. Not only do they exercise a role-modelling function, they also bear chief responsibility for structuring operational and administrative work routines and, not least, they are in a position to steer the evolution of relationships between the various social groups within the organisation. Police leaders tend to fear change, and when they do embrace it, they often try to confine it within existing frameworks. However, organisational change demands 'qualitative shifts and discontinuous breaks with past methods, mindsets, and strategies' (Kiel, 1994: 45). While police managers feel most comfortable with the 'tried and tested', they need to be more open to the uncomfortable aspects of organisational change. For this, they have to begin seeing themselves as change agents and this is not easy since it means positively welcoming uncertainty and change as opportunities to grow and learn.

One way of breaking with the past is to develop more participatory work structures that flatten the traditional police hierarchies. This can yield a number of benefits. It improves the flow of information and communication. It makes it possible for all officers, regardless of rank and function, to have a say in how the organisation really works and how change will be actualised, crucial if they are to feel motivated and committed to the process. At the same time, mutual respect and support is built through partnerships, shared visions and joint problem solving. More participatory management also has the potential to change the way the police conduct themselves in the communities they serve. Their own direct experience of the internal advantages in partnerships and joint problem solving may help them extend that appreciation to the need for comparable approaches in community policing. Internal organisational democracy spurs on external democratisation.

Police leaders are likely to worry that a flattened management structure neutralises the ranking system, which is generally regarded as highly functional, especially in public order police work (Cowper, 2004). It is an anxiety which is not entirely warranted. A distinction needs to be made between the command role of police leaders during operations and their role in organisational planning and policy formulation. It is in the first of these roles that police leaders should maintain their management prerogative. But regarding the second role, the case for participatory management is very strong. Actively enlisting the participation of rank-and-file in creating new policies and plans generates an organisational learning environment in which different kinds of knowledge and skills are valued and the broader policing vision is assimilated throughout the organisation.

Directive leadership
Contrary to what police leaders may believe, participatory management does not imply an undermining of managerial and supervisory authority. Although the participatory emphasis is important for long-lasting reform, directive leadership is indispensable in transition itself. This means close and careful supervision coupled with clear and understandable directives during operations. There is also a particular responsibility for leadership in seeing to the development of appropriate and agreed-upon performance indicators, formulated with rank-and-file participation, which are so crucial to shaping new responses during policing interventions and encouraging a sense of ownership and responsibility in the operational style of the unit.

Responsibly directive leadership, particularly in the early stages of police organisational change programmes, means that supervisors must as often as possible go out on operations with their subordinates. There are at least three reasons why this is so important: it puts supervisors in a position to provide continuous 'in the field' guidance and feedback; it permits close observation and monitoring of officer conduct, which is the prerequisite for fair and informed performance evaluation; and it creates the conditions for supervisors to play out their crucial role-modelling function – demonstrating by direct example what is meant by 'good' performance, particularly when subordinates are confused by new expectations.

Representative employee forums
Managers are not the only agents of change in police organisations. So too are rank-and-file, and both formally and informally they shape the outcomes of reform as much as do their superiors. Participatory management practices are one way of drawing all levels of the organisation into the change processes. But there are also other important ways for individual input to be incorporated, which leads us to the third area of potential for reform intervention: collective representative bodies, such

as the POP Empowerment Committee, which provide police officers with alternative forums to discuss, debate and strategise, and for that reason can be fertile terrain for the cultivation of new cultural knowledge to transform the organisational ethos. These collective bodies need not necessarily be unions or collective bargaining associations: more loosely structured forums that operate as pressure groups are likely to have at least as much significance.

The mere existence of representative forums, with the challenges they can raise, undercuts, to a degree, the police institutional hierarchy and with it the unspoken expectation of acquiescent compliance. Such forums can also serve to keep a watchful eye on police managers should they stray from the goals of transformation, particularly when it comes to representativeness and affirmative action. But there is another (perhaps more important) reason for supporting the concept of representative police employee bodies, and this relates more directly to the democratic practice of police members. For public policing to be democratised, there has to be a strong shift of emphasis from state protectionism to community needs and equitable service delivery, and that means that officers in public police agencies need to have direct experience of democratic practice and mindset within their own organisation. Police representative formations can play a key role in redefining notions of citizenship when they themselves set a priority on rights and freedoms within police organisations and on identification with members of communities that they serve (Marks and Fleming, 2004). They may often be looked on with disfavour by police managers, but if more constructively engaged with and supported, such bodies have the potential to spur on and legitimise organisational change.

New stories
We have already noted how important it is for an organisation as close-knit as the police to change the way they represent themselves in their daily discourse. Selective memories of the 'good old days' can block the inflow of understanding; new memories and stories need to be created that will transform what Shearing refers to as the 'sensibilities' of the police.

This is a subject that has been attracting some interest in the literature recently (Shearing and Ericson, 1991; Shearing, 1995; Stapley, 1996; Chan, 1997; McLaughlin and Murji, 1998), and it is worth giving it more thought as we look back on the 'story' of POP and ahead to what can be learnt from it.

Their 'stories' shape the perspective police have of the world and how they choose to act in it. They offer them 'ready-made schemas and scripts' (Chan, 1997: 70) for the roles they play out in their profession. They help them make sense of their profession. They provide justification and legitimation for what they have done and will do in the exercise of that profession. In many respects the stories and the shared memories *are* the collective identity of the police. That collective identity can also be a negatively defensive one, particularly when legitimacy and integrity are in question – as was the case for so long with the police in South Africa. The inclination is to hold onto the past more tenaciously when it stands for an epoch of apparent social control with the police keeping it all running. Writing about the British police, McLaughlin and Murji comment:

> Police 'storylines' frequently contain a strong element of nostalgia, expressing a sense of loss for a 'golden age' when things were less complicated and the world was a more law abiding place where the police were trusted and respected (1998: 374).

So the new stories must also be stories that permit the police to let go of their defensiveness: stories that reaffirm what is functional, what really works, what has real value in the work the police do. And then they may begin to think of themselves as different from the past. At the same time, they need to feel valued and supported as they reconstruct themselves collectively and individually in the change endeavour, as the psychoanalytic organisational theorists advise.

But is it feasible for an organisation, the police, actively to set about creating new stories and fostering new memories? As simple as it may sound, I would like to suggest that, yes, there is at least one way of changing the present stories and replacing the old memories, and that is to collectively and actively *celebrate* when things go conspicuously well. The instance that springs most immediately to mind is the international praise that, as we saw in Chapter 7, Durban POP earned for its truly exemplary policing of the World Conference Against Racism in September 2001. Yet these tributes were never publicly acknowledged in the unit and a golden moment was lost where more imaginative leadership could have brought the whole of the unit together for self-affirmation and celebration of work well done.

Celebrations can be learning opportunities: people remember them; they are moments when good outcomes of good work are likely to be more instinctively taken to heart and touch a deeper level than bureaucratic office directives. That is the kind of positive reinforcement that can feed the collective memory (and consolidate new directory and menu knowledge?) for approving recall when police speak of the 'good times'.

Lateral entry programmes

The old 'stories' may take a long time to fade, but they will not change fundamentally – there will not be fundamentally new stories – until there are also new people, new police men and women, to tell them. Ultimately police organisational culture will change as the social base of the organisation begins to change and, in the process, open the police to fresh minds and new schemas.

Brogden and Shearing (1993) remark that, ideally, in the South African police the middle and upper echelons need to be replaced for the 'stories' to be transformed, though they concede that this is not too likely a prospect. But they also note that it would be useful for the state police to realise that policing is not the 'sole preserve of the police' (1993: 59); it can also be done (and is) by other groups and institutions in society. In particular, they suggest, there are lessons that the state police can learn from more popular policing initiatives or traditions which would give communities greater control over social ordering; in this scenario communities would, for the most part, police themselves with the state police intervening as 'problem solvers'.

There are possibilities here which would undoubtedly produce quite radically shifted sensibilities in the state police. But there are also two fundamental problems. Firstly, when states democratise, it is *state* institutions that communities rightfully look to for better delivery. So although non-state policing activities may well continue and even spread in the wake of state democratisation (given the lack of capacity in the state police), this kind of policing should really be a last resort. Secondly, as Brogden and Shearing acknowledge, popular policing initiatives are very difficult to regulate and abuses and excesses are all too possible.

Even so, it would be a pity to dismiss this line of thinking, because there are powerful hints here of what deep-set policing schemas might begin to look like if they can be turned around. But there is an alternative starting point from which some of the same objectives can be reached without the state police vacating any of their accustomed domain.

It is very difficult (and probably quite impractical) to reshape the entire social base of a police organisation. New programmes for entry and recruitment which accompany reform will in time gradually alter the personnel profile at the lower levels. Management echelons, however, can be altered rather more speedily. My final suggestion, then, is to encourage lateral entry programmes that systematically introduce to key police management positions civilian professionals who have experience in managing, strategising and collaborating with community groups. These positions should be functional rather than exclusively policy oriented; it is in hands-on, day-to-day policing that new practices and norms must evolve, and lateral entry recruits, with fresh scripts and fresh schemas from different workplace experience and different community engagement, would need to be deployed to posts where their influence would be direct and immediate.

Lateral entry programmes may well meet with a degree of scepticism from existing personnel of whatever rank. Police officers see themselves as having 'special qualities' (McLaughlin and Murji, 1998) and a uniqueness of role not easily assumed by outsiders. Two cautions would therefore be necessary. On the one hand, lateral entry programmes should not block the career paths of officers who do perform well and are evidently committed. On the other hand, lateral entry recruits would have to undergo intensive training (both nationally and internationally) to equip them with the knowledge and skills required for their new occupation. They would also need to be sensitive to the histories and the defensive misgivings of longstanding police personnel.

*

A police organisation looks like a pretty solid fortress, built to repel would-be reformers. Yet police organisational change is by no means an impossibility. Indeed the very hierarchical, rule-bound character of police organisations, paradoxically perhaps, improves the prospect for behavioural change. But change driven from above will be shallow unless it is coupled with appropriate reforms of organisational structure and value-shift in the deep-level occupational culture of the police. So police may have to re-engineer the ways in which they go about their work, but they must also remember to celebrate the good. Then there is more than a chance that policemen and women will be excited by fresh challenges and fired by the respect they earn for themselves as members of a worthy team of colleagues – not just Robocop functionaries with knee-jerk reactions and iron fists.

Notes

Chapter 1
1. In South Africa policemen and policewomen of all ranks invariably speak of one another as 'members', rather than 'officers' – an idiosyncrasy also to be encountered in other services such as the Defence Force and to some extent shared by the lay public. In this book I sometimes conform to that usage, and sometimes to more universal usage, whichever seems appropriate.

Chapter 3
1. No comprehensive documentation on the history of public order policing in South Africa exists and the information in this chapter is consequently drawn from a range of sources: interviews, secondary literature, recent police documentation, and the Truth and Reconciliation Commission Reports. I had hoped to make use of police documentation in compiling this information but I was told by officials at SAPS Head Office that most of the relevant documentation, particularly for the years 1960–94, was destroyed during the transition period for fear they might be incriminating.
2. The Population Registration Act set out to classify all South Africans into ethnic or racial categories, and the Group Areas Act to locate (or relocate) them in corresponding residential areas. The Separate Amenities Act laid down which facilities and amenities (transport, leisure, toilets, beaches, etc.) were to be used by which racial groups. The Bantu Education Act introduced separate mass education for black people that would effectively confine them to semi-skilled labour.
3. Interview with General Marais, September 1999.
4. Interview with General Marais, September 1999.
5. Interview with Sergeant Nzimande, Chatsworth Training College, August 1997.
6. Telephonic interview with Director Fryer, Commander of the National Task Force, July 2000.
7. This was not, however, the first time the military had been called upon to act internally to assist the SAP with riot control. The SADF was deployed on alert after the 1960 Sharpeville shootings. During the 1976 Soweto uprisings the SADF was again called in to assist the SAP (Prior, 1989).
8. The State Security Council (SSC) was a cabinet committee chaired by the Prime Minister. It was responsible for directing and co-ordinating the activities of 15 inter-departmental committees. SSC policies and decisions were implemented at regional and local level by Joint Management Councils headed by the SAP and the SADF.

9. Both the 'independent' and the non-independent homelands developed their own police forces. These had close ties with the SAP and in most homelands were notorious for their brutality in suppressing unrest.
10. The war between Inkatha and the ANC led to enormous social and political disruption in Natal. By March 1989, 30 000 people had fled their homes, urban townships were divided into no-go zones; altogether some 11 600 people lost their lives in the 1980s and early 1990s (Jeffrey, 1997).
11. In July 1990 Inkatha was formally constituted as a political party (the Inkatha Freedom Party) and began to embark on major recruitment drives in KwaZulu and in Natal. This took place at the same time as the newly unbanned ANC openly campaigned for members. Rivalry for membership and resources generated violent conflict, although in many ways the clash was also ideological, with the IFP essentially a rural movement/party based on traditional values and with a historically accommodating relationship with the apartheid government. The ANC on the other hand was essentially urban and revolutionary in nature.
12. Director Coetzee [not his actual name] was later appointed as unit commander of the Public Order Police unit in Durban.
13. Brutal repression of protest continued in the 'independent' homelands. The best-documented incident is the Bisho massacre which took place on 7 September 1992, and following which the ANC once more withdrew from the negotiation process. On this day, the ANC had organised a protest march of 80 000 people who were campaigning for the opening up of areas for free political activity. Ciskei homeland troops opened fire on the marchers, killing 30 people (Truth and Reconciliation Commission, 1998: Volume 2, Chapter 7).
14. Telephonic interview with David Storey, March 1998.
15. For example, on 30 April 1998, Sifiso Nkabinde, a controversial and much-feared figure in Richmond, in the Natal Midlands, was acquitted and released from prison after being charged with nineteen politically related murders. The night prior to his release, 100 families fled the area fearing renewed violence and instability (*Mercury* 1 May 1998). This event alone, according to Director Wiggins, required, at various stages, between 600 and 1 000 officers to be deployed in Richmond to prevent disorder.
16. This was, however, not the only possible model. At least three others are internationally accepted in public order policing: a) public order policing as an integrated part of classical policing, as in Britain; b) a police/military force attached to the defence force, as in France; c) public order policing as the responsibility of an integral element of the defence force, as in the USA (Report by the Technical Team on Public Order Policing, South Africa, 27 July 1995).

Chapter 4
1. Interview with Unit Commander of POP Durban, May 1998.
2. The KwaZulu Police (KZP) were notorious for their brutally partisan and inefficient policing. They had no specialised training in crowd control or public order policing.
3. The Unit's Director shut down the RDP and Reaction Platoons in January 2001 in the interests of greater equity in the Unit.

4. Interview with Senior Superintendent Bhengu, January 2001.
5. Interview with Sergeant Ncobo, November 1999.
6. Interview with Captain Viljoen, Durban POP base, April 1988.
7. Interview with Senior Superintendent Meiring, POP Durban Base, August 1999.
8. A lower-middle class/working class area close to the Durban Central Business District.
9. An affluent inner Durban suburb.
10. A Coloured residential area; infamous for high levels of drug usage and sale as well as organised crime.
11. Maydon Wharf is a part of the Durban port complex. Durban Harbour is the busiest in South Africa.
12. An affluent, mainly white suburb 15 km from the centre of Durban.
13. Point is a mixed, working class inner-city suburb in Durban. It is a well-known crime area, especially with regard to 'victimless crimes'.
14. The hostels were initially established by industry in the 1920s. They were built as single-sex housing for Africans employed in the city. The accommodation was atrocious, but no doubt served its purpose in reducing production costs for employers. In the 1960s and 1970s government Administration Boards built more hostels for municipal workers. They still survive as cruel reminders of the apartheid era.
15. The unit was also called upon from time to time for 'special duties'. This involved deployment outside of Durban, but usually in the province, in areas of unrest. See Chapter 3, note 15.
16. Informal chat with Inspector Prem while sitting in the Information Management Department, February 2001.

Chapter 5
1. Ericson (1982) states that in his experience of conducting fieldwork in police organisations, there was often confusion about his identity as a fieldworker. Some officers thought he was an official police evaluator. In my own experience, unit members seemed to regard me as an agent of change: an 'expert' helping to develop new strategies, or a consultant to management, possibly also a trouble-shooter.
2. I spent about five hours discussing this report with the Director and two of his officers. The report was also used as a catalyst for certain changes that were later implemented in the unit. This report has never been published or distributed, either publicly or within the unit itself.
3. Holdaway (1983) writes that in participant observation there is an obligation not to cause harm: aside from the obvious consideration of not wanting to hurt those who have extended trust and hospitality, the researcher has to avoid giving any impression that sociologists cannot be trusted.
4. It is not possible for an ethnographer to record everything that is observed. Taking field notes will always be a selective process informed by the researcher's own interpretations and objectives, and by the questions that frame the study.
5. I am not comfortable using these race categorisations but they are still so current in ordinary South African discourse as to be pretty much unavoidable in referring to the everyday dynamics of Durban POP.

6. From the late 1970s onward there was a strong tradition on the part of left researchers in South Africa of making research accessible and popular, but this was not extended to those associated with the apartheid state.

Chapter 6

1. Although there were a host of other parties involved in the negotiation process, the outcome was essentially the result of negotiations between the ANC and the NP (Friedman, 1996).
2. The RDP was, however, faced with numerous problems that included foot-dragging and faltering structures in the civil service and poor co-ordination by central government. In April 1996 RDP National Office closed and the importance of the RDP document declined as emphasis shifted to fiscal discipline, free markets and investor confidence.
3. Interview with Captain Mohamed, April 1998.
4. Interview with Inspector Myeni, May 1998.
5. Interview with Platoon Commander at Chatsworth Training College, May 1998.
6. Interview with Captain Modise, only female Platoon Commander in the unit, May 1999.
7. Interview with Captain Modise, May 1999.
8. Empangeni is on the KwaZulu-Natal north coast and has been the scene of high levels of political violence, usually between groups claiming to be supporters of the ANC and those claiming to be supporters of the IFP.
9. All members of Durban POP had completed retraining by November 2000.
10. The tonfa is a type of baton. It is a preferred weapon in crowd management since it causes minimum injury. The tonfa used in South Africa is similar to the one used in Japan.
11. Interview with Senior Superintendent Meiring, August 1999, Durban POP base. At the time of the interview Superintendent Meiring was acting unit commander.
12. Interview with Sergeant Maduna, November 1999.
13. Interview with Sergeant Patel, Chatsworth Training College, April 1998.
14. Members also liked the fresh approach in the training methods. Durban POP trainers made a point of creating a relaxed and open atmosphere. They had themselves attended a Training Officers' Course where they learned about adult-based learning, group facilitation and updated lecturing techniques. They were very committed to this new training approach and four of them even signed up – at their own expense – for a graduate course in adult education at the University of Natal in 1999. Most of the trainees I interviewed were very positive about the new training.
15. Interview with Director Wiggins, March 1988.
16. Interview with Inspector Bosman, Durban POP trainer, Chatsworth Training College, February 1998.
17. This is a problem that affected the entire SAPS. In November 2001 it was reported that the police service in KwaZulu-Natal was running at half its strength, largely because of absenteeism. Provincial SAPS Commissioner Moses Khanyile attributed this to lack of resources and high casualty levels of police members on duty (*Daily News*, 9 November 2001).
18. Interview with Director Wiggins, May 1998.

Chapter 7

1. Interview with Captain Modise, April 2000.
2. Interview with Senior Superintendent Meiring, August 1999.
3. Interview with Senior Superintendent Meiring, August 1999.
4. Interview with an Inspector Gopal from the Incident Recording Information System (IRIS) at the Public Order Police Headquarters in Pretoria, May 1998. The Inspector had been in public order policing for thirteen years.
5. These incident reports are recorded on a computer in the operational room at the Durban POP base where I spent many nights and weekends reading them and printing them out. There are no printed copies of these incident recordings in the unit. I have not changed any of the language which sometimes reads rather awkwardly.
6. The 'greens' and 'reds' were rival fighting groups that materialised in 1992 in an informal settlement in the Inanda district north of Durban, clashing over scarce resources in an area between two ANC factions. The 'greens', fewer in numbers, felt marginalised by the local ANC leadership. With conflict levels escalating, an ISU base was set up nearby and there were continuous ISU patrols in the area. There were allegations at the time that the ISU had sided with the 'greens', which heightened the tension. In April 1993 the 'greens' made approaches to the IFP and later began identifying themselves as IFP supporters (Truth and Reconciliation Commission, 1998: Chapter 3, 309).
7. When policing crowds it is important to have large numbers of personnel. This gives the police a sense of security and usually reduces the potential for the use of force (Waddington, 1991). The flipside is that large numbers of police officers can also antagonise a crowd (Jefferson, 1990).
8. Recalled to me by a Sergeant while I was accompanying a section on a crime prevention operation in Umlazi, June 1999.
9. Durban POP was not the only unit policing the event. The entire security operation consisted of 16 000 security personnel including Durban City Police and the South African National Defence Force. However, Durban POP played a central role in the planning and co-ordination of the security operation.
10. The statistics here are used very tentatively. The IRIS system, which distinguishes between crowd management unrest and crowd management peaceful, was only implemented in 1997. Before this, all incidents regarded as 'illegal' (most, at that time) were defined as unrest even if no violence or damage to property was recorded. In order to create uniformity, all the statistics from January 1992 to December 1996 have been compiled and calculated by hand. This took an average of three hours work for every year calculated which I completed in the Operations Room at the Durban POP base: accuracy is not guaranteed. The IRIS team at POP Head Office also helped in the compiling of the statistics. Incident recording before 1997 was not standardised nor was it always competently done. There are no statistical records for the unit prior to 1992.
11. The Reaction Unit usually intervened in high-risk incidents. It was made up largely of white members of the unit who had a history of overzealous enforcement. This information was obtained in informal discussions with a variety of commissioned officers from the POP who were present at the time of the incident. See also Chapter 3.
12. Debriefing of crowd management incident: University of Durban-Westville on 16 May 2000. POP Headquarters, June 2000, Pretoria.
13. Thirty thousand people live in this hostel which is meant to house fifteen thousand. The

deaths are said to be the result of ongoing violence between two ethnic factions, well supplied with firearms.
14. Interview with Sergeant Mamela, June 1998.
15. Interview with Constable Prathab, May 2000. This constable was in the platoon which policed the residence at UDW and whose members shared with me the stories of the 'red bands' and the 'green bands' cited above. I noticed that as a young and 'inexperienced' member of the platoon he was excluded from the informal bantering.
16. Interview with Sergeant Ngcobo, July 1999.
17. Interview with Captain Padyachee, August 2000.

Chapter 8
1. While initially the police were to be excluded from the Labour Relations Act, in the last phases of drawing up the Act the police were included. The military and intelligences services are still excluded from the Act.
2. Interview with Captain Mohamed, Chatsworth Training College, March 1999.
3. Although these ethnographies were carried out in private companies, Wilms argues that they offer powerful suggestions for redesigning public sector organisations (1996: 258).
4. The autocratic management style of the police bureaucracy in South Africa is not simply a matter of police ethos; it has long been a characteristic of the entire South African public service (see McLennan, 1997).
5. Interview with Sergeant Mbele, August 1999.
6. Interview with Captain Naidoo, May 2000.
7. There are a number of different management layers in the unit. First, there are front-line supervisors. These are the Section Leaders and Platoon Commanders. Front-line managers/ supervisors direct the operations of the rank-and-file. Middle management refers to Platoon Commanders who both direct the rank-and-file and supervise the Section Leaders. Top management signifies the Company Commanders, Operational Commanders and the Unit Commanders. This top management layer is responsible for supervising the other managers and for establishing operating policies as well as guiding the organisation's interactions with the environment. These three management/command layers are match the 'Gold/ Silver/Bronze' system of command that Waddington refers to in his work on public order policing units, where he observes that 'the intention is that command should follow the military model, with the Gold commander setting the strategy, which is translated into tactical deployment and objectives by the Silver commander to be implemented by the Bronze commander' (1991: 142). Waddington acknowledged that there are times when this command model does not work effectively such as when Gold commanders abandon the chain of command and instruct the Bronze commanders directly. A fundamental flaw with this command model is that often Bronze and Silver commanders have to make the most sensitive and complex decisions and may not be adequately trained or empowered to do so. See the organogram in Chapter 4.
8. Interview with Director Wiggins, September 1998.
9. Interview with Senior Superintendent Meiring, October 1999.
10. Interview with Sergeant Beatrice Ngcobo, May 1999.
11. Interview with Sergeant Mbele, August 1999.

12. Interview with Sergeant Beatrice Ngcobo, May 1999.
13. Interview with Sergeant Pieterse, August 1999.
14. Interview with Captain Botha, May 1998.
15. Interview with Captain Modise, May 1999.
16. Interview with Captain Zungu, October 2001.
17. Interview with Captain Chetty, August 2000.
18. In 2001, a Performance Enrichment Process (PEP) was initiated in the public service to assess and promote job performance and delivery. In accordance with PEP every member of the police is to be accountable for their performance and to develop their skills to their best ability, with the expectation that this will help to establish a performance culture in the police. By November 2001, PEP had not been implemented in Durban POP but discussions about it were underway.
19. Interview with Captain Padyachee, March 2000.
20. Interview with Sergeant Mary Magoda, March 2000.
21. Interview with Captain Padyachee, March 2000.
22. Low morale is a pervasive problem in the SAPS. Thirty-three thousand officers left the service between 1994 and 1999, almost a quarter of the total force (Govender, 1999). See also Chapter 6, note 17.
23. Informal discussion with Sergeant Cronje, April 2000.

Chapter 9

1. The South African democracy may not be 'Western', but most of its legislation and its institutional transformation programmes are based on those of Western democracies and it is therefore appropriate to compare it with these. The literature dealing with race and gender representation in state police organisations in Africa is, moreover, extremely scant.
2. POPCRU was launched on 5 September 1989. One of the main reasons for the formation of POPCRU was to provide a voice for black police officers who by all accounts worked under extremely poor conditions in the SAP. A second reason for the formation of POPCRU was to protest the use of the police, by the government, in upholding apartheid laws and policies. The social base of POPCRU was and remains essentially black.

    Police unions were not formally recognised in South Africa until 1993. By this time, another essentially white trade union, the South African Police Union (SAPU), had been formed. Many perceived the formation of SAPU as aimed at countering the existence of POPCRU. While white police officers tended to join SAPU, by 1999, the majority of members of SAPU were also black. For more information about SAPU and POPCRU see Marks (2000b) and Cawthra (1993).
3. Interview with Inspector De Bruin, July 1999.
4. Interview with Inspector Marike Vosloo, November 2001.
5. Interview with Sergeant Mary Nene, July 1998.
6. Interview with Inspector Marike Vosloo, November 2001.
7. Interview with Captain Modise, April 2000.
8. Interview with Senior Superintendent Meiring, August 1999.
9. Interview with Captain Modise, April 2000.
10. Interview with Inspector Marike Vosloo, November 2001.

11. Interview with Sergeant De Bruin, August 2000.
12. Interview with Inspector Botha, May 1999.
13. Interview with Senior Superintendent Meiring, August 1999.
14. Interview with Inspector Gumede, November 2001.
15. Interview with Inspector Vosloo, November 2001.
16. Interview with Superintendent Desai, November 2000.
17. Interview with Director Zuma, January 2001.
18. This unit was established in late 2001. Its members are specially trained to intervene in high-risk situations such as hostage situations and bomb incidents. Most of the white members of Durban POP applied to enter the Intervention Unit.
19. Interview with Captain Mbali, November 2001.
20. Interview with Captain Moonsamy, September 2001.

Chapter 10
1. I have not included suggestions about bringing non-state actors into police governance programmes, which is another crucial ingredient for democratic police reform (Wood, 2004).

Select Bibliography

Adair, B. and Albertyn, S. (2000). Restructuring management in the public service. In G. Adler (ed.). *Public Service Labour Relations in a Democratic South Africa*. Johannesburg: Witwatersrand University Press.

Adler, G. (ed.). (2000). *Public Service Labour Relations in a Democratic South Africa*. Johannesburg: Witwatersrand University Press.

Adler, G. and Webster, E. (2000). *Trade Unions and Democratization in South Africa, 1985–1997*. New York: St. Martin's Press.

Ahrne, G. (1994). *Social Organisations: Interactions Inside, Outside and Between Organisations*. London: Sage.

Ainsworth, P. (1995). *Psychology and Policing in a Changing World*. New York: John Wiley and Sons.

Albrow, M. (1970). *Bureaucracy*. London: Pall Mall Press Limited.

Anderson, D. and Killingray, D. (1991). Consent, coercion and colonial control: policing the empire, 1830–1941. In D. Anderson and D. Killingray (eds.). *Policing the Empire: Government, Authority and Control, 1830–1940*. Manchester: Manchester University Press.

Anderson, D. and Killingray, D. (eds.). (1991). *Policing the Empire: Government, Authority and Control, 1830–1940*. Manchester: Manchester University Press.

Arensberg, C., Barkin, S., Chalmers, W., Wilensky, H., Worthy, J. and Dennis, B. (eds.). (1957). *Research in Industrial Human Relations*. New York: Harper and Row.

Babbie, E. (1989). *The Practice of Social Research*. Belmont: Wadsworth Publishing Company.

Baker, B. (2003). Policing and the rule of law in Mozambique. *Policing and Society,* 13(2): 139–158.

Banton, M. (1964). *The Policeman in the Community*. London: Tavistock.

Barnard, D. (2000). Public Order Police Durban move into the next millennium. *Servamus*, June: 5–8.

Bastion, R. (1985). Participant observation in social analysis. In R. Walker (ed.). *Applied Qualitative Research*. Aldershot: Gower Publishing Company.

Bayley, D. (1993). Accountability and control of police: lessons from Britain. In T. Bennett (ed.). *The Future of Policing: Papers Presented at the First Cropwood Round Table Conference*. Cambridge: Cropwood Conference Series.

———. (1994). *Police for the Future*. New York: Oxford University Press.

———. (1999). *Democratising the Police Abroad: What to Do and How to Do It*. New York: National Institute of Justice.

Bayley, D. and Shearing, C. (1996). The future of policing, *Law and Society Review*, 33: 585–606.
———. (2001). *The New Structure of Policing: Description, Conceptualization and Research Agenda*. Washington: United States Department of Justice.
Beckhard, R. and Harris, R. (1987). *Organisational Transitions: Managing Complex Change*. Reading, MA: Addison-Wesley Publishing Company.
Bennett, T. (ed.). (1993). *The Future of Policing: Papers Presented at the First Cropwood Round Table Conference*. Cambridge: Cropwood Conference Series.
Bennett, T.W., Devine, D.J., Hutchinson, D.B., Leeman, I., and Van Zyl Smit, D. (eds.). (1989). *Acta Juridica*. Cape Town: Juta.
Bent, A. (1974). *The Politics of Law Enforcement: Conflict and Power in Urban Communities*. Toronto: Lexington Books.
Birzer, M. (1996). Police supervisors in the 21st century. *FBI Law Enforcement Bulletin*, 65(6): 5–11.
Bittner, E. (1975). The concept of organization. In R. Turner (ed.). *Ethnomethodology*. Harmondsworth: Penguin.
———. (1980). *The Functions of the Police in Modern Society*. Cambridge: Gunn and Hain.
Blalock, H. and Blalock, A. (eds.). (1968). *Methodology in Social Research*. New York: McGraw-Hill.
Blumer, M. (ed.). (1993). *Social Research Ethics*. London: Macmillan.
Blyton, P. and Bacon, N. (1997). Recasting the organisational culture in steel: some implications of changing from crews to teams in the US steel industries. *Sociological Review*, 45(1): 79–101.
Bouwer, D. (1997). Common-law labour rights for the South African Police Service and its members in the workplace. In F. Nel and J. Bezuidenhout (eds.). *Policing and Human Rights*. Cape Town: Juta.
Bouza, A. (1990). *The Police Mystique: An Insider's Look at Cops, Crime, and the Criminal Justice System*. New York: Premium Press.
Bowling, B., Phillips, C., Campbell, C. and Docking, M. (2001). Policing and human rights: eliminating discrimination, xenophobia, intolerance and the abuse of power from police work. Paper prepared for the United Nations Research Institute for Social Development Conference on Racism and Public Policy, September, Durban.
Bozzoli, B. (1991). *The Women of Phokeng: Consciousness, Life Strategy and Migrancy in South Africa 1900–1983*. Johannesburg: Ravan Press.
Brearley, N. and King, M. (1996a). Policing social protest: some indicators of change. In C. Critcher and D. Waddington (eds.). *Policing Public Order: Theoretical and Practical Issues*. Brookfield: Avebury Publications.
———. (1996b). *Public Order Policing: Contemporary Perspectives on Strategies and Tactics*. Leicester: Perpetuity Press.
Brewer, J. (1988). The police in South African politics. In S. Johnson (ed.). *South Africa: No Turning Back*. Indiana: Indiana University Press.
———. (1990). *Ethnography*. Buckingham: Open University Press.
———. (1991). *Inside the RUC: Routine policing in a divided society*. Oxford: Clarendon Press.
———. (1994). *Black and Blue: Policing in South Africa*. Oxford: Clarendon Press.

Brewer, J., Guelke, A., Hume, I., Moxon-Browne, E. and Wilford, R. (1988). *The Police, Public Order and the State: Policing in Great Britain, Northern Ireland, the Irish Republic, Israel, South Africa, and China*. London: Macmillan.

Brewer, N. and Wilson, C. (1994). Supervisory behaviour and team performance amongst police sergeants. *Journal of Occupational and Organisational Psychology*, 67(1): 69–79.

Brogden, M. and Shearing, C. (1993). *Policing for a New South Africa*. London: Routledge.

Brookes, E. (1980). *Organisational Change: The Management Dilemma*. London: Macmillan.

Brown, J. (1993). The ad hoc task force: change made simple. *FBI Law Enforcement Bulletin*, August: 17–21.

———. (1997). Equal opportunities and the police in England and Wales: past, present and future possibilities. In P. Francis, P. Davies and V. Jupp (eds.). *Policing Futures: The Police, Law Enforcement and the Twenty-First Century*. London: Macmillan.

———. (2000). Discriminatory experiences of women police: a comparison of officers serving in England and Wales, Scotland, Northern Ireland and the Republic of Ireland. *Journal of the Sociology of Law*, 28(2): 91–185.

Brown, J. and Howes, G. (eds.). (1975). *The Police and the Community*. New York: Lexington Press.

Brown, J. and Waters, I. (1996). Force versus service: a paradox in the policing of public order? In C. Critcher and D. Waddington (eds.). *Policing Public Order: Theoretical and Practical Issues*. Brookfield: Avebury Publications.

Brown, M. (1988). *Working the Streets: Police Discretion and the Dilemmas of Reform*. New York: Garland Publishing.

Brunsson, N. and Olsen, J. (1993). *The Reforming Organisation*. London: Routledge.

Burgess, R. (1984). *In the Field: An Introduction to Field Research*. London: Unwin Hyman.

Cain, M. (1973). *Society and the Policeman's Role*. London: Routledge and Kegan Paul.

Cameron, N. and Young, W. (eds.). (1986). *Policing at the Crossroads*. Wellington: Allen and Unwin.

Cashmore, E. (1991). Black Cops Inc. In E. Cashmore and E. McLaughlin (eds.). *Out of Order: Policing Black People*. London: Routledge.

Cashmore, E. and McLaughlin, E. (1991). Introduction. In E. Cashmore and E. McLaughlin (eds.). *Out of Order: Policing Black People*. London: Routledge.

———. (eds.). (1991). *Out of Order: Policing Black People*. London: Routledge.

Cawthra, G. (1992). *South Africa's Police: From Police State to Democratic Policing*. London: Catholic Institute for International Relations.

———. (1993). *Policing South Africa: The South African Police and the Transition from Apartheid*. London: Zed Books.

———. (1997). *Securing South Africa's Democracy: Defense, Development and Security in Transition*. Basingstoke: Macmillan.

Chan, J. (1996). Changing police culture. *British Journal of Criminology*, 36(1): 109–133.

———. (1997). *Changing Police Culture: Policing in a Multicultural Society*. Melbourne: Cambridge University Press.

———. (1999). Police culture. In D. Dixon (ed.). *A Culture of Corruption: Changing an Australian Police Force*. Sydney: Hawkins Press.

Chan, J., Devery, C. and Doran, S. (2003). *Fair Cop: Learning the Art of Policing*. Toronto: University of Toronto Press.

Chattopadhyay, S. and Pareek, U. (eds.). (1982). *Managing Organisational Change*. Bombay: Oxford and IBH Publishing.
Christie, G., Petrie, S. and Timmins, P. (1996). The effect of police education, training and socialization on conservative attitudes. *The Australian and New Zealand Journal of Criminology*, 29: 299–314.
Cicourel, A. (1975). Police practice and official records. In R. Turner (ed.). *Ethnomethodology*. Harmondsworth: Penguin.
Cilliers, J. (1995). Reigning in the riot police. *Crime and Conflict*, 1: 25–28.
Cobbett, W. and Cohen, R. (eds.). (1988). *Popular Struggles in South Africa*. London: James Currey.
Constitution (interim) of the Republic of South Africa, Act 200 of 1993.
Constitution of the Republic of South Africa, Act 108 of 1996.
Couch, C. and Maines, D. (eds.). (1987). *Communication and Social Structure*. Springfield: Charles Thomas.
Cox, S. (1996). *Police: Practices, Perspectives, Problems*. Boston: Allyn and Bacon.
Cowper, T. (2004). The myth of the 'military model' of leadership in law enforcement. In Q. Thurman and J. Zhao (eds.). *Contemporary Policing: Controversies, Challenges and Solutions*. Los Angeles: Roxbury Publishing Company.
Critcher, C. and Waddington, D. (eds.). (1996). *Policing Public Order: Theoretical and Practical Issues*. Brookfield: Avebury Publications.
Crosby, F. and Clayton, S. (1990). Affirmative action and the issue of expectancies. *Journal of Social Issues*, 46(2): 61–79.
Cunningham, J.B. (1993). *Action Research and Organisational Development*. London: Praeger Press.

Daniel, J., Habib, A., and Southall, R. (2003). *State of the Nation: South Africa 2003–2004*. Pretoria: Human Science Research Council Press.
Dean, G. (1995). Police reform: rethinking operational policing. *Journal of Criminal Justice*, 23: 337–347.
Decker, S. and Smith, R. (1980). Police minority recruitment: a note on its effectiveness in improving black evaluations of the police. *Journal of Criminal Justice*, 8: 387–393.
De Haas, M. (1999). Report into Racism in the South African Police Service. Unpublished report. University of Natal, Durban.
Della Porta, D. (1993). Police operational practices and knowledge: a comparative research on the police in contemporary Europe. Research proposal for the European University Institute, Italy.
———. (1995a). Police knowledge and public order: some reflections on the Italian case. Paper presented at the International Workshop on The Policing of Mass Demonstrations in Contemporary Democracies, European University Institute, Italy.
———. (1995b). Social movements and the state: thoughts on the policing of protest. Paper presented at the Human Science Research Council Workshop on Social Movements, February, University of Natal, Durban.
———. (1998). Police knowledge and protest policing: some reflections on the Italian case. In D. Della Porta and H. Reiter (eds.). *Policing Protest: The Control of Mass Demonstrations in Western Democracies*. Minnesota: University of Minnesota Press.

Della Porta, D., Pizzorno, A. and Szakolczai, A. (1992). Police operational practices and knowledge: a comparative research on the police in contemporary Europe. Unpublished paper presented to the European University Institute, Italy.

Della Porta, D. and Reiter, H. (eds.). (1998). *Policing Protest: The Control of Mass Demonstrations in Western Democracies*. Minnesota: University of Minnesota Press.

De Lint, W. (1998). Regulating autonomy: police discretion as a problem for training. *Canadian Journal of Criminology*, July: 277–300.

Dippenaar, M. (1988). *Die Geskiedenis van die Suid-Afrikaanse Polisie, 1913–1988*. Pretoria: Promedia.

Dixon, D. (ed.). (1999). *A Culture of Corruption: Changing an Australian Police Force*. Sydney: Hawkins Press.

Dominique, O. (2003). Security-sector restructuring in Bosnia-Herzegovina: addressing the division? *Conflict, Security and Development*, 3(1): 73–95.

Downes, B. (1998). Recent literature on leading and managing change in public service organisations. *Social Science Journal*, 35(4): 657–673.

Du Toit, V. (1995). *State Building and Democratisation in South Africa*. New York: New Press.

Dutton, M. and Tianfu, L. (1993). Missing the target? Policing strategies in the period of economic reform. *Crime and Delinquency*, 39(3): 316–336.

Eldfonso, E., Coffey, A. and Grace, R. (1968). *Principles of Law Enforcement*. Toronto: John Wiley and Sons.

Ellis, R. (1991). Perceptions, attitudes and beliefs of police officers. *Canadian Police College Journal*, 15: 95–117.

Ellis, S. and Sechaba, T. (1992). *Comrades Against Apartheid: The ANC and the South African Communist Party in Exile*. Indiana: Indiana University Press.

Emerson, R., Fretz, R. and Shaw, L. (1995). *Writing Ethnographic Fieldnotes*. Chicago: University of Chicago Press.

Emsley, C. (1983). *Policing and its Context, 1750–1870*. London: Macmillan.

Ericson, R. (1982). *Reproducing Order: A Study of Police Patrol Work*. Toronto: Oxford University Press.

Etzioni, A. (1993). A socio-economic perspective on friction. In S. Sjostrand (ed.). *Institutional Change*. New York: M.E. Sharpe.

Evans, K. (1996). Managing chaos and complexity in government: a new paradigm for managing change, innovation and organizational renewal. *Public Administration Review*, 56(5): 56–61.

Evans, M. and Phillips, M. (1988). Intensifying civil war: the role of the South African Defence Force. In P. Frankel, N. Pines and M. Swilling (eds.). *State, Resistance and Change in South Africa*. London: Croom Helm.

Farrell, G. and Buckley, A. (1999). Evaluation of a UK police domestic violence unit using repeat victimization as a performance indicator. *Howard Journal of Criminal Justice*, 38(1): 42–56.

Fielding, N. (1981). *The National Front*. London: Routledge and Kegan Paul.

———. (1982). Observational research on the national front. In M. Blumer (ed.). *Social Research Ethics*. London: Macmillan.

———. (1987). Being used by the police. *British Journal of Criminology*, 27(1): 64–69.
———. (1988a). *Joining Forces: Police Training, Socialisation, and Occupational Competence*. London: Routledge.
———. (1988b). Socialisation of recruits into the police role. In P. Southgate (ed.). *New Directions in Police Training*. London: Home Office Research and Planning Unit.
———. (1989). Police culture and police practice. In M. Weatheritt (ed.). *Police Research: Some Future Prospects*. Sydney: Avebury Press.
———. (1997). Janet Chan: Changing Police Culture (Review). *Sociological Research Online*. www.socresonline.org.uk/2/2/fielding.html
Fielding, N. and Fielding, J. (1991). Police attitudes to crime and punishment. *British Journal of Criminology*, 31: 39–53.
Fillieule, O. and Jobard, F. (1998). The policing of protest in France: toward a model of protest policing. In D. Della Porta and H. Reiter (eds.). *Policing Protest: The Control of Mass Demonstrations in Western Democracies*. Minnesota: University of Minnesota Press.
Fitzgerald, P., McLennan, A. and Munslow, B. (eds.). (1997). *Managing Sustainable Development in South Africa*. Cape Town: Oxford University Press.
Fivaz, G. (1997). Press release by the National Commissioner of the SA Police, 16 October 1997. www.polity.org.za/html/govdocs/pr/1997/pr1016b.html
Fleming, J. and Lafferty, G. (2000). New management techniques and restructuring for accountability in the Australian police organisations. *Policing: An International Journal of Police Strategies and Management*, 23(2): 154–168.
Fombrun, C. (1992). *Leading Corporate Change*. New York: McGraw Hill.
Francis, P., Davies, P. and Jupp, V. (eds.). (1997). *Policing Futures: The Police, Law Enforcement and the Twenty-First Century*. London: Macmillan.
Frankel, P., Pines, N. and Swilling, M. (eds.). (1988). *State, Resistance and Change in South Africa*. London: Croom Helm.
Freund, B. (1999). The weight of history: the prospects of democratisation in South Africa. In J. Hyslop (ed.). *African Democracy in the Era of Globalisation*. Johannesburg: Witwatersrand University Press.
Friederickson, G. (2000). Can bureaucracy be beautiful? *Public Administration Review*, January/February: 47–53.
Friedman, S. (1996). Pact making and the South African transition. In S. Friedman and R. de Villiers (eds.). *Comparing Brazil and South Africa: Two Transitional States in Political and Economic Perspective*. Johannesburg: Centre for Policy Studies.
Friedman, S. and Atkinson, D. (eds.). (1994). *South African Review 7: The Small Miracle: South Africa's Negotiated Settlement*. Johannesburg: Ravan Press.
Friedman, S. and De Villiers, R. (eds.). (1966). *Comparing Brazil and South Africa: Two Transitional States in Political and Economic Perspective*. Johannesburg: Centre for Policy Studies.

Garfinkel, H. (1975). The origins of ethnomethodology. In R. Turner (ed.). *Ethnomethodology*. Harmondsworth: Penguin.
Gianakis, G. and Davis, J. (1998). Reinventing or repackaging public services? The case of community oriented policing. *Public Administration Review*, 56(7): 485–498.
Gill, P. (1994). *Policing Politics: Security, Intelligence and the Liberal Democratic State*. London: Frank Cass.

Glanz, L. (ed.). (1993). *Managing Crime in the New South Africa: Selected Readings.* Pretoria: Human Science Research Council Press.

Glaser, D. (2001). *Politics and Society in South Africa.* London: Sage Publications.

Global Security.org. (n.d.). Casspir. www.globalsecurity.org/military/world/rsa/casspir/htm

Goldsmith, A. (2003). Policing weak states: citizen safety and state responsibility. *Policing and Society,* 13(1): 3–21.

Goldstein, H. (1990). *Problem Oriented Policing.* New York: McGraw-Hill.

Goldstone Commission. (1991). Press Release by Mr Justice R.J. Goldstone. 6 December. Pretoria.

Goldstone, R.J. (1990). Report of the Commission on Inquiry into Incidents at Sebokeng, Boipathong, Lekoa, Sharpeville, and Evaton. Johannesburg.

Govender, D. (1999). Motivation and the police manager. *People Dynamics,* July.

Greenhill, N. (1981). The value of sociology in policing. In D. Pope and N. Weiner (eds.). *Modern Policing.* London: Croom Helm.

Gregory, F. (1985). The British police system: with special reference to public order policing. In J. Roach. and J. Thomaneck (eds.). *The Police and Public Order in Europe.* London: Croom Helm.

Grest, J. (1988). The crisis of local government in South Africa. In P. Frankel, N. Pines and M. Swilling (eds.). *State, Resistance and Change in South Africa.* London: Croom Helm.

Hain, P. (ed.). (1980). *Policing the Police.* London: John Calder.

Halan, J. and Austin, J. (1981). The role of police in post-colonial sub-Saharan Africa. *Police Studies,* 4: 21–27.

Halford, S. and Savage, M. (1995). Restructuring organizations, changing people: gender and restructuring in banking and local government. *Work, Employment and Society,* 9(1): 97–122.

Hall, S. and Jefferson, T. (1976). *Resistance through Rituals.* London: Hutchinson.

Hansson, D. (1989). Trigger happy? An evaluation of fatal police shootings in the greater Cape Town area from 1984–1986. In T.W. Bennett et al. (eds.). *Acta Juridica.* Cape Town: Juta.

Hansson, D. and Van Zyl Smit, D. (eds.). (1990). *Towards Justice? Crime and State Control in South Africa.* Cape Town: Oxford University Press.

Harrington, J. (1999). Rigidity of social systems. *Journal of Political Economy,* 107(1): 40–64.

Hawkins, H. and Thomas, R. (1991). White policing of black populations: a history of race and social control in America. In E. Cashmore and E. McLaughlin (eds.). *Out of Order: Policing Black People.* London: Routledge.

Haysom, N. (1989). Policing the police: a comparative survey of police control mechanisms in the United States, South Africa and the United Kingdom. In T.W. Bennett et al. (eds.). *Acta Juridica.* Cape Town: Juta.

———. (1990). Vigilantism and the policing of African townships: manufacturing violent stability. In D. Hansson and D. van Zyl Smit (eds.). *Towards Justice? Crime and State Control in South Africa.* Cape Town: Oxford University Press.

Helen Suzman Foundation. (n.d.). Police promotions are designed to sow racial divisions. www.hsf.org.za/Briefing_10/Indians_under_fire/Indians_under_fire.htm

Hendrickx, E. and Van Ryckeghem, D. (1999). Conflict in society: policing in partnership? Community policing and public order policing, an integrated approach. Paper presented at the Centre for the Study of Violence and Reconciliation, 24 June.

Hendry, J. (1999). Cultural theory and contemporary management organization. *Human Relations*, 52(5): 557–579.

Herbert, S. (1996). Morality in law enforcement: chasing 'bad guys' with the Los Angeles Police Department. *Law and Society Review*, 30(4): 799–818.

———. (1997). *Policing Space: Territoriality and the Los Angeles Police Department*. Minneapolis: University of Minneapolis Press.

———. (1998). Police subculture reconsidered. *Criminology*, 36(2): 343–369.

———. (2001). 'Hard Charger' or 'Station Queen'? Policing and the masculinist state. *Gender, Place and Culture,* 8(1): 55–71.

Hertzog, S. (2000). Is there a distinct profile of police officers accused of violence? The Israeli case. *Journal of Criminal Justice*, 28: 457–471.

Heuns, C., Van Ryckeghem, D. and Hendrickx, E. (1998). Crowd management in a democratic society: the community policing option. Paper presented at the International Conference on Public Order Police, 16–18 December, Kwa-Maritane, South Africa.

Heymann, P. (1992). *Towards Peaceful Protest in South Africa*. Pretoria: Human Science Research Council.

Hills, A. (2000). *Policing Africa: Internal Security and the Limits of Liberalisation*. London: Rienner.

Hochstedler, E. and Conley, J. (1986). Explaining underrepresentation of black officers in city police agencies. *Journal of Criminal Justice*, 14: 319–328.

Hogg, M. and Terry, D. (2000). The dynamic, diverse and variable faces of organizational identity. *Academy of Management Review*, 25(1): 121–140.

Hoggarth, T. (1993). Worker support for organizational and technical change: workplace industrial relations in United Kingdom manufacturing – the case study evidence. *Work, Employment and Society,* 7(2): 189–212.

Holdaway, S. (1983). *Inside the British Police*. Oxford: Basil Blackwell.

———. (1989). Discovering structure: studies of the British police occupational culture. In M. Weatheritt (ed.). *Police Research: Some Future Prospects*. Sydney: Avebury Press.

———. (1991). Race relations and police recruitment. *British Journal of Criminology*, 31(4): 365–383.

———. (1994). Recruitment, race and the police subculture. In M. Stephens and S. Becker (eds.). *Police Force, Police Service: Care and Control in Britain*. London: Macmillan.

Huggins, M. (1998). Brazilian police violence: legacies of authoritarianism in police professionalism, a study of torturers and murderers. Paper presented at the Legacies of Authoritarianism Conference, Madison, WI.

Huggins, M. and Gleebeck, M. (2003). Women studying violent male institutions: cross gendered dynamics in police research on secrecy and danger. *Theoretical Criminology*, 7(3): 363–387.

Human, P. and Horwitz, F. (1992). *On the Edge: How the South African Business Organisation Copes with Change*. Cape Town: Juta.

Hyslop, J. (1988). School student movements and state education policy: 1972–87. In W. Cobbett and R. Cohen (eds.). *Popular Struggles in South Africa*. London: James Currey.

———. (1999). African democracy in the era of globalisation. In J. Hyslop (ed.). *African Democracy in the Era of Globalisation*. Johannesburg: Witwatersrand University Press.

———. (ed.). (1999). *African Democracy in the Era of Globalisation*. Johannesburg: Witwatersrand University Press.

Institute of Criminology, University of Cape Town. (1992). Crowd management: civilian and police conduct. Submission to the Goldstone Commission of Enquiry regarding the Prevention of Public Violence and Intimidation.

Jaime-Jimenez, O. and Reinares, F. (1998). The policing of mass demonstrations in Spain: from dictatorship to democracy. In D. Della Porta and H. Reiter (eds.). *Policing Protest: The Control of Mass Demonstrations in Western Democracies.* Minnesota: University of Minnesota Press.

Jansen, J. (2003). Mergers in South African higher education: theorising change in transitional contexts. *Politikon*, 30(1): 27–57.

Jefferson, T. (1990). *The Case Against Paramilitary Policing.* Philadelphia: Open University Press.

Jeffery, A. (1991). *Riot Policing in Perspective.* Cape Town: South African Institute of Race Relations.

———. (1997). *The Natal Story: 16 Years of Conflict.* Johannesburg: Institute of Race Relations.

Jehn, K., Northcraft, G. and Neale, M. (1999). Why differences make a difference: a field study of diversity, conflict and performance in workgroups. *Administrative Science Quarterly*, December.

Johanson, J. (2000). Intraorganisational influence. *Management Communication Quarterly*, February.

Johnson, S. (1989). The soldiers of Lethuli: youth in the politics of resistance in South Africa. In S. Johnson (ed.). *South Africa: No Turning Back.* Indiana: Indiana University Press.

———. (ed.). (1989). *South Africa: No Turning Back.* Indiana: Indiana University Press.

Johnson, T., Misner, G. and Brown, L. (1981). *The Police and Society: An Environment for Collaboration and Confrontation.* New Jersey: Prentice Hall.

Johnston, L. (1988). Controlling police work: problems of organizational reform in large public bureaucracies. *Work, Employment and Society*, 2(1): 51–70.

Jones, T., Newburn, D. and Smith, D. (1996). Policing and the idea of democracy. *British Journal of Criminology*, 36(2): 182–198.

Kaminsky, R. (1993). Police minority recruitment: predicting who will say yes to an offer for a job as a cop. *Journal of Criminal Justice*, 24: 395–409.

Karis, T. and Carter, G. (1977). *From Protest to Challenge: A documentary History of African Politics in South Africa 1882–1964*, Stanford: Hoover Institution Press.

Keel, R. (1999). Ethnomethodological perspective (on crime and deviance). In *Encyclopedia of Criminology and Deviance.* London: Taylor and Francis.

Keith, M. (1991). Policing a perplexed society? No-go areas and the mystification of police-black conflict. In E. Cashmore and E. McLaughlin (eds.). *Out of Order: Policing Black People.* London: Routledge.

———. (1993). *Race, Riots and Policing: Lore and Disorder in a Multi-Racist Society.* London: University College of London.

Kelman, S. (2000). Making change. *Government Executive*, January.

Kiel, L. (1994). *Managing Chaos and Complexity in Government: A New Paradigm for Managing Change, Innovation, and Organisational Renewal.* San Francisco: Jossey-Bass.

Killingray, D. and Clayton, A. (1989). *Khaki and Blue: Military and Police in British Colonial Africa*. Athens, Ohio: Ohio University Press.
King, R. and Wincup, E. (eds.). (2000). *Doing Research on Crime and Justice*. Oxford: Oxford University Press.
Klandermans, B., Roefs, M. and Olivier, J. (2001). *The State of the People: Citizens, Civil Society and Governance in South Africa, 1994–2000*. Pretoria: Human Science Research Council.
Klinck, E. (2001). Transformation and social security in South Africa. Paper published by Friederich Ebert Stiftung South Africa Office, June, Johannesburg.
Klockars, C. and Mastrofsky, S. (1991). *Thinking About Police: Contemporary Readings*. New York: McGraw-Hill.
Koci, A. (1998). Reform of the police in Hungary and Lithuania: empirical findings on the policing of public order. *The European Journal of Social Sciences*, 11(3): 307–315.
Kraska, P. (1999). Questioning the militarization of the U.S. police: critical versus advocacy scholarship. *Policing and Society*, 9(2): 141–156.
Kraska, P. and Kappeler, V. (1997). Militarizing American police: the rise and normalization of paramilitary units. *Social Problems*, 44(1): 1–18.
Kraska, P. and Paulsen, D. (1997). Grounded research into U.S. paramilitary policing: forging the iron fist inside the velvet glove. *Policing and Society*, 7: 253–270.
Kuykendall, J. and Roberg, R. R. (1982). Mapping police organizational change. *Criminology*, 20(2): 241–256.

Labour Relations Act, 66 of 1995.
LAPD Board of Inquiry Final Report. (2001). Public Report on Rampart Area Corruption Incident. www.lapdonline.org/pdf_files/pc/boi_pub.pdf
Laurence, P. (1999). Deadly force. *Focus*, August: 29–35.
Lawrence, A. (2000). Codetermination in post-apartheid South Africa? *Politikon* 27(1): 117–132.
Lawrence, P. (1990). Why organizations change. In S. Mohrman, G. Morhman, G. Ledford, T. Cummings and E. Lawler (eds.). *Large Scale Organisational Change*. San Francisco: Jossey-Bass.
Lazarsfield, P. (1949). The American soldier: an expository review. *Public Opinion Quarterly*, 13.
Lea, J. (2000). The Macpherson Report and the question of institutional racism. *The Howard Journal*, 39(3): 219–233.
Le Bon, G. (1960). *The Crowds: A Study of the Popular Mind*. New York: Garland Publishers.
Ledford, G., Mohrman, S., Mohrman, A. and Lawler, E. (1990). The phenomenon of large scale organizational change. In S. Mohrman, G. Mohrman, G. Ledford, T. Cummings and E. Lawler (eds.). *Large Scale Organisational Change*. San Francisco: Jossey-Bass.
Lee, R. (1995). *Dangerous Fieldwork*. Qualitative Research Methods Series No. 34. Thousand Oaks, CA: Sage.
Leggett, T. (2002). Performance measures for the South African Police Service: Setting the benchmarks for service delivery. *Transformation*, 49: 55–85.
Levin, N., Ngubeni, K. and Simpson, G. (1994). Meeting the challenge of change? Notes on policing and transition in South Africa. Occasional paper written for the Centre for the Study of Violence and Reconciliation, May.

Levine, C. (1985). Police management in the 1980s: from decrementalisation to strategic thinking. *Public Administration Review*, November: 691–700.

Lodge, T. (1983). *Black Politics in South Africa since 1945*. Johannesburg: Ravan Press.

———. (1991). Rebellion: the turning of the tide. In T. Lodge and B. Nasson (eds.). *All Here and Now: Black Politics in South Africa in the 1980s*. Cape Town: David Phillip.

———. (2001). South African politics and collective action, 1994–2000. In B. Klandermans, M. Roefs and J. Olivier (eds.). *The State of the People: Citizens, Civil Society and Governance in South Africa, 1994–2000*. Pretoria: Human Science Research Council.

Lodge, T. and Nasson, B. (eds.). (1991). *All Here and Now: Black Politics in South Africa in the 1980s*. Cape Town: David Phillip.

Los Angeles Police Department. (2000). Board of Inquiry Final Report into the Rampart Scandal. Los Angeles.

Lumb, R and Breazeale, R. (2002). Police officer attitudes and community policing implementation: developing strategies for durable organisational change. *Policing and Society*, 13(1): 91–106.

Lundman, R. (ed.). (1980). *Police Behaviour: A Sociological Perspective*. New York: Oxford University Press.

Mackay, P., Cameron, N. and Young, W. (1986). Legislative reform and police behaviour: the decriminalization of public drunkenness. In N. Cameron and W. Young (eds.). *Policing at the Crossroads*. Wellington: Allen and Unwin.

Mahoney, A. (1999). Choosing a future. *Association Management*, 51(7).

Maier, M. and Messerschmidt, J. (1998). Commonalities, conflict and contradictions in organizational masculinities: exploring the gendered genesis of the Challenger disaster. *Canadian Review of Sociology and Anthropology*, 33(3): 325–344.

Mamdani, M. (1995). Making sense of the political impasse in South Africa. Paper presented at the Codesria General Assembly, Dakar, 26 June – 2 July.

Mandela, N. (1996). Address given on the occasion of Mandela's acceptance of an honorary Doctorate of the University of Stellenbosch, Stellenbosch, South Africa, October.

Manganyi, N. (1990). Crowds and their vicissitudes: Psychology and law in the South African courtroom. In N. Manganyi and A. du Toit (eds.). *Political Violence and the Struggle in South Africa*. London: Macmillan.

Manganyi, N. and Du Toit, A. (eds.). (1990). *Political Violence and the Struggle in South Africa*. London: Macmillan.

Mangham, I. (1979). *The Politics of Organisational Change*. Westport: Greenwood Press.

Manning, P. (1977). *Police Work: The Social Organisation of Policing*. Cambridge, MA: MIT Press.

———. (1982). Organisational work: structuration of environments. *British Journal of Sociology*, 33: 118–148.

———. (1987a). The police occupational culture in Anglo-American societies. In V. Stretcher, L. Hoover and J. Dowling (eds.). *Encyclopedia of Police Science*. Warsaw: Gower Press.

———. (1987b). *Semiotics and Fieldwork*. London: Sage.

———. (1988). *Signifying Calls and the Police Response*. Cambridge, MA: MIT Press.

Manwaring-White, S. (1983). *The Policing Revolution: Police Technology, Democracy, and Liberty in Britain*. Brighton: The Harvester Press.

Marais, E. (1993a). Paramilitarism must go. *DSA in Depth*, August/September.

———. (1993b). The police-community relationship: the Natal conflict and the prospects for peace. In L. Glanz (ed.). *Managing Crime in the New South Africa: Selected Readings*. Pretoria: Human Science Research Council Press.

———. (1994). *Policing in 1994: A Perspective*. Johannesburg: Graduate School of Public and Development Management, University of the Witwatersrand.

Marais, H. (1998). *South Africa's Limits to Change: The Political Economy of Transformation*. London: Zed Books.

Maré, G. (1999). Race thinking and thinking about race in South Africa: non-racialism in the struggle against apartheid. Paper presented at the Conference of the African Studies Association of the Australasian and the Pacific, University of Western Australia, Perth.

———. (2001). Race counts in contemporary South Africa: 'an illusion of ordinariness'. *Transformation*, 47: 75–93.

———. (2003). The state of the state: contestation and race reassertion in a neo-liberal terrain. In J. Daniel, A. Habib and R. Southall. (eds.). *State of the Nation: South Africa 2003–2004*. Pretoria: Human Sciences Research Council Press.

Maré, G. and Hamilton, G. (1987). *An Appetite for Power: Buthelezi's Inkatha and South Africa*. Johannesburg: Ravan Press.

Marenin, O. (1996). *Policing Change, Changing Police*. New York: Garland Publishing.

Marks, M. (1993). Organisation, identity and violence amongst activist Diepkloof youth, 1984–1993. Masters dissertation, University of the Witwatersrand.

———. (1996). New motives, new methods: policing in KwaZulu Natal. *Crime and Conflict*, 7: 9–13.

———. (1997). Changing police, policing change: the case of KwaZulu Natal. *Society in Transition*, 28(1–4): 54–69.

———. (1998). Policing for democracy: a case for paramilitary policing. *Crime and Conflict*, 11: 15–18.

———. (1999). Changing dilemmas and the dilemmas of change: transforming the Public Order Police unit in Durban. *Policing and Society*, 8(2): 157–179.

———. (2000a). Crash and burn: LAPD and the Rampart Scandal. *Crime and Conflict*, 20: 20–23.

———. (2000b). Transforming police organizations from within: police dissident groupings in South Africa. *British Journal of Criminology*, 40(4): 557–573.

———. (2000c). Labour relations in the SAPS. In G. Adler (ed.). *Public Service Labour Relations in a Democratic South Africa*. Johannesburg: Witwatersrand University Press.

———. (2001). *Young Warriors: Youth Politics, Identity and Violence in South Africa*. Johannesburg: Witwatersrand University Press.

Marks, M. and Fleming, J. (2004). The untold story: the regulation of police labour rights and the quest for police democratisation. Paper presented at the International Employment Relations 12th Annual Conference, 5–8 July, Capricorn Coast, Australia.

Martin, C. (1996). The impact of equal opportunities policies on the day-to-day experiences of women police constables. *British Journal of Criminology*, 36(4): 510–528.

Marx, G. (1976). Alternative measures of police performance. http://web.mit.edu/gtmarx/www/alt.html

———. (1998). Some reflections on the democratic policing of demonstrations. In D. Della Porta and H. Reiter (eds.). *Policing Protest: The Control of Mass Demonstrations in Western Democracies*. Minnesota: University of Minnesota Press.

Mastrofski, S. and Uchida, C. (1993). Transforming the police. *Journal of Research in Crime and Delinquency*, 30(3): 330–358.

Mastrofski, S., Ritti, D. and Richard, R. (1994). Expectancy theory and police productivity in DUI enforcement. *Law and Society Review*, 28(1): 113–149.

Maykut, P. and Morehouse, R. (1994). *Beginning Qualitative Research: A Philosophic and Practical Guide*. London: The Falmer Press.

McBeth, J. (1993). Clean sweep: senior officers fired in effort to reform police. *Far East Economic Review*, 13 May: 13, 22.

McCaul, C. (1988). The wild card: Inkatha and contemporary black politics. In P. Frankel, N. Pines and M. Swilling (eds.). *State, Resistance and Change in South Africa*. London: Croom Helm.

McConville, M. and Shepherd, D. (1992). *Watching Police, Watching Communities*. London: Routledge.

McLaughlin, E. and Murji, K. (1998). Resistance through representation: 'storylines', advertising and Police Federation campaigns. *Policing and Society*, 8(4): 367–399.

McLennan, A. (1997). Into the future: restructuring the public service. In P. Fitzgerald, A. McLennan and B. Munslow (eds.). *Managing Sustainable Development in South Africa*. Cape Town: Oxford University Press.

Meyer, M. (1979). *Change in Public Bureaucracies*. London: Cambridge University Press.

Miller, S. and Fredericks, M. (1994). *Qualitative Research Methods: Social Epistemology and Practical Enquiry*. New York: Peter Lang Publishing.

Mills, A. (1998). Toward an agenda of radical organizations. *Canadian Review of Sociology and Anthropology*, 33(3): 281–299.

Mohrman, A., Mohrman, S., Ledford, G., Cummings, T. and Lawler, E. (eds.). (1990). *Large Scale Organisational Change*. San Francisco: Jossey-Bass.

Mohrman, S., Ledford, G. and Mohrman, A. (1990). Conclusion: what have we learned about large scale organisational change? In A. Mohrman, S. Morhman, G. Ledford, T. Cummings and E. Lawler (eds.). *Large Scale Organisational Change*. San Francisco: Jossey-Bass.

Moir, P. and Eijkman, J. (eds.). (1992). *Policing Australia: Old Issues, New Perspectives*. Melbourne: Macmillan.

Moir, P. and Moir, M. (1992). Community policing and the role of community consultation. In M. Moir and J. Eijkman (eds.). *Policing Australia: Old Issues, New Perspectives*. Melbourne: Macmillan.

Moore, E. (2001). Emerging legal constraints on affirmative action in police agencies and how to adapt to them. *Journal of Criminal Justice*, 29: 11–19.

More, H. (1984). Organisational intervention: reaction to reality. *Journal of Police Science and Administration*, 11(2).

Morgan, R. and D. Smith. (1989). *Coming to Terms with Policing*. London: Routledge.

Morrel, R. (ed.). (2001). *Changing Men in Southern Africa*. Pietermaritzburg: University of Natal Press.

Mufamadi, S. (1994). Formulating a policing vision in the spirit of our constitution. Media statement by the Minister of Safety and Security, 25 May, Cape Town. www.polity.org.za/govdocs/pr/1994/pr0525.html

Mulcahy, A. (2000). Policing history: the official and organizational memory of the Royal Ulster Constabulary. *British Journal of Criminology*, 40: 68–87.

Muller, J. and Cloete, N. (1987). The white hands: academic social scientists, engagement and struggle in South Africa. *Social Epistemology*, 1(2): 141–154.

Nadler, D. and Tushman, M. (1990). Leadership for organizational change. In S. Mohrman, G. Mohrman, G. Ledford, T. Cummings and E. Lawler (eds.). *Large Scale Organisational Change*. San Francisco: Jossey-Bass.
Naidoo, K. (1989). Internal resistance in South Africa: the political movements. In S. Johnson (ed.). *South Africa: No Turning Back*. Indiana: Indiana University Press.
Neild, R. (1999). From national security to citizen security: civil society and the evolution of public order debates. Paper written for the International Centre for Human Rights and Democratic Development, USA.
———. (2000). Democratic police reforms in war-torn societies. *Journal of Conflict, Security and Development*, 1: 21–43.
Nel, F. and Bezuidenhout, J. (eds.). (1997). *Policing and Human Rights*. Cape Town: Juta.
North, D. (1993). Institutional change: a framework of analysis. In S. Sjostrand (ed.). *Institutional Change*. New York: M.E. Sharpe.
North Yorkshire Police Authority (n.d.). The North Yorkshire Policing Trust. www.northyorkshire.police.uk/policingplan/page07.htm

Ogbonna, E. and Harris, L. (1998). Managing organisational culture: Compliance or genuine change? *British Journal of Management*, December: 28–41.
Olivier, J. and Ngwane, R. (1995). Marching to a different tune. *Crime and Conflict*, (4): 9–16.
Olson, D. (1998). Improving deadly force decision making. *FBI Law Enforcement Bulletin*, February: 1–9.
O'Rawe, M. and Moore, L. (1997). *Human Rights on Duty: Principles for Better Policing – International Lessons for Northern Ireland*. Belfast: Committee on the Administration of Justice.

Passerini, L. (1980). Italian working class culture between the wars: consensus to fascism and work ideology. *International Journal of Oral History*, 1(1).
Patel, I. (2000). Democratising the public service: codetermination, workplace democratization and transformation. In G. Adler (ed.). *Public Service Labour Relations in a Democratic South Africa*. Johannesburg: Witwatersrand University Press.
Pease, K. (1988). Methodological developments. *British Journal of Criminology*, 28(2): 70–76.
Pederson, J. and Sorensen, J. (1989). *Organisational Cultures in Theory and Practice*. Sydney: Avebury Press.
Pike, M. (1985). *The Principles of Policing*. Hong Kong: Macmillan.
Plasket, C. (1989). Subcontracting the dirty work. In T.W. Bennett et al. (eds.). *Acta Juridica*. Cape Town: Juta.
Policy Co-ordination and Advisory Service (PCAS). (2003). Toward a ten year review: synthesis report on implementation of government programmes. Discussion document, Presidency Office of the Government of South Africa, Cape Town.
Pope, D. and Weiner, N. (eds.). (1981). *Modern Policing*. London: Croom Helm.
Posel, D. (1990). Symbolising violence: state and media discourse in television coverage of township protest, 1985–7. In N. Manganyi and A. du Toit (eds.). *Political Violence and the Struggle in South Africa*. London: Macmillan.
———. (1991). *The Making of Apartheid 1948–1961: Conflict and Compromise*. Oxford: Clarendon Press.

―――. (2001). What's in a name? Racial categorisations under apartheid and their afterlife. *Transformation*, 47: 50–75.

Prenzler, T. (1995). Equal employment opportunity and policewomen in Australia. *The Australian and New Zealand Journal of Criminology*, 28: 258–277.

Prior, A. (1989). The South African Police and the counter-revolution of 1985–1987. In T.W. Bennett et al. (eds.). *Acta Juridica*. Cape Town: Juta.

Public Order Police (SAPS). (1996). Public Order Police Policy Document on Crowd Management, December.

―――. (2000). Debriefing of Crowd Management Incident: University of Durban Westville on 16 May 2000. June, Pretoria.

Punch, M. (1975). Research and the police. In J. Brown and G. Howes (eds.). *The Police and the Community*. New York: Lexington Press.

―――. (1986). *The Politics and Ethics of Fieldwork*. Hollywood: Sage.

―――. (2003). Summary remarks of the International Police Conference at Kentucky University, 12–14 June.

Punch, M. (ed.). (1983). *Control in the Police Organisation*. Cambridge, MA: MIT Press.

Pustintsev, B. (2000). Police reform in Russia: obstacles and opportunities. *Policing and Society*, 10(1): 79–91.

Radelet, L. (1986). *The Police and the Community*. New York: Macmillan.

Rauch, J. (1991). The limits of police reform. *Indicator South Africa*, 8(4): 17–20.

―――. (1993). State, civil society and police reform in South Africa. Paper presented at the International Society of Criminology Conference, August, Budapest.

―――. (2000). Policereform and South Africa's transition. Paper presented at South African Institute of African Affairs conference, 24–25 October, Johannesburg.

Rauch, J. and Storey, D. (1998). The policing of public gatherings and demonstrations in South Africa 1960–1994. Paper published by the Centre for the Study of Violence and Reconciliation, Johannesburg.

Ray, G. (1995). From Cossack to trooper: manliness, police reform and the state. *Journal of Social History*, 28: 565–587.

Reiner, R. (1988). British criminology and the state. *British Journal of Criminology*, 28(2): 138–158.

―――. (1992a). *The Politics of the Police*. London: Harvester Wheatsheaf.

―――. (1992b). Police research in the United Kingdom: a critical review. In M. Tonry and N. Morris (eds.). *Crime and Justice: A Review of Research*. Chicago: University of Chicago Press.

―――. (1998). Policing protest and disorder in Britain. In D. Della Porta and H. Reiter (eds.). *Policing Protest: The Control of Mass Demonstrations in Western Democracies*. Minnesota: University of Minnesota Press.

―――. (2000). Police research. In R. King and E. Wincup (eds.). *Doing Research on Crime and Justice*. Oxford: Oxford University Press.

Reiter, H. (1998). Police and public order in Italy, 1944–1948: the case of Florence. In D. Della Porta and H. Reiter (eds.). *Policing Protest: The Control of Mass Demonstrations in Western Democracies*. Minnesota: University of Minnesota Press.

Report by the Technical Team on Public Order Policing, South African Police Service, July 1995.

Report on investigation into recent public order management in the Western Cape, 30 August 1996. Report compiled by a team of police officers and David Storey, consultant to the Secretariat of Safety and Security.
Republic of South Africa. (1994). Regulation of Gatherings Act, Act no. 205 of 1993. Government Gazette, 343(15446). Cape Town: Government Printer.
Reuss-Ianni, E. (1983). *Two Cultures of Policing: Street Cops and Management Cops.* New Brunswick, NJ: Transaction Books.
Rippy, K. (1990). The ins and outs of implementing change. *The Police Chief,* April.
Roach, J. and Thomaneck, J. (eds.). (1985). *The Police and Public Order in Europe.* London: Croom Helm.
Roberg, R., Kuykendall, J. and Novak, K. (2002). *Police Management.* Los Angeles: Roxbury Publishing Company.
Robertson, S. and Seneviratne, S. (1995). Outcomes of planned organizational change in the public sector: a meta-analytic comparison to the private sector. *Public Administration Review,* 55(6): 547–558.
Rock, P. (1988). The present state of criminology in Britain. *British Journal of Criminology,* 28(2): 188–199.
Rodgers, D. (2001). Making danger a calling: anthropology, violence and the dilemmas of participant observation. Working paper for the Crisis States Programme at the London School of Economics and Political Science, University of London.
Rollo, J. (1980). The Special Patrol Group. In P. Hain (ed.). *Policing the Police.* London: John Calder.
Rosenbaum, D. and Lurigo, A. (1994). An inside look at community policing reform: Definitions, organizational change, and evaluation findings. *Crime and Delinquency,* 40(3): 299–314.
Rothschild, J. (2000). Creating a just and democratic workplace: more engagement, less hierarchy. *Contemporary Sociology,* January: 193–213.

Sackman, S. (1991). *Cultural Knowledge in Organizations.* Newbury Park, CA: Sage.
Savage, S. (2003). Tackling tradition: reform and modernisation of the British police. *Contemporary Politics,* 9(2): 172–184.
Sayles, L. (1957). Work group behaviour and the larger organization. In C. Arensberg, S. Barkin, W. Chalmers, H. Wilensky, J. Worthy and B. Dennis (eds.). *Research in Industrial Human Relations.* New York: Harper and Row.
Scharf, W. and Cochrane, R. (1993). *World Factbook of Criminal Justice Systems: South Africa.* Washington: US Bureau of Statistics.
Schein, E. (1996). Culture: the missing concept in organisational studies. *Administrative Science Quarterly,* 41(2): 229–240.
———. (1997). *Organizational Culture and Leadership.* San Francisco: Jossey-Bass.
Schnetler, J. (1997). Internal climate study. Pretoria: South African Police Service Research Department.
Schrager, S. (1983). What is social in oral history? *International Journal of Oral History,* 4(2): 76–98.
Schutte, L. (1997). New training approaches: exploring the paradigm shift. In P. Fitzgerald, A. McLennan and B. Munslow (eds.). *Managing Sustainable Development in South Africa.* Cape Town: Oxford University Press.

Scott, S., Lane, G. and Vicki, R. (2000). Fluid, flaccid and distinctive? In search of a definition of organizational identity. *Academy of Management Review*, 25(1).

Seekings, J. (1988). Political mobilization in the black townships of the Transvaal. In P. Frankel, N. Pines and M. Swilling (eds.). *State, Resistance and Change in South Africa*. London: Croom Helm.

Seleti, Y. (2000). The public in the exorcism of the police in Mozambique: challenges of institutional democratization. *Journal of Southern African Studies*, 26(2): 349–354.

Shaw, M. (1994). Point of order: policing the transition. In S. Friedman and D. Atkinson (eds.). *South African Review 7: The Small Miracle: South Africa's Negotiated Settlement*. Johannesburg: Ravan Press.

Shearing, C. (1992). Reflections on police management practices. Discussion paper (No. 12) written for the Royal Canadian Mounted Police External Review Committee, Ottawa.

———. (1995). Transforming the culture of policing: thoughts from South Africa. *The Australian and New Zealand Journal of Criminology*, Special Issue: 44–56.

Shearing, C. and Ericson, R. (1991). Culture as figurative action. *British Journal of Sociology*, 42: 481–506.

Silverman, J., Anderson, N. and Patterson, F. (1999). Organizational culture. *Organisational Psychology*, 27(1).

Sjostrand, S. (ed.). (1993). *Institutional Change*. New York: M. E. Sharpe.

Skolnick, J. (1975). *Justice Without Trial: Law Enforcement in Democratic Society*. New York: John Wiley and Sons.

Smelser, N. (1962). *Theory of Collective Behaviour*. New York: Free Press of Glencoe.

Smit, B. and Botha, C. (1990). Democracy and policing: an introduction to paradox. *Acta Criminologica*, 3(1): 36–45.

Smith, R. (ed.). (1982). *An Introduction to Social Research: A Handbook of Social Science Methods*, Vol. 1. Cambridge: Bellinger.

Smith, V. (1989). On organizational culture. *Contemporary Sociology*, 22(3).

Solomos, J. and Racket, T. (1991). Policing and urban unrest: problem constitution and policy responses. In E. Cashmore and E. McLaughlin (eds.). *Out of Order: Policing Black People*. London: Routledge.

South African Human Rights Commission. (1999). Inquiry into Racism in the SAPS Vryburg District, 30 November.

South African Police Service Act, 68 of 1995.

South African Police Service. (1996). Public Order Police Policy Document on Crowd Management. Pretoria.

———. (1997). Credo for Affirmative Action, 22 October.

Southgate, P. (1987). Behaviour in police-public encounters. *The Howard Journal*, 26: 153–163.

———. (1988). *New Directions in Police Training*. London: Home Office Research and Planning Unit.

Stadler, A. (1987). *The Political Economy of Modern South Africa*. Cape Town: David Phillip.

Standfest, S. (1996). Police supervisors and stress. *FBI Law Enforcement Bulletin*, May: 7–11.

Stapley, L. (1996). *The Personality of the Organisation: A Psycho-dynamic Explanation of Culture and Change*, New York: Free Association Books.

Stephens, M. and Becher, S. (eds.). (1994). *Police Force, Police Service: Care and Control in Britain*. London: Macmillan.

Steytler, N. (1989). Policing 'unrest': the restoring of authority. In T.W. Bennett et al. (eds.). *Acta Juridica*. Cape Town: Juta.

——. (1990). Policing political opponents: death squads and cop culture. In D. Hansson and D. van Zyl Smit (eds.). *Toward Justice? Crime and State Control in South Africa*. Cape Town: Oxford University Press.

Stokes, L. and Scott, J. (1996). Affirmative action and selected minority groups in law enforcement. *Journal of Criminal Justice*, 24(1): 29–38.

Strangleman, T. and Roberts, I. (1999). Looking through the window of opportunity: The cultural cleansing of workplace identity. *Sociology*, 33(1): 47–68.

Stretcher, V. Hoover, L. and Dowling, J. (eds.). (1987). *Encyclopedia of Police Science*. Warsaw: Gower Press.

Swilling, M. (1988). The United Democratic Front and township revolt. In W. Cobbett and R. Cohen (eds.). *Popular Struggles in South Africa*. London: James Currey.

Sykes, G. (1986). Automation, management, and the police role: the new reformers? *Journal of Police Science and Administration*, 14(1): 24–30.

Sykes, R. and Brent, E. (1983). *Policing: A Social Behaviourist Perspective*. New Jersey: Rutgers University Press.

Taylor, M. (1995). White backlash to workplace affirmative action: peril or myth? *Social Forces*, 73(4): 1385–1414.

Thomaneck, J. (1985). Police and public order in the Republic of Germany. In J. Roach and J. Thomaneck (eds.). *Police and Public Order in Europe*. London: Croom Helm.

Thomas, J. and Marquart, J. (1987). Dirty information and clean conscience: communication problems in studying 'bad guys'. In C. Couch and D. Maines (eds.). *Communication and Social Structure*. Springfield: Charles Thomas.

Thompson, P. and McHugh, D. (1990). *Work Organisations: A Critical Introduction*. London: Macmillan.

Thurman, Q. and Zhao, J. (eds.). (2004). *Contemporary Policing: Controversies, Challenges and Solutions*. Los Angeles: Roxbury Publishing Company.

Tonry, M. and Morris, N. (eds.). (1992). *Crime and Justice: A Review of Research*. Chicago: University of Chicago Press.

Truth and Reconciliation Commission. (1998). Truth and Reconciliation Commission Report. Cape Town.

Turner, R. (ed.). (1975). *Ethnomethodology*. Harmondsworth: Penguin.

Uys, S. (1989). The Afrikaner establishment. In S. Johnson (ed.). *South Africa: No Turning Back*. Indiana: Indiana University Press.

Vanagunas, S. and Elliot, J. (1980). *Administration of Police Organizations*. London: Allyn and Bacon.

Van Buskirk, W. and McGrath, D. (1999). Organisational cultures as holding environments: a psychodynamic look at organizational symbolism. *Human Relations* 52(6): 805–832.

Van der Merwe, W. (1994). Managing political unrest. Unpublished paper for the Institute for Security Studies at the University of Pretoria.

Van der Spuy, E. (1989a). Literature on the police in South Africa: an historical perspective. In T.W. Bennett et al. (eds.). *Acta Juridica*. Cape Town: Juta.

———. (1989b). Recent trends in police studies. *South African Sociological Review*, 1(1): 52–64.

———. (1990). Political discourse and the history of the South African Police. In D. Hansson and D. van Zyl Smit (eds.). *Towards Justice? Crime and State Control in South Africa*. Cape Town: Oxford University Press.

———. (2001). Crime and its discontents: recent South African crime control and policing responses. Unpublished paper.

Van Heerden, T.J. (1982). *Introduction to Police Science*. Pretoria: University of South Africa.

Van Hoek. F. and Bossuyt, J. (1993). Democracy in sub-Saharan Africa: the search for a new industrial setup. *Africa Development Review*, June.

Van Kessel, W.M.J. (2001). Transforming the South African Police Service: the changing meaning of change. Paper presented at the South African Sociological Association congress, July, University of Pretoria.

Van Maanen, J. (1972). Pledging the police: a study of selected aspects of recruit socialization in a large urban police department. Prepared for the Office of Naval Research, Vancouver: National Technical Information Service.

———. (1982). On the ethics of fieldwork. In R. Smith (ed.). *An Introduction to Social Research: A Handbook of Social Science Methods*, Vol. 1. Cambridge: Ballinger.

———. (1983). The boss: first line supervision in an American police agency. In M. Punch (ed.). *Control in the Police Organisation*. Cambridge, MA: MIT Press.

———. (1988). *Tales of the Field: On Writing Ethnography*. Chicago: University of Chicago Press.

———. (1995). *Representations in Ethnography*. London: Sage.

Van Maanen, J., Manning, P. and Miller, M. (1995). Series editors' introduction. In R. Lee. *Dangerous Fieldwork*, Qualitative Research Methods Series No. 34. Thousand Oaks, CA: Sage.

Van Ryckeghem, D., Hendrickx, E. and Heuns, C. (1998). Conflicts in society: the police as partner? Policing public order-disorder: a study investigating the limits of traditional frames of reference and those of community policing. Belgian Federal Police. Unpublished manuscript.

Vollmer, I., Peper, J. and Boolsen, F. (1951). *Police Organization and Administration*. Sacramento: California State Department of Education.

Waddington, P. A. J. (1991). *The Strong Arm of the Law: Armed and Public Order Policing*. Oxford: Clarendon Press.

———. (1993). Dying in a ditch: the use of police powers in public order. *International Journal of the Sociology of Law*, 21: 335–353.

———. (1998). Controlling protest in contemporary historical and comparative perspective. In D. Della Porta and H. Reiter (eds.). *Policing Protest: The Control of Mass Demonstrations in Western Democracies*, Minnesota: University of Minnesota Press.

———. (1999a). Police (canteen) subculture. *British Journal of Criminology*, 39(2): 287–309.

———. (1999b). Swatting police paramilitarism: a comment on Kraska and Paulsen. *Policing and Society*, 9(2): 125–140.

Wainwright, D. and Smith, N. (1978). *Management in the Police Service: First Line Management for Police Officers*. London: Barry Rose Ltd.

Walker, R. (ed.). (1985). *Applied Qualitative Research*. Aldershot, UK: Gower Publishing Company.
Wardrop, J. (1989). Riding the whole Soweto: Soweto flying squad and the representations of the field. Paper presented at the History Seminar Programme, March, University of Natal, Durban.
Washo, B. (1984). Effecting planned change within a police organization. *The Police Chief*, November: 33–35.
Weatheritt, M. (ed.). (1989). *Police Research: Some Future Prospects*. Sydney: Avebury Press.
Webster, E. (1995). Beyond the boundaries: experimenting with organisational change in the South African workplace. Occasional paper for the Sociology of Work Unit, University of the Witwatersrand.
Weitzer, R. (1993). Transforming the South African Police. *Police Science*, Spring:1–10.
———. (2000). White, black or blue cops? Race and citizen assessment of police officers. *Journal of Criminal Justice*, 28: 313–324.
Westmarland, L. (2001). Blowing the whistle on police violence: gender, ethnography and ethics. *British Journal of Criminology*, 41(3): 523–536.
White, W.F. (1995). *Street Corner Society: The Structure of an Italian Slum*. Chicago: University of Chicago Press.
White Paper on Human Resource Management in the Public Service, December 1997.
White Paper on Safety and Security, 1998.
White Paper on the Transformation of the Public Service, Notice 1227 of 1995.
White Paper on the Transformation of Public Service Delivery (Batho Pele), Notice 1459 of 1997.
Wiatrowski, M. (1999). Community policing in democratic societies: towards a human rights perspective in policing. Paper presented to the American Society of Criminology, November.
Wicks, D. (1980). Organisational structure as recursively constructed systems of agency and constraint: compliance and resistance in the context of structural conditions. *Canadian Review of Sociology and Anthropology*, 33(3): 369–390.
Wilkinson, T. (1989). *All Change at Work: The Human Dimension*. London: Institute of Personnel Management.
Williams, E. (2003). Structuring in community policing: institutionalizing innovative change. *Police Practice and Research*, 4(2): 119–129.
Willis, P. (1977). *Learning to Labour*. London: Routledge.
Wilms, W. (1996). *Restoring Prosperity: How Workers and Managers are Forging a New Culture of Cooperation*. New York: Times Books.
Wilson, J.Q. (1968). *Varieties of Police Behaviour: The Management of Law and Order in Eight Communities*. Cambridge: Harvard University Press.
Winslow, D. (1998). Misplaced loyalties: the role of military culture in the breakdown of discipline in Peace Operations. *Canadian Review of Sociology and Anthropology*, 33(3): 344–367.
Winslow, S., Hobbs, D., Lister, S. and Hadfield, P. (2001). Get ready to duck: bouncers and the realities of ethnographic research on violent groups. *British Journal of Criminology*, 41: 536–548.
Winter, M. (1998). Police philosophy and protest policing in the Federal Republic of Germany, 1960–1990. In D. Della Porta and H. Reiter (eds.). *Policing Protest: The Control of Mass Demonstrations in Western Democracies*. Minnesota: University of Minnesota Press.

Wood, J. (2004). Cultural change in the governance of security. *Policing and Society*, 14(1): 31–48.
Wooldridge, D. and Cranko, P. (1997). Transforming public sector institutions. In. P. Fitzgerald, A. McLennan and B. Munslow (eds.). *Managing Sustainable Development in South Africa*. Cape Town: Oxford University Press.
Woolgar, S. (1988). *Knowledge and Reflexivity*. London: Sage.
Worden, R. (1989). Situational and attitudinal explanations of police behaviour: a theoretical reappraisal and empirical assessment. *Law and Society Review*, 23(4): 667–711.

Young, J. (1988). Radical criminology in Britain: the emergence of a competing paradigm. *British Journal of Criminology*, 28(2): 159–183.
Young, M. (1991). *Inside Job: Policing and Police Culture in Britain*. Oxford: Oxford University Press.

Zhao, J. and Lovrich, N. (1998). Determinants of minority employment in American municipal police agencies: the representation of African American officers. *Journal of Criminal Justice*, 26(4): 267–277.

Index

absenteeism 136–137, 259 n.17
abuse by police viii, 3 *see also* violence
accountability of police 143
activists, anti-apartheid 106
affirmative action 62, 67, 95, 136–137, 183, 216–229, 236, 238–239, 244, 248, 252
    SAPS Credo, 1997 221, 229
African National Congress (ANC) 34, 36, 54–59, 61, 62, 76, 80, 113–114, 146, 174, 257 n.13
    conflict with Inkatha 55, 56, 59, 146, 174, 257 nn.10, 11
    unbanning 54
Afrikaner Weerstandsbeweging (AWB) 56–57
Afrikaners 19, 36, 217
Aids World Conference, 2000 156
ammunition, live 152, 158, 160
Angola 40
apartheid vii, 8, 32, 34, 36, 40, 47, 57, 246, 248
Area Crime Combating Unit xii, 9, 249
arms 35, 55–58, 63
    police 35, 46, 49–50, 52, 57, 84, 97, 99, 127, 162, 203, 245
    see also weapons
arrests 52, 130, 167, 206, 208, 209, 220, 232
authoritarianism 2, 3, 4, 9, 29, 187, 189–190, 247
authority, police 136, 172

Bantu Education 34
Bantu Education Act, 1953 34, 256 n.2
Bantu Education, Department of 39
Batho Pele principle 183–184
Bayley, D. 10, 17, 26, 185, 199, 206
Belgium, Gendarmerie 125, 131
Best Value Performance Indicators 206
bike unit 69, 198, 213
Bill of Rights 119, 182
Bisho massacre 257 n.13
Black Consciousness Movement 40, 44
Black Local Authorities Act, 1983 46
Black Officers' Forum (BOF) 223, 239
Blair, Sir Ian vii
Boipatong massacre, 1992 59–60
border duty 37
Bosnia-Herzegovena 3
boycotts 34, 46, 96
Brazil 3, 107
Brewer, J. 17, 89, 220
briefing and de-briefing 126, 145, 151, 195–196, 203, 210, 247
British police *see* police, British
Brixton riots 44–45
Brogden, M. 19, 24, 51, 217, 220, 254
Brown, Jennifer 218, 228
bullets, rubber 46, 50, 147, 156, 162
bureaucracy 14–16, 183, 185, 208

Cain, M. 95
career prospects 136–137, 208, 211–213, 220, 227, 238, 255

Casspirs 31–32, 58, 144
Cawthra, G. 220, 262 n.2
celebrations 253
Chan, Janet vii–viii, 9, 14, 21–23, 26–27, 144, 157, 170, 181, 195, 215, 217, 229, 244, 252
China, Cultural Revolution 35
Christopher Commission of Enquiry 5
Cillie Report 42
City Police, Durban 137, 208
Code of Conduct 59
communication 199, 239, 250
community orientation 2, 5, 7–8, 143, 151, 169, 177, 216, 244–245, 250, 252, 255
community relations 45, 59, 60, 72, 95, 117, 126, 134, 136, 139, 142–179, 186, 215
Community Resources Against Street Hoodlums (CRASH) 5
community support officers (CSOs) 6
conduct, police 24, 59 *see also* culture, police
Congress of South African Trade Unions (Cosatu) 53, 61, 157
Constitution, South Africa, 1996 61, 114, 116–117, 119, 151, 182, 221, 241
corruption, Mozambique 3–4
counter-insurgency 43, 47, 50, 52, 70, 127
Counter-Insurgency Unit 51
counter-revolution 113
courts, kangaroo 99, 164
CRASH *see* Community Resource Against Street Hoodlums
crime viii, xii, 47, 63, 83, 97, 206, 249
  organised 4
  prevention 9, 33, 58, 75, 77–81, 127, 163–168, 195, 202–204, 209–210, 231, 245–246
Criminal Law Amendment Act, 1953 34
Criminal Procedures Act, 1977 47
crowd control 58, 60, 63, 64, 75–82, 119–132, 136, 144–146, 151–156, 158, 170–171, 176, 195, 202, 210, 243

crowd management 244–246, 249, 260 n.10
  unrest 158–159
  see also crowd control
cultural knowledge 26–27, 157, 160, 170, 195, 217, 235, 244–249
  axiomatic 22, 26, 195, 244–245
  dictionary 195, 234, 240, 245
  directory 195, 245, 254
  recipe 195, 245
culture
  police vii–viii, 9, 16–24, 180, 229–240, 244, 254–255
  change 21–23, 26–30, 180, 215, 244

De Klerk, F.W. 54, 56, 59
deaths from police action 55, 156, 158, 160
Defence Force *see* South African Defence Force
Defiance Campaign 34
Della Porta, D. 21–22, 116, 144, 157, 170
demilitarisation 7–8, 187–188, 244
democracy 62–65, 241, 244, 250, 252, 254
demonstrations 7–8, 34–36, 50, 60–61, 64, 75, 78, 117–119, 148–149, 152, 156, 158, 243
  student 160–163
detention 47, 49, 51–52
disaster support 75
discipline 177, 180, 184, 187–191, 207, 212, 228, 247
discrimination 239 *see also* race representation
dogs, police 41
drugs 163, 209, 235
  raids 79, 81, 96, 100, 164, 165, 202
drugs *and* crime 5

efficiency, police 115
El Salvador 3
employment contracts 183
Empowerment Committee, POP 67, 190, 193, 239–240, 244, 252

Index

equal opportunity 219, 221, 228, 239
equipment 43, 49, 195, 203, 231
Ericson, R. 122, 252

faction fights 147–148, 150, 260 nn.6, 13
field of policing 23, 27, 144, 157, 170, 215, 229, 244
Fielding, N. 19–20, 70, 132
firearms *see* arms
Fivaz, G. 180
France, riots 35
funerals 48, 52, 78, 144

gatherings 46–47, 56, 61–62 *see also* Internal Security Act, 1982
Gatherings Act *see* Regulation of Gatherings Act, 1993
gender 27, 64, 67, 106, 183, 216–218, 221, 223–229, 240, 245, 248
Golden Triangle 60
Goldstein, H. 27–30, 185–186, 194, 214
Goldstone Commission 59–62
Goldstone, Judge R. 118
Group Areas Act, 1950 34, 36, 256 n.2
Guatamala 3
guns 101, 156, 166
 AK47s 146
 stolen 208, 232
 trade 54
 Uzis 49, 99
 see also arms
Gwala, Harry 44

habitus 23, 26–27, 215
Haysom, N. 50
hegemony 4, 35–36, 40
helmets 162
Herbert, S. 20, 128–129, 245
Heymann, Phillip 118
hierarchy 178, 184–185, 187, 192, 240, 247, 250, 252, 255

organisation 14, 28
 racial viii, 239
hijackings 99
Holdaway, S. 17, 109, 111, 123, 238, 258 n.3
homelands 50, 257 nn.9, 13
hostels 54, 55, 80–81, 167, 202, 258 n.14, 260 n.13
Human Resource Management in the Public Service, White Paper, 1997 183, 204–205
human rights 3–4, 45, 54, 55, 115, 119, 143, 159, 195, 246, 248
Hungary, police 3

incentives 208–210
informers 50, 101
injuries
 in violence 148, 149, 156, 158, 160, 243
 to police 160–161, 167, 197
 to protesters 49, 57, 144, 158, 160–162
 see also violence
Inkatha 50, 53, 55, 56, 174, 257 n.10
Inkatha Freedom Party (IFP) 54, 55, 59, 61, 76, 77, 80, 146, 257 n.11, 260 n.6
intelligence 69, 75, 151, 162
Internal Security Act, 1982 46–47
Internal Stability Division (ISD) 8, 57–60, 62–64, 66, 70, 73, 81, 148, 243
Internal Stability Unit 146, 149, 260 n.6
Irish Republican Army (IRA) 39
Israel 39, 43

Jansen, Jonathan 242
Jefferson, T. 35, 39, 74, 119, 184, 186, 223–224
job description 207–208, 210
Job Reservation and Separate Amenities Act, 1953 34

Kiel, S. 250
King, Rodney 5
Kwazulu Police Force 66

labour relations, democratisation   182–183, 244
Labour Relations Act, 1995   182–183, 197, 261 n.1
leadership   10, 24, 29, 182, 194–215, 242, 247, 251
liberation movements   36, 40, 51, 149
Lithuania, police   3
Los Angeles Police Department (LAPD)   5

management   10, 24, 27–28, 131, 180–215, 238–239, 246, 249–252, 255
  participatory   28–30, 179, 181, 184–188, 191–194, 247, 250–251
  top-down   9, 15, 24, 179, 185–186, 239, 246–247
Mandela, Nelson   1, 36
Marais, Hein   113
Marks, Monique   vii–x, 13, 52, 54, 183–184, 221
media   157, 176
Metropolitan Police Service, London   vii
militarism   8, 13, 14, 33, 35, 40, 139, 186, 191, 237
minorities, treatment by police   219
Mobile Units   50, 52, 73
morale   136–137, 186, 196–199, 207, 211, 262 n.22
motivation   136, 211, 214, 228, 250
Mozambique   3–4, 40
Municipal Police   51
murder   167
  political   257 n.15 *see also* African National Congress, conflict with Inkatha
muti murders   150

National Party   7, 34, 36, 113, 116
National Peace Accord, 1991   58–59
negotiation
  police, skills   45, 50, 58, 125–126, 162, 186, 195

with protesters   50, 61, 145–146, 245
Nield, Rachel   4–5
Non-Aligned Movement Summit, 1998   155
Nyalas   31–32, 58, 173, 234

Operation Palmiet   47

Pan Africanist Congress (PAC)   36
paramilitary   63, 81, 127, 131, 132, 155, 237, 247–248
pass laws   34–36
Performance Enrichment Process   262 n.18
performance evaluation   181, 183–184, 199, 204–211, 214, 246–247, 251
police
  British   5–6, 32, 35, 39, 44–45, 206, 253
  culture   vii–viii, 9, 16–24, 180, 229–240, 244, 254–255
  change   21–23, 26–30, 180, 215, 244
Police Act, 1958   49
Police and Prisons Civil Rights Union (POPCRU)   2, 182, 222–223, 262 n.2
Police Federation, British   6
Police Services Act, 1995   63
Policing Performance Assessment Framework   206
Policy Co-ordination and Advisory Service (PCAS)   242
POP   *see* Public Order Police
POPCRU   *see* Police and Prison Civil Rights Union
Population Registration Act, 1950   34, 256 n.2
poverty   5, 63, 98
pragmatism of the police   18
Prevention of Public Violence and Intimidation Act, 1991   59
privatisation   13
productivity   199, 228, 239 *see also* performance evaluation
protection, equipment   98, 152, 162

protests   34–57, 61, 63, 117, 145, 146, 148–149, 155–158, 171, 197, 200–202, 206, 243, 257 n.13
   Arab   39
Provincial Intervention Unit   237, 263 n.18
public order   32, 45, 65, 70, 81, 116–126, 146, 194–195, 243 *see also* riot control
Public Order Police (POP)   vii–x, 6–11, 14, 21, 63–64, 66–82, 117, 125, 130
Public Order Police, Durban
   activities   76–79, 154–155, 160–178, 258 n.15
   composition, racial   66–67
   democratising   185–194, 236–240
   duties   69, 75, 151–157, 245
   ranks   82
   restructuring   236–240
   structure   68–70, 216, 229–230, 233, 240, 261 n.7
   transformation   116–141, 142–179, 243 *see also* under topic, e.g. leadership; management
Public Order Police Policy Document   118–124, 129–131, 151, 239
Public Order Police Units
   Germany   134
   South Africa   63, 258 n.15 *see also* Public Order Police, Durban
   Spain   134
Public Order Policing, Technical Team   63–64, 75, 118, 125, 133–134, 257 n.16
Public Safety Act, 1953   34, 38
public service, service delivery   184, 186
Public Service, South Africa, transformation   114–118, 182–183, 241–242
Punch, Maurice   84, 243
punishment   34

race   106–108, 211
   attitude difference   152
   conflict   39, 45, 63, 77, 233
   relations   229, 234–236, 248
   representation   64, 66–73, 137, 143, 216, 220–223, 229–240, 243, 248
racism   2, 5, 7, 27, 33, 72, 183, 195–196, 212–213, 217–223, 231–236, 239–240, 245, 248
   Commission of Enquiry   222
rank   28–30, 67–68, 82, 185–186, 207, 216, 229–230, 243–244, 250 *see also* hierarchy
rape   5, 98, 147, 164–165
Rauch, J.   37, 49
Reaction Unit   43, 52, 57, 69, 74, 160, 237, 257 n.3, 260 n.11
Reconstruction and Development Programme (RDP)   114, 231–232, 237, 257 n.3, 259 n.2
recruits   133–141, 254–255
reform, police resistance   6 *see also* transformation
Regulation of Gatherings Act, 1993   61, 126, 151, 159, 162
Reiner, R.   viii, 16–19, 22, 70–71, 112, 170, 186, 249
representivity   218–229, 239, 244, 251–252
resistance politics   40
resources   242 *see also* equipment
re-training   125–126, 178, 245 *see also* training
retrenchment   66, 77
right wing   56
riot(s)
   Detroit   35
   France   35
riot control   31–33, 37, 39–43, 58, 126–128, 256 n.7
   Britain   44,
   South Africa   46–51, 82 *see also* crowd control
Riot Units
   Britain   39, 44–45

South Africa   8, 42–43, 50, 52–57, 60, 64–66, 70, 73, 243
Riotous Assembly Act, 1956   34–35, 38
robbery, armed   100
Robocops   10, 28, 146, 186, 196, 255
Royal Ulster Constabulary   172–173, 213
Russia, post-communist   3

sabotage   39
Sackman, S.   22
safety and security   117
Safety and Security, Department of   221
Safety and Security Green Paper, 1994   7
Safety and Security Portfolio Committee   222
Safety and Security White Paper, 1998   221
SAPS   see South African Police; South African Police Service
Scarman Report, 1981   44–45
Schein, E.   20–22, 181
security   11, 205–206
segregation, racial   34, 36
segregation laws   33 see also apartheid
self-defence   127
Separate Amenities Act, 1953   34, 256 n.2
service delivery, equity   244, 252
Seven Day War, 1990   54–55
sexism   240 see also gender
Sharpville   36, 256 n.7
Shaw, M.   54
Shearing, C.   10, 19, 24, 51, 176, 180, 217, 220, 254
shields   52, 126, 128, 162
skills   130, 131, 134, 175, 183, 208, 247, 255
Skolnick, J.   16
South African Communist Party (SACP)   34, 61, 157
South African Defence Force   47–48, 197, 256 n.7
South African Police   vii, 32–34, 61
    transformation   ix, 7, 32, 62, 65, 116–118, 143, 216–229

South African Police Service   62
South African Police Service Act, 68 of 1995   62, 117, 151
South African Police Strategic Plan   7
South African Police Union (SAPU)   182–183, 262 n.2
Soweto uprisings, 1976   41, 44, 256 n.7
Special Constables   51
Special Weapons and Tactics (SWAT)   35, 39, 225
Stadler, Alf   40
State of Emergency, 1985   48–49, 51
State of Emergency, 1986   51–52
State Security Council (SSC)   48, 256 n.8
stereotyping   18, 234–236, 240, 246, 248
Storey, David   37, 49, 63
stories   13–14, 41, 47–48, 74–75, 127, 144, 159–160, 173–175, 252–254
strikes   183
    Durban   44
    police   197
student unrest   160–163, 173–175, 178, 192–193, 199–203, 245
supervision   24, 184–185, 194–204, 245, 247
    see also management
Suppression of Communism Act, 1950   38
survival courses   127–128
SWAT units   see Special Weapons and Tactics
Swilling, Mark   40

taxies   77, 78, 80
    violence   158
teamwork   133
tear gas   43, 46, 49, 52, 127, 147, 156, 162, 174
terrorism   13, 39
Terrorism Act, 1967   36–37, 44
townships   46, 48, 50, 100, 107, 127, 174, 224, 245
    faction fighting   146

police units   50
security   52
violence   54–55, 146–147, 150, 174, 257 n.10
trade unions   40, 182
training   viii, xi, 8, 42–43, 45, 50–52, 58, 65, 81, 125–141, 151, 162, 170, 176–177, 183, 189, 196, 221, 233, 239, 244, 247, 255, 259 n.14
   blacks   220, 223
transformation, police   vii–xii, 14–15, 27, 170, 178, 181, 187, 219, 249–255
   Hungary   3
   Lithuania   3
   Russia   3
   South Africa   1–3, 9–10, 54, 66, 115, 125–141, 143, 152, 176, 195, 229–240, 244–255
   see also affirmative action
transformation, public service
   South Africa   113–118, 125, 143
Transformation of the Public Service, White Paper, 1995   114–115, 220
Transformation of Public Service Delivery, White Paper, 1997   183
treason trials   35, 44
tribalism   237 *see also* faction fights
Trust Feed massacre   53
Tswete, Steve   168–169

Umkhonto we Sizwe (MK)   36, 39
unemployment   40, 248
uniforms   58, 244
United Democratic Front (UDF)   46, 53–54, 56
United States, police, paramilitary   81
unrest   *see* crowd control
Urban Areas Act, 1923   33

Van der Spuy, E.   33
Van Maanen, John   85, 94, 112, 139

vehicles
   armoured   31, 43, 59, 84, 144, 203
   stolen   99, 209–210, 232
vigilantes   50, 53
violence   46, 55, 81, 96, 102–103, 131, 149, 158, 164, 171, 202
   police   103, 124, 195
      Brazil   107
      Britain   44–45
      Los Angeles   5
      Russia   3
      South Africa   viii, 2–3, 42, 44, 47–52, 57, 126, 144–149, 151–152, 158, 160–163, 165–166, 202, 245, 257 n.13
   political   124, 259 n.8 *see also* African National Congress, conflict with Inkatha
   prevention   58–59
   township   54–55, 146–147, 150, 174, 259 n.8

Waddington, P.A.J.   194–195, 247
wages   142, 220, 231
weapons   80–81, 130, 147, 167–168, 202, 228
   police   31, 43, 59, 126–127, 146, 148, 151, 162, 259 n.10
   stolen   206, 208–210
   training   52
Weberianism   14–15
Wilms, W.   28, 180, 187
Winslow, D.   102–103
women   105–107
   police officers   ix, 2, 68, 106, 216–221, 223–229, 248
      duties   224
   see also gender
World Aids Conference, 2000   156–157
World Conference Against Racism (WCAR)   157, 253

Zulu(s)   109, 235, 236–237